FOOD HEALTH

Research Methods for Anthropological Studies of Food and Nutrition

Published in Association with the Society for the Anthropology of Food and Nutrition (SAFN) and in Collaboration with Rachel Black and Leslie Carlin

Volume I
Food Research: Nutritional Anthropology and Archaeological Methods
Edited by Janet Chrzan and John Brett

Volume II
Food Culture: Anthropology, Linguistics, and Food Studies
Edited by Janet Chrzan and John Brett

Volume III
Food Health: Nutrition, Technology, and Public Health
Edited by Janet Chrzan and John Brett

Food Health

Nutrition, Technology, and Public Health

Edited by
Janet Chrzan and John Brett

berghahn
NEW YORK • OXFORD
www.berghahnbooks.com

Published in 2017 by
Berghahn Books
www.berghahnbooks.com

Library of Congress Cataloging-in-Publication Data

Names: Chrzan, Janet, editor. | Brett, John A., editor.
Title: Food health : nutrition, technology, and public health / edited by Janet
    Chrzan and John A. Brett.
Description: New York : Berghahn Books, 2017. | Series: Research methods for
    anthropological studies of food and nutrition ; Volume III | Includes
    bibliographical references and index.
Identifiers: LCCN 2016049181 (print) | LCCN 2016053040 (ebook) |
    ISBN 9781785332913 (hardback : alk. paper) | ISBN 9781785332920 (ebook)
Subjects: LCSH: Nutritional anthropology—Research—Methodology. | Public
    health—Research—Methodology. | Food habits—Research—Methodology.
Classification: LCC GN407 .F67 2017 (print) | LCC GN407 (ebook) |
    DDC 306.4072—dc23
LC record available at https://lccn.loc.gov/2016049181

British Library Cataloguing in Publication Data

A catalogue record for this book is available from the British Library.

ISBN 978-1-78533-291-3 hardback
ISBN 978-1-78920-525-1 paperback
ISBN 978-1-78533-292-0 ebook

Contents

List of Tables and Figures   vii

Introduction to the Three-Volume Set *Research Methods for Anthropological Studies of Food and Nutrition*   1
Janet Chrzan

Introduction to *Food Health: Nutrition, Technology, and Public Health*   7
Janet Chrzan

Research Ethics in Food Studies   13
Sharon Devine and John Brett

Section VII. Public Health and Nutrition

Chapter 1. Introduction to Public Health Nutrition Methods   29
Ellen Messer

Chapter 2. Identifying and Using Indicators to Assess Program Effectiveness: Food Intake, Biomarkers, and Nutritional Evaluation   42
Alyson Young and Meredith Marten

Chapter 3. Ethnography as a Tool for Formative Research and Evaluation   54
Gretel H. Pelto

Chapter 4. Methods for Community Health Involvement   71
David A. Himmelgreen, Sara Arias-Steele, and Nancy Romero-Daza

Chapter 5. Understanding Famine and Severe Food Emergencies   91
Miriam S. Chaiken

Chapter 6. Food Activism: Researching Engagement, Engaging
Research   106
   Joan Gross

Chapter 7. Food Praxis as Method   118
   Penny Van Esterik

Section VIII. Technology and Analysis

Chapter 8. Using Technology and Measurement Tools in Nutritional
Anthropology of Food Studies   127
   John Brett

Chapter 9. Mapping Food and Nutrition Landscapes: GIS Methods for
Nutritional Anthropology   134
   Barrett P. Brenton

Chapter 10. Photo-Video Voice   154
   Appendix: Key Steps in Designing a Photo-Video Voice Study   162
   Helen Vallianatos

Chapter 11. Digital Storytelling: Using First-Person Videos about Food
in Research and Advocacy   165
   Marty Otañez

Chapter 12. Accessing and Using Secondary Quantitative Data from
the Internet   181
   Appendices: Secondary Data Sources Relevant to Anthropological
      Food and Nutrition   194
   James Wilson and Kristen Borre

Chapter 13. Using Secondary Data in Nutritional Anthropology
Research: Enhancing Ethnographic and Formative Research   203
   Kristen Borre and James Wilson

Chapter 14. Designing Food Insecurity Scales from the Ground Up:
An Introduction and Working Example of Building and Testing
Food Insecurity Scales in Anthropological Research   217
   Craig Hadley and Lesley Jo Weaver

Index   232

Tables and Figures

Tables

4.1. Community Action Research and Community-Based Research Methods   75

4.2. Participatory Action Research and Participatory Rural Appraisal   78

5.1. Examples of Organizations that Address Famine and Food Emergencies   95

12.1. Nutrition, food, and agricultural institutional websites that provide secondary data and publications that can be used in research   192

13.1. A comparison of percent household food stamp recipients among selected geographic regions (2006–2010)   210

14.1. Candidate food insecurity scale items discovered during qualitative work in Bangladesh   219

14.2. Sample of the full data set used for the analyses in the chapter (contact authors for full data set)   222

14.3. Regression Results for Food Insecurity Model   226

Figures

3.1. An Ecological Model of Food and Nutrition   64

11.1. We Are What We Eat: One Family's Quest for a Healthy Home   178

13.1a and b. Estimated household data on food stamp/SNAP recipients by census tracts, downloaded as a comma separated value (CSV) file and metadata describing the field names for the worksheet.   209

13.2. Comparison of percent households receiving food stamps between selected Kentucky geographic areas and Jefferson county census tracts.   210

13.3. Map showing the distribution of percent census tract households receiving food stamps in Jefferson County, Kentucky, 2006 to 2010   211

Introduction to the Three-Volume Set
Research Methods for Anthropological Studies of Food and Nutrition

Janet Chrzan

These three volumes provide a comprehensive examination of research design and methods for studies in food and nutrition anthropology. Our goal is to provide a resource that bridges the biocultural or nutritional focus that traditionally characterized nutritional anthropology and the broad range of studies widely labeled as the anthropology of food, and food studies. The dramatic increase in all things food in popular and academic fields over the last two decades, accompanied by vast changes in technology, has generated a diverse and dynamic set of new methods and approaches to understanding the relationships and interactions people have with food. Earlier methods books tended toward the biocultural perspective of nutritional anthropology (e.g., Pelto, Pelto, and Messer 1989; Quandt and Ritenbaugh 1986) while more recent volumes have focused on food studies (e.g., MacBeth and MacClancy 2004; Belasco, 2008; Miller and Deutsch 2009) and applied work (e.g., den Hartog, Van Staveren and Brouwer 2006). The rapidly evolving field of food studies has generated a host of new perspectives and methods from a wide variety of academic backgrounds, many of which include anthropological theories and research designs. Because of the expansion of the field and the recent rise of food studies, we saw a need for a comprehensive reference volume to guide design and research across the full spectrum of food, diet, and nutrition studies.

The set has eight sections, each of which can almost stand alone as a food methods volume for a particular subdiscipline of anthropology. Just as nutritional anthropology and studies in the anthropology of food benefit from a four-field, contextualized approach, this volume assumes that research in food systems and nutrition relies upon four subdisciplines in order to effectively study the importance of food within human societies. Therefore, in addition to sections covering biological/nutritional, sociocultural, linguistic, and archeological anthropology methods, we have included sections on public health/applied nutrition, food studies, technology, and statistics. Each section is anchored by an introductory chapter that chronicles the history of the study of food within that area of research or practice and provides a comprehensive discussion of previous studies that have helped to define current work. By examining where we have been in relation to what we are doing and where we are going, each section seeks to define how current and future research can choose, adopt, and adapt the best methods to ensure high-quality outcomes. Each section is designed to provide readers with the background sources necessary for a fully comprehensive understanding of the use of methods for that area of study—a "pointing to" of studies and practitioners that have defined the field so that the reader has a good understanding of what is necessary to conduct respectable food research using methods germane to that area of anthropology. The individual chapters provide case studies and examples of how these methods have been used by other social scientists.

The chapters within each section form a complementary packet covering most of the major methods generally used by practitioners within each subdiscipline. We have included what might be called standard methods in the various subdisciplines (e.g., participant observation, ethnographic interviewing, excavation techniques, site surveying, etc.) but have expanded this focus with specialized techniques and approaches that have emerged or become popular more recently, such as digital storytelling, GIS, bone chemistry, and the use of biomarkers. The authors write about the methods and research design for their topics from their own research experience, outlining how they thought through their research questions, designs, data collection, and in some cases analysis. These volumes are meant to be a primary resource for research about food for not only the beginning student but also graduate students as well as research and teaching professionals who desire a better understanding of how their peers have tackled specific questions and problems. Each author follows a similar outline, with a short introduction to the method and its antecedents (covering key background/ historical literature and essential readings where applicable) followed by current discussions and uses of the method, including the gray literature where applicable (e.g., material from the FANTA projects, FAO, Gates Foundation, etc.) and then discussion of analysis and research design considerations, concluding with the references cited and further readings. The sections on further reading include key historical volumes, reviews, monographs, software links, and so on for background or more in-depth exploration.

The eight sections were divided into three volumes by clustering areas of anthropological research that are linked conceptually and methodologically. The first volume contains ethics, nutritional anthropology and archeological methods, studies that are often biological in focus. The second volume is mostly sociocultural, covering classic social anthropology, linguistic anthropology, and food studies. We felt that research in food studies was more frequently rooted in social processes and disciplines such as history, journalism, and sociology and thus belonged amongst the allied anthropological fields. The final volume folds the more applied research paradigms together with public health anthropology and finishes with a section on technology and statistical analysis. Clearly, this last volume could be paired with one or the other volumes to provide a comprehensive overview of allied methods, as applied anthropology and technology are utilized in biological/archeological fields as well as socio-cultural, linguistic, and food studies research and practice. By breaking these three volumes into sections we hope to provide a comprehensive overview of methods related to food research, one that allows faculty, students, and researchers to purchase the volume(s) best suited to their subdiscipline and research interests.

A final word concerns research design. These volumes have no chapter dedicated to research design for two reasons: one, the topic is far too large to be adequately covered in one or even two chapters, and two, each chapter includes some aspect of research design. Clearly, research design will differ between biological and sociocultural studies, even if the philosophy of each is derived from classic anthropology theory. However, each author was asked to provide foundational examples of research design in their field in order to create a comprehensive core bibliography for research design and methods in food and nutritional anthropology and food studies. That bibliography is given here, along with a second bibliography for Rapid Assessment Procedures and Focused Ethnographic Studies.

Food/Nutritional Anthropology and Food Studies: Research Design and Methods

Albala, Ken, ed. 2013. *Routledge Handbook to Food Studies.* New York: Routledge.

Axinn, William, and Lisa Pearce. 2006. *Mixed Method Data Collection Strategies.* Cambridge: Cambridge University Press.

Belasco, Warren. 2008. *Food: The Key Concepts.* New York and Oxford: Berg.

Bernard, H. Russell. 2011. *Research Methods in Anthropology: Qualitative and Quantitative Approaches,* 5th ed. Lanham, MD: AltaMira Press.

den Hartog, Adel P., Wija A. van Staveren, and Inge D. Brouwer. 2006. *Food Habits and Consumption in Developing Countries.* Wageningen, The Netherlands: Wageningen Academic Publishers.

Dufour, Darna L., and Nicolette I. Teufel. 1995. Minimum Data Sets for the Description of Diet and Measurement of Food Intake and Nutritional Status. In *The Comparative Anal-*

ysis of Human Societies: Toward Common Standards for Data Collection and Reporting, ed. Emilio F. Moran, 97–128. Boulder, CO: Lynne Rienner.

Edge, John T. 2013. *The Larder: Food Studies Methods from the American South.* Athens, GA: University of Georgia Press.

Gibson, Rosalind. 2005. *Principles of Nutritional Assessment,* 2nd ed. Oxford: Oxford University Press.

Johnston, Francis, ed. 1987. *Nutritional Anthropology.* New York: Alan R. Liss.

Kedia, Satish, and John van Willigen. 2005. *Applied Anthropology: Domains of Application.* Westport, CT: Praeger.

Kiefer, Christie W. 2006. *Doing Health Anthropology: Research Methods for Community Assessment and Change.* New York: Springer.

Macbeth, Helen, and Jeremy MacClancy. 2004. *Researching Food Habits: Methods and Problems.* New York: Berghahn Books.

Margetts, Barrie, and Michael Nelson. 1997. *Design Concepts in Nutritional Epidemiology,* 2nd ed. Oxford: Oxford University Press.

Mead, Margaret. 1945. *Manual for the Study of Food Habits.* Washington, DC: National Research Council.

Miller, Jeff, and Jonathan Deutsch. 2009. *Food Studies: an Introduction to Research Methods.* Oxford and New York: Berg.

Murcott, Anne, Warren Belasco, and Peter Jackson, eds. 2013. *The Handbook of Food Research.* London and New York: Bloomsbury.

Pellett, P. L. 1987. Problems and Pitfalls in the Assessment of Human Nutritional Status. In *Food and Evolution: Toward a Theory of Human Food Habits,* ed. Marvin Harris and Eric Ross, 163-180. Philadelphia: Temple University Press.

Pelto, Gretel, Pertti Pelto, and Ellen Messer. 1989. *Research Methods in Nutritional Anthropology.* Tokyo: United Nations University.

Pelto, Pertti. 2013. *Applied Ethnography: Guidelines for Field Research.* Walnut Creek, CA: Left Coast Press.

Pelto, Pertti, and Gretel Pelto. 1978. *Anthropological Research: The Structure of Inquiry.* Cambridge: Cambridge University Press.

Quandt, Sara, and Cheryl Ritenbaugh, eds. 1986. *Training Manual in Nutritional Anthropology.* Washington, DC: American Anthropological Association.

Scrimshaw, Susan C. M., and Elena Hurtado. 1987. *Rapid Assessment Procedures for Nutrition and Primary Health Care: Anthropological Approaches to Improving Programme Effectiveness.* Tokyo: United Nations University and New York: UNICEF.

Shamoo, A., and D. Resnik. 2009. *Responsible Conduct of Research,* 2nd ed. New York: Oxford University Press.

Sobo, Elisa J. 2009. *Culture and Meaning in Health Services Research.* Walnut Creek, CA: Left Coast Press.

Sutton, Mark Q., Kristin D. Sobolik, and Jill K. Gardner. 2010. *Paleonutrition.* Tucson: University of Arizona Press.

Thursby, Jacqueline S. 2008. *Foodways and Folklore.* Westport, CT: Greenwood Folklore Handbooks.

Ulijaszek, Stanley. 2005. *Human Energetics in Biological Anthropology.* Cambridge Studies in Biological and Evolutionary Anthropology 16. Cambridge: Cambridge University Press.

Ulijaszek, Stanley, and S. S. Strickland. 1993. *Nutritional Anthropology: Biological Perspectives.* Littlehampton: Smith-Gordon.

VanderWerker, Amber M., and Tanya M. Peres. 2010. *Integrating Zooarchaeology and Paleoethnobotany: A Consideration of Issues, Methods and Cases.* New York: Springer.

Weiss, William, and Paul Bolton. 2000. *Training in Qualitative Research Methods for NGOs and PVOs: A Trainer's Guide to Strengthening Program Planning and Evaluation.* Baltimore, MD: Center for Refugee and Disaster Studies, Johns Hopkins University School of Public Health. http://www.jhsph.edu/research/centers-and-institutes/center-for-refugee-and-disaster-response/publications_tools/publications/_pdf/TQR/tg_introduction.pdf.

Rapid Assessment Procedures and Focused Ethnographic Studies

Beebe, James. 2001. *Rapid Assessment Process: An Introduction.* Lanham, MD: AltaMira Press.

———. 2014. *Rapid Qualitative Inquiry: A Field Guide to Team-Based Assessment.* Lanham, MD: Rowman and Littlefield.

Blum L., P. J. Pelto, G. H. Pelto, & H. V. Kuhnlein. 1997. *Community Assessment of Natural Food Sources of Vitamin A.* Boston: International Nutrition Foundation.

Catholic Relief Services. n.d. *Rapid Rural Appraisal/Participatory Rural Appraisal Manual.* http://www.crsprogramquality.org/storage/pubs/me/rrapra.pdf.

Catley, Andrew, John Burns, Davit Abebe, and Omeno Suji. 2008. Participatory Impact Assessment: A Guide for Practitioners. Feinstein International Center, Friedman School of Nutrition Science and Policy, Tufts University (in English, Spanish, or French). http://fic.tufts.edu/assets/Part_Impact_10_21_08V2.pdf.

Chaiken, Miriam S. 2011. Using Qualitative Methods in Save the Children Programs and Research: A Training Manual. Washington, DC: Save the Children.

Chaiken, Miriam S., J. Richard Dixon, Colette Powers, and Erica Wetzler, 2009. Asking the Right Questions: Community-Based Strategies to Combat Hunger. *NAPA Bulletin* 32(1): 42–54.

GERANDO: Community Based Disaster Risk Management; Facilitator's Manual. 2011. http://www.wvi.org/disaster-risk-reduction-and-community-resilience/publication/gerando-community-based-risk-reduction.

Gittelsohn, J., P. J. Pelto, M. E. Bentley, K. Bhattacharyya, and J. Russ. 1998. *Ethnographic Methods to Investigate Women's Health.* Boston: International Nutrition Foundation.

Gove, S., and G. H. Pelto. 1994. Focused Ethnographic Studies in the WHO Programme for the Control of Acute Respiratory Infections. *Medical Anthropology* 15: 409–24.

Pelto, Gretel H., and Margaret Armar-Klemesu. 2014. *Focused Ethnographic Study of Infant and Young Child Feeding 6–23 Months: Behaviors, Beliefs, Contexts and Environments. Manual for Conducting the Study, Analyzing the Results, and Writing a Report.* Global Alliance for Improved Nutrition (GAIN). http://www.hftag.org/resources/all-resources/ (select "Demand Generation for Home Fortification", then "Focused Ethnographic Study").

Pelto, G. H., M. Armar-Klemesu, J. Siekmann, and D. Schofield. 2013. The Focused Ethnographic Study: Assessing the Behavioral and Local Market Environment for Improving the Diets of Infants and Young Children 6 to 23 Months Old and Its Use in Three Countries. *Maternal & Child Nutrition* 9: 35–46.

Pelto, G. H., and S. Gove. 1994. Developing a Focused Ethnographic Study for the WHO Acute Respiratory Infection Control Programme. In *Rapid Assessment Procedures: Qualitative Methodologies for Planning and Evaluation of Health Related Programmes,* ed. N. S. Scrimshaw and G. R. Gleason, 215–26. Boston: International Nutrition Foundation.

Scrimshaw, Nevin S., and Gary R. Gleason, eds. 1992. *Rapid Assessment Procedures: Qualitative Methodologies for Planning and Evaluation of Health Related Programmes.* Boston: International Nutrition Foundation for Developing Countries (INFDC). http://archive.unu.edu/unupress/food2/UIN08E/UIN08E00.HTM.

Scrimshaw, S., and E. Hurtado. 1987. *Rapid Assessment Procedures for Nutrition and Primary Health Care.* Tokyo: UNU.

Smith, Madeleine, Geoff Heinrich, Linda Lovick, and David Vosburg. 2010. *Livelihoods in Malawi: A Rapid Livelihoods Assessment Using the Integral Human Development Conceptual Framework.* http://www.crsprogramquality.org/storage/pubs/general/Malawi-Assessment-low.pdf.

Introduction to *Food Health: Nutrition, Technology, and Public Health*

Janet Chrzan

Introduction, Research Design, and Ethics

This volume, the third in the three-volume set **Research Methods for Anthropological Studies of Food and Nutrition,** begins with a discussion of the volume followed by a chapter on research ethics by Sharon Devine and John Brett. Their chapter will be reproduced in all three volumes because ethics must be understood by all researchers, and a consideration of the ethics of methods used to collect, analyze, store, and publish must be an essential and initial element of the planning of any project. In their chapter they expand the idea of research ethics beyond publication and permissions to include the ethics of study design, recruitment, enrollment, and obtaining informed consent. They present a brief history of the research problems that led to the current ethics regulation requirements as well as a primer on the principles that guide ethical research: respect for persons, beneficence, and justice. They conclude with two short case studies highlighting application of these ethical principles in hypothetical food studies.

Volume and Section Overviews: Volume Three, Sections Seven and Eight

Section Seven: Public Health and Nutrition

It is probably fair to state that many nutritional anthropologists are interested in and involved with public health interventions. Indeed, many of the earlier chapters in this volume have outlined research projects that contain elements of public health and nutritional outreach, often embedded within a research paradigm focused on biocultural patterns of health and well-being in individuals and groups. This section explicitly examines the methods and theory behind public health and interventionist nutritional anthropology from perspectives as diverse as famine relief, food praxis, and ethics. Readers will note that the authors of these chapters employ many of the methods discussed earlier in this volume, though often adapted for assessment and field-based programming. Public health/nutrition is a framework that introduces the cultural and the biological into public health and community perspectives, a perspective much in vogue due to the growing popularity of global health studies.

Ellen Messer introduces this section, first tracing the history of the intersection of food and nutrition research and policy development starting in the 1990s, and following with a discussion of how the anthropological differs from other academic/outreach approaches, such as those of psychological and standard public health. She then details her experiences teaching these differing methods in policy courses and concludes with reflections on how anthropologists can incorporate public health into their research and outreach. The next chapter, by Alyson Young and Meredith Marten, describes how health indicators can be used to assess program effectiveness. They focus on dietary intake, biomarkers and overall nutritional health evaluation, starting with a discussion of how nutritional epidemiologists establish baselines and assess effectiveness. They introduce monitoring strategies for programming, and then explore methods including dietary diversity measures, biomarkers, and nutritional analyses in the field. They conclude with a thoughtful review of how to choose a laboratory for sample analysis and a description of statistical analysis for these kinds of projects. Gretel Pelto's essay describes how focused ethnographic studies (FES) can be used in nutrition interventions and program development. Similar in some ways to rapid assessment, focused ethnography is a mixed-methods approach that investigates a specific set of questions or issues for which data and insights are required in a relatively short time. The first half of the chapter provides the theoretical background and methodology of FES, discusses the need for emic and etic perspectives, and describes the ethnographic techniques used in the field. Pelto then provides three case studies from her own work developing and using FES, including assessment and intervention with regard to acute respiratory infections in children, vitamin A deficiency, and infant and young child nutrition.

The remaining contributions in this section focus clearly on community involvement, ethics, and the philosophy of intervention. David Himmelgreen, Sara Arias-Steele, and Nancy Romero-Daza describe methods for ensuring participation in nutrition programming with the goal of including community in planning, research, and implementation. They analyze the pros and cons of a variety of methods including community action research (CAR), community based research (CBR), participatory action research (PAR), and participatory rural appraisal (PRA). In addition to a discussion of these methods, the authors also provide a description of the ideas and goals of community participation as well as two case studies of their use of participatory methods in anthropological research. Miriam Chaiken's chapter provides insights into famine recognition, measurement, and relief by highlighting the changes in assessment and intervention that have occurred in the last several decades. Her comprehensive review of the theory and methods of famine assessment includes famine early warning systems (FEWS), organizations that respond to famines, and a discussion of resources available to those who wish to become better informed and involved. She also discusses the problems sometimes created by famine response and the realization among planners that famine is often an ongoing problem rather than a discrete event. Assessment measurements and indicators of long-term hunger and decreased community resilience are elucidated and analyzed. In conclusion, she provides a comprehensive list of organizations and how they work with famine that is sure to be an excellent starting point for understanding the complexities of hunger and famine in the world today.

A similar ethos of "getting things done" infuses the treatment of food activism in the next chapter, written by Joan Gross. She documents the growing arena of organizations seeking to promote changes in food access, production, or use. The chapter begins with an explanation of differing organizations' scale, focus (mission), and types of action, and then discusses the topics and subjects that can be pursued when investigating such organizations. Gross provides examples of ethnographic methods she has used, including participant observation, textual analysis, and what she terms "participant participation." The latter involves acting with the group as a fellow activist, and she discusses the roles that the anthropologist can effectively (and ethically) perform in such a capacity. Penny Van Esterik also examines food advocacy, but through a slightly different lens. She discusses how action involving food—what she terms food praxis—is appropriately incorporated into academic research and how such actions alter the nature of the academic endeavor. She argues that food activism and academic research are often kept separate even though many if not most nutritional anthropologists regard food praxis as central to their lives as professionals and community members. Van Esterik explores the ethical methodology of such integrated food work and suggests that because it blurs boundaries between research and advocacy, it needs to be more robustly contemplated by researchers in nutrition and food studies. In particular, we must think carefully about how information is disseminated and how it might affect community members. Together, the chapters included in this section break new ground in understanding how we think through and conduct our research and food work, and provide a roadmap for nutritional anthropologists—whether students or established professionals—who aim to effectively and ethically use academic skills for community intervention and programming.

Section Eight: Technology and Analysis

The final section focuses on technology and analysis and is meant as a companion to the earlier sections. John Brett introduces the technology section with a brief review of the technological changes that have occurred within the last two decades, describing how they have altered and expanded anthropologists' study of food use, diet, and nutrition. New technological possibilities have also altered how research is designed and conducted, and have caused some degree of confusion for researchers as constant innovation and development sometimes make the choices of programs and protocols seem overwhelming. Brett explains how to think through the use of technology during the design phase of research and provides information on where and how to find programs suitable for anthropological research in food. Finding and using technology is a primary focus in all of the chapters that follow, starting with Barrett Brenton's chapter on using Geographic Information Systems (GIS) for nutritional anthropology. GIS methods have enormous potential to improve the analysis of the spatial complexity of food system and nutrition research because the inclusion of layers of information allows for robust data collection and integration. Brenton reviews the theories and capacities that shape GIS, its potential for field use, and applications for qualitative and quantitative analyses. He compares and contrasts GIS systems available to researchers, both free and fee-based, and provides a list of web resources for planning and implementation that will aid those interested in GIS. He concludes with a case study of use of GIS to map food deserts and an analysis of how such technologies can allow for community participation in research and implementation. Another participatory method using technology is photo- and videovoice, described by Helen Vallianatos. Recording ethnographic data on film is not new, but the relative simplicity of digital cameras has made doing so ever easier. In this chapter, Vallianatos provides an overview of the method, discusses the theoretical uses and goals of photo- and videovoice, and describes the history of its use by anthropologists.

Digital storytelling is a first-person video with narration and personal photographs and video created by individuals around topics of importance to them. Marty Otañez describes how such videos are made, what utility they have in ethnographic work, and how to conduct a workshop in order to create meaningful digital stories. He reminds the reader that these videos, which are not simply movies of an interview but are created and constructed by individuals, are "a method and process for sharing our own stories and using our skills to create a platform for community collaborators to make their own visual narratives." Otañez discusses the ethics of such creations, especially in light of social media platforms and the sharing of personal narratives within communities.

Kristen Borre and James Wilson have co-authored two chapters on using secondary quantitative datasets to add to and contextualize ethnographic research.

They begin with an introduction to what is available and how to access it; provide a list of key websites and portals, including the gray literature and datasets available from NGOs, government agencies, and international multilateral groups such as the FAO and WHO. They discuss the type and scope of information and data available, and describe the nature of what is available, especially the ties to place and time that allow robust GIS models to be built. Finally, they provide a GIS case study alongside an explanation of statistical considerations for research design and analysis. Their second chapter focuses more specifically on using nutrition datasets during research planning, implementation, and analysis. They present a compendium of sources and discuss both their strengths for nutritional anthropology research and examples of how combining secondary and primary research allows for greater scope in design, planning, and policy work.

The final chapter contains a lesson in statistics via a case study of food insecurity. Authors Craig Hadley and Lesley Jo Weaver discuss the theory and history of food insecurity research, paying particular attention to the difficulty of collecting accurate measurements. They then use a case study from their work in Tanzania to take the reader through assessment, analysis, statistics, and measures of reliability. They also contribute an important analysis of food insecurity scales and measures of association that test relationships between food security and other biological and sociocultural variables. Also embedded in this chapter is information on where and how to find statistical software and how to choose the appropriate program for research.

Research Ethics in Food Studies

Sharon Devine and John Brett

Why Ethics Are Important

Imagine that someone approaches you at a shopping center and asks if you would mind answering a few questions about what you eat. You answer the questions— what time you usually eat; how many meals you typically eat in a day; the types of foods you eat; and whether you consider yourself of average weight. Later you find out a research study has published your answers together with your photograph. The analysis suggests that you are overweight and that your nutritional intake could explain your deviation from ideal weight. Most people in this situation would be surprised and perhaps angry that by answering a few generic questions they wound up enrolled in a research study, and that personally identifiable information was in the public domain as a result.

Our research results are only as good as the information provided by those we study, and a trusting and respectful relationship is the basis for obtaining in-depth and nuanced information. Therefore compliance with ethical principles and the regulatory structures that support them should be a professional virtue of researchers (DuBois 2004). The question is, how do we ensure that research is conducted ethically? First, we must be aware of the historical background of ethical lapses that led to the development of principles embodied in research regulations. Second, we must incorporate ethical principles into our research designs from the very beginning.

History of Ethical Lapses in Research

A lengthy history of research studies raising ethical concerns led up to the adoption of federal regulations for protection of human subjects in the United States.

A favorite argument of social scientists is that federal regulations governing research were designed to curb biomedical researchers (Heimer and Petty 2010; Hammersley 2009; Hamilton 2005). However, the impetus for ethical principles and regulations is not solely a result of ill-advised medical studies. A brief description of key episodes in the history of ethical lapses makes clear that ethical concerns apply as much to social science as to medical studies. Each of the examples described in this chapter has been explored in depth, and at the end of the chapter references are provided for those who wish to learn more. In hindsight concerns with these studies might appear obvious, but the facts, context, and nuances of each are often complex, sometimes contradictory, and documentation may be sketchy or lost to history. The purpose of this list is not to condemn so much as to present a number of studies, done over a long period of time, from which lessons for contemporary ethics have been extracted.

- Reed Commission/Yellow Fever (1900–1901). This research occurred as part of the U.S. occupation of Cuba after the Spanish-American War. Yellow fever was devastating occupation forces at the time, and it was unclear how it was transmitted. Suspected modes included contact with an infected person, contact with infected objects such as clothing or blankets, and transmission via mosquitoes. Army personnel and other volunteers were offered $100 in gold to participate in the study and be exposed to blankets used by infected persons, transfused with blood from an infected person, or bitten by mosquitoes. The study was carefully designed and implemented at great expense. Notes of Major Walter Reed, who conducted the study, state that written informed consent was obtained from the volunteers (Lederer 2008; Baxby 2005).
- Tuskegee Syphilis Study (1932–1972). The U.S. Public Health Service, working with the Tuskegee Institute, investigated the natural history of syphilis to justify treatment programs for blacks. Six hundred men volunteered for the study: 399 with syphilis, 201 without. The volunteers were poor, most were illiterate, and none knew anything about syphilis. The study included routine blood tests, spinal taps, as well as autopsies. The men were told they were being treated for "bad blood." They were offered free hot meals, clinic visits, and burial insurance, which was of great importance to this group. In 1943 penicillin was accepted as curative for syphilis, but it was not offered to the men in the study, which continued to observe the study participants without treating them until 1972 (Katz and Warren 2011; Reverby 2009; Jones 1993).
- Radiation Experiments (1944–1994). People were intentionally exposed to fallout from nuclear bomb testing events and told that the fallout was not harmful, even though scientists involved in the testing knew differently.

In some instances people were injected with plutonium to see what would happen (U.S. Department of Defense 1994a, 1994b).

- Willowbrook Study (1956). Willowbrook was a school for the intellectually challenged. Healthy children were injected with a virus causing hepatitis to study the natural history of the disease and eventually test a vaccine. Parental consent was obtained (Robinson and Unruh 2008; Rothman 1982).
- Milgram Obedience Study (1961). Milgram wanted to investigate the psychology of people who follow the directions of an authority figure, even when they are told to do cruel and unethical things. Participants were told the study was investigating learning and memory. They were asked to give what appeared to be increasingly harmful electric shocks to a fake "subject" if the subject performed incorrectly on a memory test. Participants were not told the real purpose of the study (how long people would follow orders) or that the shocks were fake until their participation was over. At this debriefing, many experienced extreme psychological distress (Nicholson 2011; McArthur 2009).
- Tearoom Trade Study (1970). A graduate student conducted a study of homosexual behavior in public restrooms. While functioning as a "watch queen" outside the restroom to sound the alert at any police presence, he recorded car license numbers to locate names and addresses of subjects. He then went to their homes and misrepresented himself to interview subjects about their lives (Warwick 1973).
- Zimbardo Prisoner Study (1971). College students were recruited for a two-week experiment to determine whether personality or situational differences cause conflict between guards and prisoners. The students took the California Personality Inventory and interviewed with the study team. The most normal, average, and healthy students on all dimensions were invited to participate and divided into guards and prisoners. The guards met for a general orientation and to formulate rules for proper prisoner behavior. The prisoners were arrested by the local police and brought to the site in handcuffs. The study was stopped after six days when the simulation seemed real and the guards became abusive. About half of the prisoners left the study before it ended due to severe emotional or cognitive reaction (McLeod 2008; Savin 1973; Zimbardo 1973).
- Havasupai Origins Study (1990–2003). Members of the Havasupai tribe provided DNA samples to researchers from Arizona State University beginning in 1990 for studies of diabetes. Other researchers at the university later used these samples to study mental illness and theories about the tribe's geographical origins. The results of the study about origins conflicted with the tribe's origin beliefs. The scope of the informed consent was disputed. Ultimately unused samples were returned to the tribe, and the university

paid $700,000 to settle a lawsuit brought by the tribe (Garrison and Cho 2013; Reardon and TallBear 2012).

Types of Ethical Concerns in Food Studies

Many involved in food studies might argue that ethical concerns, especially of the type that led to the creation of the regulations applicable to human subject research, are unlikely to arise in their work. And yet, because food is so central to life—and in many cases to our sense of identity and place in the world—study topics can easily raise ethical issues if they are not appropriately addressed.

- Stigma can attach to studies of overweight, obesity, and eating disorders, as noted in the scenario that introduces this chapter.
- Belief systems of certain groups of people may conflict with the taking of blood samples or body measurements.
- Cultural norms may be offended by judgments about body image.
- Communities may be negatively impacted by studies of action anthropology such as advocating breastfeeding or studies of food security.

In short, almost any study can raise ethical issues. Therefore, ethical principles should be the foundation of the design and operation of all studies so as to minimize ethical lapses, protect human subjects, and obtain valid research results.

What Makes a Study Ethical?

Nuremberg Code

The Nuremberg Code and the Helsinki Declaration are international statements of aspirational principles for ethical research. The Nuremberg Code was proposed as a result of the war crimes trials held in Nuremberg, Germany, after the end of World War II (Nuremberg Military Tribunals 1949). The trial verdict against one of the doctors accused of unlawfully conducting medical experiments during the war incorporated ten principles that were later labeled the Nuremberg Code. These ten principles address the record in the trials of experiments done on captives who were not able to consent to or dissent from participation in experiments, many of which had little if any scientific value when weighed against the risk to subjects. A common defense was that the experimenter was following orders of superiors. The ten principles in the code are:

1. Each subject must give voluntary consent, based on comprehension of the study, its procedures, and the risks associated with participation in the

experiment. This is a personal duty of any researcher involved in obtaining informed consent—it cannot be delegated.

2. The experiment should be designed to produce results for the good of society and not be random or unnecessary.
3. The experiment should be based on scientific knowledge and previous animal studies, if appropriate.
4. The experiment should avoid unnecessary physical and psychological suffering and injury.
5. No experiment should be done if there is reasonable belief that death or disabling injury would occur.
6. The degree of risk should never exceed the potential humanitarian benefit.
7. Researchers must prepare for and provide facilities to address even remote possibilities of injury, disability, or death.
8. Only scientifically qualified persons may conduct experiments on humans.
9. A human subject must have the liberty to refuse to continue with an experiment.
10. The scientist in charge of the experiment must terminate any experiment, at any stage, if the scientist has probable cause to believe that the experiment might lead to injury, disability, or death of any human subject.

Declaration of Helsinki

In 1947, representatives of twenty-seven medical associations from around the world created the World Medical Association, an open forum for discussions about medical ethics, medical education, and socio-medical topics with the purpose of reaching international consensus and guidance. In 1964, the World Medical Association adopted the Declaration of Helsinki—Ethical Principles for Medical Research Involving Human Subjects (World Medical Association 1964). It incorporates the same principles as the Nuremberg Code and adds others that broaden interests to be protected and provide procedural safeguards:

1. It is the right of human subjects to protect their privacy and confidentiality of private information.
2. Research proposals should address funding, sponsors, institutional affiliations, conflicts of interest, and incentives to subjects.
3. Research proposals must be reviewed and monitored by an independent committee.
4. Research on a vulnerable population or community may be justified only if it is responsive to the needs and priorities of the population or community and there is a reasonable likelihood that the vulnerable group stands to benefit from the results of the research.

5. Clinical trials must be registered in a publicly accessible database before recruitment of any subject.
6. Ordinarily, subjects must consent to collection, analysis, storage, or reuse of identifiable human materials or data. Waiver of consent may be granted only by the independent review committee.
7. The welfare of animals used for research must be respected.
8. Research must respect harm to the environment.
9. Authors, editors, and publishers have ethical duties regarding the publication of results of human subjects research.

Belmont Report and Federal Regulations

Certain states and countries adopted the Nuremberg Code into law, but neither it nor the Declaration of Helsinki has the authority of federal law in the United States. However, in 1974, prompted largely by revelations about the Tuskegee Syphilis Study, Congress authorized the National Commission for the Protection of Human Subjects of Biomedical and Behavioral Research, as part of the National Research Act, to recommend ethical principles for research with human subjects. In 1979, the predecessor of the Department of Health and Human Services published the report of the national commission. Called the Belmont Report, this document organizes its discussion of ethics in research around three principles: respect for persons, beneficence, and justice (U.S. Department of Health and Human Services 1979). It draws heavily from both the Nuremberg Code and the Declaration of Helsinki. These principles were embodied in federal regulations in the 1980s. In 1991, fourteen other federal agencies adopted the same federal regulations, codified as 45 C.F.R. Part 46 and known today as the "Common Rule" (U.S. Department of Health & Human Services 2009, n.d. [List]). The regulations also established a requirement for independent review by an institutional review board (IRB) in many circumstances. A study may need permission from multiple IRBs—university, tribe, and country (or regional IRBs if the study is international). IRBs in the United States apply the regulations that are based on the Belmont Report and any other regulations applicable to the study under review. All researchers should use the Belmont principles as their touchstone for ethical research whether or not they are required to get approval from an IRB.

Respect for persons

Respect for persons requires that research involving human subjects must protect their autonomy, privacy, and confidentiality; avoid coercion; and provide additional protection for vulnerable populations. Autonomy demands that a person be in control of her or his life and not suffer from diminished self-worth and independence as a result of participating in research. Thus respect requires that human subjects provide informed consent to research that is not obtained through coercion or undue influence. This principle of respect requires that subjects receive sufficient information about a study—its purpose, why they are being recruited, what they will be asked to do, potential harms, potential benefits, alternatives to being in the study, and information about confidentiality—so that they can understand what is being asked and their consent is truly voluntary. Although these elements of informed consent are usually embodied in a document, informed consent is a process. Different methods of communication may be used and should accommodate subjects' levels of understanding. The informed consent process should include methods to test each subject's comprehension of the study.

Respect for persons requires that any compensation for study participation be compensatory for the time of participation and not unduly influence the decision to participate. If the payment constitutes an inducement, then consent is not voluntary. Therefore payment is not considered a benefit for participation in a study and may not be considered in the analysis of risk and benefit.

Consent may be waived by the IRB if full waiver of consent is necessary to accomplish the goals of the research, risks are no more than minimal, and there is an adequate plan to debrief subjects if appropriate, including when deception is involved (45 CFR 46.116). The regulations require a showing that the waiver is necessary for the validity of the research; waivers are not granted simply because it is inconvenient or more expensive to obtain informed consent. Waiver of consent may be appropriate for the review of pre-existing medical records when it is impracticable to reach all subjects to ask for their consent or when study design requires information from consecutive medical records. Waiver of signature may be appropriate in cultures where signing a document is culturally inappropriate under the circumstances, when the signature is the only link identifying the subject to the study and identification of participation in the study could increase risk, or when the study collects information for which written consent is not normally obtained (45 CFR 46.117).

Some individuals may have diminished autonomy and therefore receive additional protections against coercion or undue influence. Certain groups are specifically addressed as "vulnerable" in the federal regulations: minors (45 CFR 46.401–409); pregnant women, fetuses, and neonates (45 CFR 46.201–207); and prisoners or other institutionalized persons (45 CFR 46.301–306). Other groups that may be considered vulnerable to coercion include decisionally challenged persons and those in other situations subject to coercion or undue influence. Situational and institutional coercion can occur when someone is asked to be in a study by their treating physician or professor, or when a person feels obligated to participate because the community feels that participation is important. There are mechanisms for obtaining consent from appropriate third parties when the subject is not capable of giving his or her own consent. These mechanisms, such as parental consent, legally authorized representatives, and proxies, can be complex because they are governed by federal regulation and sometimes also by state law.

Protection of privacy and confidentiality originates in the concept of respect for persons. The harm that results from an invasion of privacy or breach of confidentiality is a social harm because it can compromise reputation, financial status, employability, or insurability. Although often conflated, privacy and confidentiality address different concepts. Privacy is the desire to control access to oneself and comes into play when considering methods to contact and recruit subjects, the research setting, and methods of data collection. Confidentiality applies to the way information is handled, managed, and stored once a person is enrolled in a study. Here researchers should consider how information is protected, what limitations affect access to information, and how to collect the least amount of information necessary for the study.

Beneficence

Ethical research maximizes benefits and minimizes risks, as researchers have an obligation to protect subjects from harm. The principle of beneficence comes from the Hippocratic Oath: "I will do no harm or injustice." Harm in the context of research includes not just physical harm, but also psychological and social harm, which may apply to the individual or the community. Brutal or inhumane treatment of human subjects is never morally justified.

Application of the principle of beneficence requires an assessment of potential risks and benefits to assure that the balance is always in favor of potential benefits. Subjects may participate in studies that will provide no direct or immediate benefit to them so long as the risks are minimal and there is the potential for societal benefit. The higher the risk and the more remote the benefit, the harder the questions of balancing risks and benefits. When assessing risk, it is important to consider both probability and magnitude of risk. A risk may be common but low or very uncommon but very damaging. Studies need not be risk free, but researchers should design their studies to minimize risk. The principle of beneficence necessarily implicates study design. A poorly designed study that is unlikely to generate data to answer the research question posed has no benefit to subjects or to society. Researchers should always consider whether human subjects are necessary. And if the study proposes to include vulnerable subjects, the researcher should justify why they are necessary for the study.

Justice

The principle of justice requires that the benefits and burdens of research be distributed equitably in society. Injustice occurs when one group is unduly burdened with research risks and another group receives benefits. One of the reasons prisoners are identified as a vulnerable population and given additional regulatory protections, aside from the potential for coercion as a captive population, is that historically they have borne unequal burdens of research with no prospect of enjoying the benefits. Selecting classes of subjects because they are convenient, compromised, marginalized, or easily manipulated raises questions of justice. Injustice also occurs when one group is denied access to benefits to which they are entitled, as in the Tuskegee Syphilis Study. Another example of injustice includes the groups of people who are selected for study. For many years most pharmaceutical research was conducted using Caucasian males. Women and people of color were not routinely included in research. Today federally funded studies prohibit researchers from excluding subjects on the basis of gender, race, or ethnicity unless exclusion is required based on the question being studied, so that benefits of the research may accrue to all groups.

Other Sources of Ethical Principles and Rules

The Common Rule, as embodied in federal regulations, is not the only source of ethical rules for research. The Department of Health and Human Services administers the Health Insurance Portability and Accountability Act (HIPAA) (U.S. Department of Health and Human Services n.d. [Health Information Privacy]), which protects personal health information. HIPAA is complex and applies to "covered entities." The Food and Drug Administration, Department of Veterans Affairs, Department of Education, and Department of Defense all have regulations governing aspects of research under their auspices (U.S. Department of Health & Human Services n.d. [List]). In addition, many professional associations, such as the American Anthropological Association (American Anthropological Association 2012), Society for Applied Anthropology (Society for Applied Anthropology n.d.), and the American Sociological Association (American Sociological Association n.d.), have codes of conduct that include ethical standards for research. In general, all of these bodies apply principles consistent with or based on the principles in the Belmont Report, but they may have more protective requirements or specific processes that apply to research within their domains. Researchers should familiarize themselves with all applicable sources of ethical principles before designing their studies.

Application of Principles

There is usually little disagreement on the ethical principles for research, but their application in practice is often much more nuanced than a mere recitation of the rules. The following two case studies raise various ethical questions. Each is followed by a brief identification of ethical issues and considerations.

Case 1

Researchers wish to study the dietary practices of a community of Native Americans living on a tribal reservation in the United States. The study is designed to identify attitudes and understanding of the healthfulness of foods in the diet; journal actual consumption by individuals and families; collect weight, height, and medical histories; and correlate the findings with concerns about BMI and diabetes. Some information will be confirmed by comparing it with Indian Health Service medical records of subjects. The study is exploratory and will inform interventions designed to reduce obesity and diabetes among those living on the reservation. The tribal council is enthusiastic about the study and wants it to be in the nature of community-based participatory research including the use of tribal research assistants, data collectors, and analysts.

Issues

Respect for persons
- There is the potential for coercion of individuals in light of tribal support. Can individual members safely exercise their autonomy and say no? Will the tribal council demand to know who has agreed to participate and who has not? What if the tribe has a long history of communal decision making that binds the group? Do you impose Western ideals of individual autonomy? First, it is important to understand the cultural values of the tribe or group and discuss all proposed procedures with the community and the IRB to identify any nuances in their application. Then consider whether you need to institute procedures to reduce the potential for coercion. For example, researchers might make clear that they will not provide any information about the identity of those who enroll or decline to participate to the tribal council to protect the privacy of individual participants.
- There is the potential for inadvertent release of confidential information. As part of the community-based approach, research assistants and data collectors will be members of the community. Procedures to train assistants and data collectors should emphasize the need for absolute confidentiality of information obtained. Personally identifiable data should be entered immediately into encrypted databases and recorded in such a way that data cannot be linked back to individuals or coded in a way that makes identification without the code very difficult. Any paper records should be destroyed as soon as possible.

Beneficence
- All researchers should be trained in cultural sensitivity, including respect for cultural norms around body image to assure appropriate interaction with

subjects and reporting of findings in a nonjudgmental, nonstigmatizing manner.

Justice
- Concerns about justice could arise if there is divergence of understanding about the scope of the research between the researchers and the community. For example, the community may expect that interventions will be immediately forthcoming while researchers understand that the current study is a pilot and that there is no funding for interventions at this time.

Process
- There may be multiple IRB stakeholders: researchers' institutions, the tribe, and the Indian Health Service. HIPAA may apply. Community-based research is, by definition, fluid and dynamic, requiring lots of work, time, and patience to manage the review process.

Case 2

Researchers wish to conduct action research into breastfeeding in a lesser-developed country. The study wishes to catalog women's decision making around breastfeeding to identify cultural norms and tie breastfeeding to infant and child health outcomes. The community where this is to occur is poor and has a variety of breastfeeding practices. Women come to live with their husband's family; the culture is strongly patriarchal.

Issues

Respect for persons
- When looking at women's decision making, the very process of getting informed consent may influence choices. If women choose not to breastfeed, they may not want to discuss it or may feel that they are "bad mothers." In this situation, researchers might consider requesting permission from the IRB to engage in minor deception, for example by describing the study as one of infant/child heath generally, without mentioning that the focus of the study is breastfeeding (technically, this is a request to waive consent to omit the true purpose of the study). This type of waiver for minor deception is justifiable if telling people about the focus of the study would tend to skew the results.
- In a patriarchal society it may be appropriate to assure that men understand and approve of the research, even if men will not be subjects. Knowing the culture and its norms is key.

Beneficence
- Women who face or have experienced sexual abuse may have strong emotional attitudes, unknown to the researcher. As with all research, it is important to know the culture and its norms so that appropriate probes and safeguards can be used to protect vulnerable subjects, so as not to cause additional harm from participation in the study.
- If it is reasonable to expect that the researcher may identify cases of neglect from inadequate or inappropriate breastfeeding, the team should consider how to handle such instances in advance.

Sharon Devine, PhD, JD is Research Assistant Professor at the University of Colorado Denver, where she teaches, conducts research, and co-chairs the social and behavioral panel of the Colorado Multiple Institutional Review Board. Before joining academia, she practiced corporate and compliance law.

John Brett is retired faculty in the Department of Anthropology, University of Colorado Denver. He received his PhD from the Joint Program in Medical Anthropology at the University of California San Francisco and Berkeley in 1994. His primary research interests focus on food systems, food security and food justice, and microfinance as a development enterprise.

References

45 C.F.R. 46.116.

45 C.F.R. 46.117.

45 C.F.R. 46.201–207.

45 C.F.R. 46. 301–306.

45 C.F.R. 46.401–409.

American Anthropological Association. 2012. AAA Statement on Ethics-Principles of Professional Responsibility. http://ethics.aaanet.org/category/statement/. Accessed 30 August 2016.

American Sociological Association. n.d. ASA Code of Ethics. http://www.asanet.org/about/ethics.cfm. Accessed 30 August 2016.

Baxby, Derrick. 2005. Walter Reed and Yellow Fever. *Epidemiology & Infection* 133(Supp. 1): S7–8.

DuBois, James M. 2004. Is Compliance a Professional Virtue of Researchers? Reflections on Promoting the Responsible conduct of Research. *Ethics & Behavior* 14(4): 383–395.

Garrison, Nanibaa' A., and Mildred K. Cho. 2013. Awareness and Acceptable Practices: IRB and Researcher Reflection on the Havasupai Lawsuit. *American Journal of Bioethics Primary Research* 4(4): 55–63.

Hamilton, Ann. 2005. The Development and Operation of IRBs: Medical Regulations and Social Science. *Journal of Applied Communication Research* 33(3): 189–203.

Hammersley, Martyn.2009. Against the Ethicists: On the Evils of Ethical Regulation. *Journal of Social Research Methodology* 12(3): 211–225.

Heimer, Carol A., and JuLeigh Petty. 2010. Bureaucratic Ethics: IRBs and the Legal Regulation of Human Subjects Research. *Annual Review of Law and Social Science* 6: 601–626.

Jones, James H. 1993. *Bad Blood: The Tuskegee Syphilis Experiment.* New York: Free Press.

Katz, Ralph V., and Reuben Warren, eds. 2011. *The Search for the Legacy of the USPHS Syphilis Study at Tuskegee.* Lanham: Lexington Books.

Lederer, Susan E. 2008. Walter Reed and the Yellow Fever Experiments. In *Oxford Textbook of Clinical Research Ethics,* ed. Ezekiel J. Emanuel and Christine Grady et al., 9–18. Oxford: Oxford University Press.

McArthur, Dan. 2009. Good Ethics Can Sometimes Mean Better Science: Research Ethics and the Milgram Experiments. *Science and Engineering Ethics* 15: 69–79.

McLeod, Saul. 2008. Zimbardo-Stanford Prison Experiment. *Simply Psychology.* http://www.simplypsychology.org/zimbardo.html. Accessed 30 August 2016.

Nicholson, Ian. 2011. "Torture at Yale": Experimental Subjects, Laboratory Torment and the "Rehabilitation" of Milgram's "Obedience to Authority." *Theory & Psychology* 21(6): 737–761.

Nuremberg Military Tribunals. 1949. Trials of War Criminals before the Nuremberg Military Tribunals under Control Council Law No. 10, V.2, 181–182. https://history.nih.gov/research/downloads/nuremberg.pdf. Accessed 30 August 30 2016.

Reardon, Jenny, and Kim TallBear. 2012. "Your DNA Is *Our* History": Genomics, Anthropology, and the Construction of Whiteness as Property. *Current Anthropology* 53(S5): S233–S245.

Reverby, Susan M. 2009. *Examining Tuskegee: The Infamous Syphilis Study and Its Legacy.* Chapel Hill: University of North Carolina Press.

Robinson, Walter M., and Brandon T. Unruh. 2008. The Hepatitis Experiments at the Willowbrook State School. In *Oxford Textbook of Clinical Research Ethics,* ed. Ezekiel J. Emanuel and Christine Grady et al., 80–85. Oxford: Oxford University Press.

Rothman, David J. 1982. Were Tuskegee & Willowbrook "Studies in Nature"? *Hastings Center Report* 12(2): 5–7.

Savin, H. B. 1973. Professors and Psychological Researchers: Conflicting Values in Conflicting Roles. *Cognition* 2(1): 147–149.

Society for Applied Anthropology. n.d. Statement of Ethics and & Professional Responsibilities. http://www.sfaa.net/about/ethics/. Accessed 30 August 2016.

U.S. Department of Defense. 1994a. Report on Search for Human Radiation Experiment Records 1944-1994, V.1. http://archive.defense.gov/pubs/dodhre/Narratv.pdf. Accessed 30 August 2016.

U.S. Department of Defense. 1994b. Report on Search for Human Radiation Experiment Records 1944-1994, V.2. http://archive.defense.gov/pubs/dodhre/Volume2.pdf. Accessed 30 August 2016.

U.S. Department of Health and Human Services. 1979. Ethical Principles and Guidelines for the Protection of Human Subjects Research (The Belmont Report). http://www.hhs.gov/ohrp/humansubjects/guidance/belmont.html. Accessed 30 August 2016.

———. 2009. Federal Policy for the Protection of Human Subjects ("Common Rule"). 45 C.F.R. 46. http://www.hhs.gov/ohrp/humansubjects/guidance/45cfr46.html. Accessed 30 August 2016.

———. n.d. Health Information Privacy. http://www.hhs.gov/ocr/privacy/hipaa/understanding/index.html. Accessed 30 August 2016.

————. n.d. List of U.S. federal agencies that have signed onto the Federal Policy for the Protection of Human Subjects ("Common Rule"). http://www.hhs.gov/ohrp/humansubjects/commonrule/index.html. Accessed 30 August 2016.

Warwick, Donald P. 1973. Tearoom Trade: Means & Ends in Social Research. *Hastings Center Studies* 1(1): 27–38.

World Medical Association. 1964, as amended. WMA Declaration of Helsinki-Ethical Principles for Medical Research Involving Human Subjects. http://www.wma.net/en/30publications/10policies/b3/. Accessed 30 August 2016.

Zimbardo, Philip G. 1973. On the Ethics of Intervention in Human Psychological Research: With Special Reference to the Stanford Prison Experiment. *Cognition* 2(2): 243–256.

SECTION
VII

Public Health and Nutrition

CHAPTER 1

Introduction to Public Health Nutrition Methods

Ellen Messer

In the 1990s, food and nutrition research and policy rediscovered and affirmed the value of qualitative inquiry and its concepts and methods. While not abandoning their priority emphases on metrics (detailing the nutrient composition of foods, biochemical and clinical measures of malnutrition and health, scientific classifications of soils, micro-organisms, and environmental and biological constraints on agricultural production; and used in economic analyses of food markets or value chains), food and nutrition professionals welcomed complementary qualitative information to provide background and fill gaps in understandings about the causes of malnutrition and the factors affecting outcomes and participation rates in community-based interventions.

This chapter situates anthropological approaches within this social-science domain. Its first part compares and contrasts several non-anthropological approaches and textbooks showcasing approaches from sociology, human development, public health, psychology, and education. The second part describes my experiences presenting multiple different anthropology methodological courses to graduate students at the Friedman School of Nutrition Science and Policy at Tufts University and integrating anthropological methods into multiple food-policy courses for graduate students in the Gastronomy–Food Studies program at Boston University. The final discussion synthesizes and reflects on these findings, and suggests ways forward for food and nutrition.

Background

Qualitative Methods (QM)

Qualitative inquiry is used by sociologists, social and educational psychologists, and other social scientists to elucidate human behaviors, motivations, and experiences that do not lend themselves easily to quantitative formulation or analysis. It is defined, most simply, as research that uses not numbers but words to communicate information and meanings, and may incorporate additional visual or auditory images or recordings to enhance credibility and authenticity. Less universally accepted subsidiary definitions add emphasis on constructed or interpretive over empirical or objective information and meanings, inductive over deductive reasoning, and purposeful over statistically valid sampling. Qualitative research results are organized to "tell a story" rather than test hypotheses, and often include highly contextualized "thick description" that illuminates a particular case rather than a single example of a more general case that is more broadly applicable to explain other cases.

To make the story compelling, valid, and believable, researchers ordinarily follow rigorous guidelines in research design; population and sample selection; and techniques of data collection, recording, organization, analysis, reporting, and write-up. As in quantitative studies, they conform to ethical standards: to do no harm, and if possible, to do some good. In all cases involving research with human subjects, studies must first win approval from the local institutional review board (IRB) that vets research involving human subjects. They must also ensure that subjects give informed consent to participation, and then follow an IRB-approved research protocol that protects subject privacy and well-being.

These basic QM theoretical and operational procedures are outlined and presented with greater elaboration, illustrative examples, and practice exercises in regularly updated textbooks geared to educational psychology (Creswell 2013), health sciences, reflexive sociology or the social sciences more generally (Denzin and Lincoln 2002), and anthropology (Bernard 2011). These textbooks and guides (e.g., Creswell 2013) distinguish at least five approaches to qualitative research, each grounded in a particular philosophical tradition that can be applied to anthropology of food and nutrition studies. A first is narrative or textual analysis, which analyzes thematic content of interview, focus group, and documentary (including policy) evidence to identify factors influencing food systems, intake, and policy. The second (and most familiar to anthropologists) is ethnography, which draws on methods of participant and other kinds of observation; formal and informal interviews; spatial, temporal, and social mapping; and documentary evidence, including literature and the arts, to produce a thick description conveying in-depth understandings of nutrition within a particular cultural context. Ethnography, especially ethno-nutritional and ethno-medical studies, which try to present the local point of view, is sometimes combined with a third approach, phenomenology, which uses in-depth interviews, focus groups, and texts to interpret individual "experiential" meanings that potentially provide more detailed and insightful guides to understanding food and nutrition behaviors and culture change.

A fourth type of qualitative research moves from thematic and comparative analysis and interpretation of particular texts or historical or ethnographic examples, to build more general understandings. This approach is labeled "grounded theory," the term Mintz (1985) uses to characterize his landmark political-economic, cultural-historical study of sugar consumption. "Case studies," according to these textbook definitions, constitute a fifth approach, in which researchers focus on analysis of some unique feature of interest in a single or delimited set of studies. Some examples might be case studies of reduction in tortilla consumption among Mexican urban and rural populations responding to spiking food prices, or the study of overweight in relation to alleged obesogenic environmental factors in particular contexts.

Choices of questions and research framework, in turn, shape choices in research design, population selection, sampling frames, strategies and field methods for data collection, and then data organization, analysis, and representation. Anthropological ethnographies are best known for opportunistic or intentional sampling, long- or short-term observation and participant observation, structured but informal and open-ended interview formats, and very careful crafting of field notes and cultural categories of record.

Anthropologists with linguistic skills in the local idiom who spend months or longer periods of time with study populations are also more likely to design studies that record and compare "cognized" and "operational" environments. In simple terms, the questions anthropologists ask seek to construct environmental categories, understandings of ecological relationships, food and nutritional values, and disease causation and symbolism from both insider and outsider perspectives. What are the goals or goal ranges of particular behaviors? How do locals understand "food insecurity," especially in relation to particular modes of livelihood? What do locals perceive as significant differences between "famine that kills" or "great hunger" as contrasted with seasonal or periodic hunger?

Particularly sociologists and anthropologists also incorporate reflexivity, which means that researchers consider, over all stages of research, the possible distortions introduced into their observations and analyses by their personal backgrounds and working assumptions. Researchers considering the colonial legacy of food insecurity in sub-Saharan Africa, for example, reflect on this heritage and how it influences both historical and contemporary nutrition findings (e.g., Moore and Vaughn's [1994] reconsideration of Richards's [1939] food ethnography). In multiple writings, Escobar (1995) has critiqued the way nutrition science and economic-development policies influence and distort the categories that nutritional and development anthropologists use to frame studies of malnutrition in technical, rather than social or political-economic terms. There are also local cultural, less political implications; for example, a researcher who expects that most food is consumed at shared hearth meals might fail to follow individuals, particularly children but also adolescents and adults, who supplement their nutrient intakes everywhere and whenever they can.

The final step is the writing, combined with other non-metrical modes of representation that communicate findings. These end points raise important questions about evaluation and validation; that is, about how effectively qualitative researchers "tell their story," and whether their conclusions can be accepted, translated, and transformed into policy, advocacy, or practice. In food and nutrition studies, the most effective formats often interweave qualitative and quantitative accounts. They might use ethnographic reconnaissance—some combination of observation and key informant interviews—to design quantitative survey instruments to identify types and distributions of nutrition problems; and then use ethnographic techniques to qualify findings about the causes of malnutrition or poor diets. The Institute of Nutrition of Central America and Panama's (INCAP) historic studies of the synergies between malnutrition and infection in Guatemalan indigenous villages and coastal *fincas* illustrate the value of such combined quantitative and qualitative techniques (e.g., Scrimshaw and Cosminsky 1991).

Reports on environmental deterioration, nutrition education, and dietary change can be authenticated with photographs and appropriately contextualized individual quotations, persuasively showing how these lead to the author's summary points and conclusions. Stone (pers. comm.), in his U.S. (St. Louis, Missouri), Indian, and world food-policy writings, uses photographs very effectively to substantiate his analysis of hyperbole used on all sides of pro- and anti-GMO campaigns (see http://pages.wustl.edu/stone/publications for examples). Qualitative research, including individual testimonies, outcries for assistance, and photographs, can enliven survey results on the impact of food-stamp benefit cuts by depicting the settings, and, with permission, the respondents. Such qualitative results give a target audience a sense of presence at the study site, thereby adding to the sense of the report's reliability, authenticity, and usefulness for advocacy.

Anthropological participatory qualitative research is also increasingly used to document and reflect on the dynamics of anti-hunger, community food-security; sustainable agriculture; and "slow food" agencies (e.g., DeLind 1999; Gross 2014).

Anthropological Contributions to Qualitative Methods Trainings

Anthropological QM trainings include additional readings and focused fieldwork exercises that introduce models for constructing thicker ethnographic contexts and understandings, and allow for practice of basic QM skills for data collection, recording, analysis, and write-up. Nancy Scheper-Hughes's incisive "Demography without Numbers" (1997), as a case in point, bears witness to and establishes the ethnographer's moral obligation to report injustice, as she lashes out against the approaches and claims of UNICEF and other international development agency programs. Her thick description of impoverished Brazilian favela households, where poverty challenges maternal love, communicates both the circumstances that discourage child survival and parental acceptance of child mortality as an unavoidable fact of life and death. Her longer ethnography, *Death Without Weeping* (1993), is a passionate political-economic indictment of official child survival, mortality, and malnutrition data, which deflect attention from the political-economic causes of poverty and death.

Kalofonos' report "All I Eat Is ARVs: The Paradox of AIDS Treatment Interventions in Central Mozambique" (2010) showcases a multilevel, multi-institutional, multi-voice account of how Mozambique's contradictory food-insecurity and AIDS relief policies push hungry AIDS sufferers to forgo their meds so as to raise infection levels to a point where they can qualify for emergency food. The essays collected in *The Global Food Crisis: Anthropological Insights into an Age-Old Problem* (Himmelgreen 2009) offer a wide range of perspectives on local- to summit-level responses to the 2007–2008 world food price crisis, providing opportunities to discuss particular anthropological framings and understandings of inequality, injustice, structural violence, and food insecurity. These essays use a mix of ethnographic methods to advocate for fairer, more effective food-security policies that will address the structural violence documented in these circumstances, and also make greater effort to break the links between food insecurity and infections. They also describe social-organizational and institutional dynamics, including NGO and development agency competitiveness, that sometimes contribute to paradoxical outcomes.

Intrinsic to doing such studies are ethnographic methods and especially focus groups within anthropological rapid assessment procedures that have been developed to address specific public health challenges such as diarrheal disease (Scrimshaw and Hurtado 1987) and a wider array of food and agriculture, water, hygiene, and nutrition issues (Scrimshaw and Gleason 1992). Both long-term and rapid anthropological ethnographic methods address such specialized topics as time allocation, which can be practiced using comparative methods of research design and data entry formats (Messer 1989); local concepts of biological and water resources, and culturally relative notions of scarcity, which can be practiced through food plant, and water-usage and distribution exercises; and symbolic analysis of branding and quality claims, based on food labels, which also lend themselves to classroom practical exercises and discussions.

The key to using QM, with or without added anthropological emphasis, is practice. In most QM courses, term-long projects provide opportunities for hands-on learning of all the skills, from research questions to preliminary data collection and analysis. These projects often are not exclusively anthropological. For example, in one of my courses students self-selected work in one of two groups. One group used key informant interviews, observations, and participant observation at La Leche League meetings to explore facilitators and barriers to a local baby-friendly hospital initiative. The second combined multiple forms of observation and interviews to map progress on an initiative for healthy corner stores. Prior to these activities they had taken the steps of defining the research questions, reviewing the literature, selecting research methods, undertaking IRB training, and writing a research proposal. This course is anthropological in that it features my own background and introductions to readings, a lack of emphasis on QM definitions and jargon, additional anthropology readings, and certain practical exercises and emphases, such as time allocation, that use anthropological formats.

Integrating Anthropology into Liberal Arts Food Policy Courses

Similar comments apply to my design of three "food policy" courses for the Boston University Metropolitan College Gastronomy–Food Studies program: "World Food Systems and Policy," "U.S. Food Policy and Cultural Politics," and "Local to Global Food Values: Policy, Practice, and Performance." Each of these courses features my particular anthropologist's lens on food systems, which systematically covers the ecology of food systems, market economy of food choices and access, cultural food preferences and social distribution rules, and nutritional and health consequences. They also follow my particular take on food-value chains and food choices, which integrate a symbolic space-time-person analytical framework. Roughly a third of the readings are by anthropologists, and there is a strong emphasis on analyzing local-to-global connections. They are all interdisciplinary courses, but a strong anthropological flavor pervades the structure and content. In contrast to the QM course, the food policy courses prioritize quantitative evidence for science and policy alongside qualitative evidence and methods. They critically examine world and U.S. hunger, food insecurity, and nutrition numbers, as well as the evidence-based policies they support.

Students in the world food policy course select, then become expert on, a particular (developing) country. They write two papers. The first presents the food-security situation and related food policies in that country, with special focus on one important food crop and one important cash crop, and on the way food policies reflect a "food first" or "comparative advantage" policy orientation. The second examines that country's experience through needs-based (Millennium and Sustainable Development Goals) versus rights-based (human right to food, food sovereignty) lenses. At midterm and the end of the term, students share their findings in ways that enable all to discern certain regional patterns or trends.

The readings are organized along the lines of the "hunger typology" of food shortage (availability) at the national level, food poverty (food security) at the household level, and food deprivation (malnutrition) at the individual level, with additional attention to anthropologists' food systems and political economists' food-value chains. In each section of the course, about a third of the readings are by interdisciplinary anthropologists whose research focuses mostly on the "missing" level of community-based food and nutrition, which is a key part of the anthropologist's food-systems framework (Messer 1996).

In the U.S. course, students select a particular food or agricultural commodity and become expert in official USDA and other government agencies, NGO, and trade association policies surrounding that crop, including state-level regulations and producer-marketer associations. As in the world food systems course, the assignments encourage students to think in comparative political, economic, cultural, and ethnobotanical terms. In addition, most weeks include basic anthropological readings on topics such as diagnosing hunger vulnerability, child nutrition and feeding, determinants of nutritional intake, and human rights advocacy.

The "Overviews and Histories" section of the U.S. food policy course introduces three types of framework—that is, the anthropological food systems, food chain, and dietary structure and content frameworks—and their key proponents. Readings integrate, for example, Margaret Mead's and other anthropologist-folklorists' historic studies of American food habits, anthropologists' participant observation–based applied, advocacy, and activist studies of farmers' markets, community-supported agriculture, organic farming and food marketing, and food-security councils across all course sections, with special emphasis on cultural politics and community-based sustainability directives and food-system transformations.

These ethnographic case studies deepen the nutrition advocate's critique of U.S. government operations, special-interest group lobbying, and the distortions they introduce into national nutrition policies (Nestle 2013), and thicken investigative journalists' accounts of the dynamics intrinsic to the currently broken U.S. food system (Roberts 2009). They provide detailed and thoughtfully analyzed, comparative evidence of local food and organic food experiences (e.g., Winne 2008; DeLind and Bingen 2007)—which can be compared with environmental advocates' appeals for a "meso-level" or "middle way" (e.g., Ackerman-Leist 2013) that can dispel doomsday scenarios of unsustainability and point the way toward processes—and of factors that demonstrably link grassroots demands for food justice and food sovereignty to county, state, and national food politics, more or less successfully. Such multilevel analyses are a contribution of holistic anthropology in general, and food studies in particular.

Anthropology of Food and Nutrition

In contrast to these interdisciplinary gastronomy food-policy courses, my anthropology of food and nutrition (AFN) courses develop basic anthropological concepts and methods for graduate students principally trained in nutrition sciences, statistics, and economics. Here the principal audiences are non-anthropologists who might have only limited background, so the overall objectives are to help them appreciate anthropology as a holistic discipline, master basic terms of analysis and discourse, and learn how to access bibliographic data bases and navigate the literature. Related aims are to help them identify anthropology's U.S. and international institutional structures and access anthropological professional networks addressing their particular thematic and topical concerns. Engaging with anthropological methodologies and methods (techniques) in each of these areas can increase understanding of the quantitative and qualitative methods used by anthropologists; our standards of data collection, analysis, and interpretation; and ethical quandaries.

After browsing the outlines, objectives, course requirements, and readings of the hundreds of theoretical, historical, applied, and advocacy syllabi on the (2012) Syllabi for Nutritional Anthropology Courses (SNAC) website, I settled on an ambitious four-field, graduate-level introduction to anthropological concepts and methods, summarized in the first seven weeks, and then a transition to special topics in food and nutritional anthropology for the remainder. The end product explores the value anthropology adds to food and nutrition studies, with reference to historical literature reviews (Messer 1984; Mintz and Dubois 2002) and more recent collections (Dufour, Goodman, and Pelto 2013).

Opening overviews introduce not only four-field, multiple sociocultural approaches, but also evolving reflexive, policy-engaged, advocacy, public, and activist approaches connected to theoretical, applied, and practice perspectives. As a biocultural anthropologist, ethnobotanist, and ethnographer who has studied time allocation and also works in policy environments, I emphasize these special methodological areas and the challenges of studying "up" to understand food-policy institutional cultures and dynamics. For those who have no background in social and cultural anthropology, Monaghan and Just's (2000) "Very Short Introduction," with its illustrative examples from their personal fieldwork experiences in Indonesia and Mexico, brilliantly encapsulates the basic questions and field methods associated with anthropological ethnographic inquiry and comparative method. For human co-evolutionary biology in relation to diet and food systems, Wrangham's (2009) *Catching Fire: How Cooking Made Us Human* refers to primary nonhuman primate and ethnographic materials to debate fundamental questions about the significance of meat eating, cooking, and hearths in human evolution, and also in basic questions of sexual division of labor and human classification, relevant to social constructions of gender and race.

These discussions on biocultural evolution of diet and cuisine carry into the next week's discussion, which consider Katz and Voigt's (1986) ancient Near Eastern beer and Mesoamerican alkali-processing of maize articles, and Flannery's writings (e.g., 1968) on systems theory and the origins of agriculture in the ancient Near East and Mesoamerica, with their emphases on broad-spectrum re-source procurement, seasonality, and scheduling. These themes are also treated in Lee and DeVore's (1968) classic analysis of diverse food resource foraging among Kalahari hunters and gatherers, who very skillfully gain a livelihood in what otherwise appears to be a resource-scarce environment.

Unfortunately, Wrangham and Katz and Voigt share the disadvantage of lacking the evidence to back up their compelling evolutionary claims and attractive logical arguments. In the former case, archaeological evidence fails to document that mastery of fire and cooking by *Homo erectus* provided the "fuel" that favored evolution of modern *Homo sapiens* with larger brains, streamlined digestion, and enhanced cultural capacities. In the latter, the archaeological record shows seeds, pots, and straws that likely were used to ferment and then strain and drink "liquid bread" as fuel for social and cultural developments. But documentation of human mastery of beer-making microbes comes only later, whereas Katz and Voigt (1986) assert that grain fermentation for beer likely preceded bread. Both writings, however (and more constructively), provide carefully constructed contexts for lively debates about the biocultural evidence and logic that are germane to discussions of the ongoing evolution of agriculture, diet, nutrition, and cuisine, which are central themes in AFN theory and method.

The next four weeks cover, critically, different kinds and modes of classic (food) ethnography and anthropology—social, cultural, economic, ecological, cognitive, and symbolic—and their critics. Such pairings include Moore and Vaughn's (1994) critique of Richards's (1939) classic food ethnography of the Bemba (in colonial Northern Rhodesia, now Zambia). Richards constructed an argument that asserts the Bemba were hungry because the colonial political-economy had drawn essential male labor to distant mines. Absent the males to cut down trees to clear new areas for cultivation, women were left embedded in cycles of seasonal and continuing hunger and malnutrition. Moore and Vaughn, on the basis of additional historical documentary and later ethnographic evidence, assert that Bemba in fact had gardens, and that women were less dependent on male labor than Richards implied. They situate the epidemiology of Bemba malnutrition in the larger context of colonial political-economic disruptions.

Analogously, Indonesianists (e.g., Dunham, Dewey, and Cooper 2009) raise searing questions about Geertz's use or abuse of historical data to formulate his concept of "agricultural involution," his reconstruction of Indonesia's agricultural economy, and the agricultural outlook that divides inner (Java) and outer island economies between rice and cash crops (see Geertz 1963). They contest Geertz's characterization of the local response to Dutch colonial landholding rules, taxation, and trade as "agricultural involution" with shared poverty as an alternative to agricultural intensification and economic growth. On the basis of careful reading of primary sources combined with thorough ethnographic reconnaissance, his critics find that Geertz's interpretation of the colonial "rice versus cash-crop" agricultural past, which gave rise to his speculations about the agricultural present and future, prove to be only questionably grounded in data. His working idea of nonintensive agricultural investments producing subsistence without growth, however clever, engaging, or profound, is not verifiable in Indonesia.

Both these cases offer compelling contexts in which to ponder the selective uses or abuses of ethnographic and historical data, and generalizations that can be made from interpretations based on them at particular or later points in time. Should anthropologists emphasize cultural and processual similarities or differences? What are their respective advantages or disadvantages? Both cases also provide excellent opportunities to reflect on the ethical dilemmas of doing fieldwork in colonial or other sensitive political environments; reflexivity in ethnographic and historical studies; and the quandaries they raise in qualitative research more generally—how to tell and validate a coherent and compelling story explaining the complex causes of food insecurity and malnutrition.

Such questions arise over and over as anthropologists, adopting different material, cognitive, symbolic, or advocacy approaches, train their anthropological lens on possible motivations for food-related practices, such as the respect paid to India's sacred cattle (Harris 1966), Papua New Guinea highlanders' periodic pig feasts (Rappaport 1967); particular industrialized and developing country farmers' and consumers' adoption, acceptance or rejection of GMOs (Stone 2002), and the internal and external trajectories of various nutritional transitions, including new core dietary items such as sugar (Mintz 1985) and globalized fast food (Watson 2006).

In each case, readers are encouraged to situate the researchers in cultural context. What is their background? What personal professional factors favored their particular approach and choice of ethnographic study? With whose permission and under whose authority did they work? Who did they talk to (e.g., what was their sampling design, did they speak the local language or work through interpreters), and how have their findings been translated into policy or practice? The answers give insight into the evolving AFN field, as well as the researcher's possible biases or blinders. Researchers should also ask these questions as they review the anthropological literature on particular topics as background to a research project.

Such questions are also relevant for reviews of studies based on rapid ethnographic methods (Scrimshaw and Hurtado 1987; Scrimshaw and Gleason 1992). Such rapid and participatory methods (covered elsewhere in this volume) seek to thicken descriptions of local understandings of subjects like barriers to primary health-care utilization, priority development concerns, diarrheal disease, or the relative advantages or disadvantages of particular agricultural technology changes. Critics assert that data collected through such methods lack cross-cultural comparability because they convene local, usually opportunistic respondents individually or in groups. The responses, moreover, may be keyed to local conditions and idioms, which means they are neither subject to validation nor generalizable. In fast-working contexts they therefore raise the same kinds of questions that pertain in longer-term studies, namely how to validate evidence collected under selective circumstances and what caveats are needed to organize and interpret it. In all, such information may still come closer than other methods to illuminating local understandings and responses to interventions and planned or unplanned change.

Ellen Messer (PhD, University of Michigan) is a biocultural anthropologist specializing in food, security, religion, and human rights. She is the former director of the World Hunger Program at Brown University and has also taught food and nutrition courses at Yale University, Tufts University's School of Nutrition Science and Policy, the Sustainable International Development program at the Heller School of Social Policy and Management at Brandeis University, and Boston University's Gastronomy–Food Studies program. She has authored numerous books and articles on topics of food and nutrition science and policy, including *The Human Right to Food as a US Nutrition Concern, 1976–2006* (2007), "Food Systems and Dietary Perspective: Are Genetically Modified Organisms the Best Way to Ensure Nutritionally Adequate Food?" in *Indiana Journal of Global Legal Studies* 9(65) (2001–2002), and "Anthropological Perspectives on Diet" in *Annual Review Anthropology* (1984).

References

Ackerman-Leist, P. 2013. *Rebuilding the Foodshed: How To Create Local, Sustainable, Secure Food Systems.* White River Junction, VT: Chelsea Green.

Bernard, H. Russell. 2011. *Research Methods in Anthropology. Qualitative and Quantitative Approaches. 5ᵗʰ edition.* Lanham, Maryland: Altamira Press.

Creswell, John. 2013. *Qualitative Inquiry and Research Design. Five Approaches.* Thousand Oaks, CA: Sage.

DeLind, Laura. 1999. "Close Encounters with a CSA: The Reflections of a Bruised and Somewhat Wiser Anthropologist." *Agriculture and Human Values* 16: 3–9.

DeLind, Laura, and Jim Bingen. 2007. "Be Careful What You Wish For: Democratic Challenges and Political Opportunities for the Michigan Organic Community." In *Remaking the North American Food System,* ed. C. Clare Hinrichs and Thomas Lyson, 298–314. Lincoln: University of Nebraska Press.

Denzin, Norman K., and Yvonna S. Lincoln, eds. 2002. *The Qualitative Inquiry Reader.* Thousand Oaks, CA.: Sage

DuFour, Darna L., Allan H. Goodman, and Gretel H. Pelto, eds. 2013. *Nutritional Anthropology: Biocultural Perspectives on Food and Nutrition.* 2nd ed. New York: Oxford University Press.

Dunham, S Ann., Alice G. Dewey, and Nancy I. Cooper, eds. 2009. *Surviving against the Odds: Village Industry in Indonesia.* With foreword by Maya Soetoro-Ng, and afterword by Robert W. Hefner. Durham, NC: Duke University Press.

Escobar, Arturo. 1995. *Encountering Development: The Making and Unmaking of the Third World.* Princeton, NJ: Princeton University Press

Flannery, Kent V. 1968. Archaeological Systems Theory and Early Mesoamerica. Reprinted in *Prehistoric Archaeology,* ed. Stuart Struever, 80–100 (Garden City, NY: Natural History Press, 1971).

Geertz, Clifford. 1963. *Agricultural Involution: The Processes of Ecological Change in Indonesia.* Berkeley: University of California Press.

Gross, Joan. 2014. Food Activism in Western Oregon. In *Food Activism: Agency, Democracy and Economy.* Carole Counihan and Valeria Siniscalchi, eds. New York: Bloomsbury, pp. 15–30.

Harris, Marvin. 1966. The Cultural Ecology of India's Sacred Cattle. *Current Anthropology* 7(1): 51–66

Himmelgreen, David, ed. 2009. The Global Food Crisis: Anthropological Insights into an Age-Old Problem. *National Association for Practicing Anthropologists Bulletin* 32.

Kalofonos, Ippolytos. 2010. All I Eat Is ARVs: The Paradox of AIDS Treatment Interventions in Central Mozambique. *Medical Anthropology Quarterly* 24(3): 363–380.

Katz, Solomon H., and Mary M. Voigt. 1986. "Bread and Beer: The Early Use of Cereals in the Human Diet." *Expedition* 28(2): 23–34.

Lee, Richard B., and Irven DeVore, eds. 1968. *Man the Hunter.* New York: Aldine de Gruyter.

Messer, Ellen. 1984. "Anthropological Perspectives on Diet." *Annual Review of Anthropology* 13: 205–249.

———. 1989. The Relevance of Time Allocation Methodologies in Nutritional Anthropology: The Relationship of Time and Household Organization to Nutrient Intake and Status. In *Research Methods in Nutritional Anthropology.* G.Pelto, P. Pelto, and E. Messer, eds. Tokyo: United Nations University Press

———. 1996. Hunger Vulnerability from an Anthropologist's Food Systems Perspective. In *Transforming Societies, Transforming Anthropology,* ed. Emilio Moran, 165–210. Ann Arbor: University of Michigan Press.

Mintz, Sidney. 1985. *Sweetness and Power: The History of Sugar.* New York: Penguin Books.

Mintz, Sidney, and Christine DuBois. 2002. The Anthropology of Food and Eating. *Annual Review of Anthropology* 31: 99–119.

Monaghan, John, and Peter Just. 2000. *Social and Cultural Anthropology: A Very Short Introduction.* Oxford: Oxford University Press.

Moore, Henrietta, and Meagan M. Vaughn. 1994. *Cutting Down Trees: Gender, Nutrition, and Agricultural Change in a Northern Province of Zambia, 1890–1990.* New York: Heinemann.

Nestle, Marion. 2013. *Food Politics: How the Food Industry Influences Nutrition and Health.* 10th ed. Berkeley: University of California Press.

Rappaport, Roy A. 1967. Ritual Regulation of Environmental Relations Among a New Guinea People. *Ethnology* 6(1): 17–30.

Richards, Audrey. 1939. *Land, Labour, and Diet in Northern Rhodesia: An Economic Study of the Bemba Tribe.* London: G. Routledge.

Roberts, Paul. 2009. *The End of Food?* Rev. ed. New York: Houghton-Mifflin.

Scheper-Hughes, Nancy. 1993. *Death Without Weeping: The Violence of Everyday Life in Brazil.* Berkeley: University of California Press.

————. 1997. Demography Without Numbers. In *Anthropological Demography: Toward a New Synthesis,* ed. David Kerzer and Thomas Fricke, 201–222. Chicago: University of Chicago Press.

Scrimshaw, Mary, and Sheila Cosminsky. 1991. Impact of Health on Women's Food Procurement Strategies on a Guatemalan Plantation. In *Diet and Domestic Life in Society,* ed. Anne Sharman, Janet Theophano, Karen Curtis, and Ellen Messer, 61–89. Philadelphia: Temple University Press.

Scrimshaw, Nevin S., and Gary Gleason, eds. 1992. *Rapid Assessment Procedures: Qualitative Methodologies for Planning and Evaluation of Health Programmes.* Boston, MA: International Nutrition Foundation for Developing Countries.

Scrimshaw, Susan, and Elena Hurtado. 1987. *Rapid Assessment Procedures for Nutrition and Primary Health Care: Anthropological Approaches to Improving Programme Effectiveness.* Tokyo: United Nations University Press.

Stone, Glenn. 2002. Both Sides Now: Fallacies in the Genetic-Modification Wars, Implications for Developing Countries, and Anthropological Perspectives. *Current Anthropology* 43(4): 611–630.

Watson, James, ed. 2006. *Golden Arches East: McDonald's in Asia.* 2nd ed. Stanford, CA: Stanford University Press.

Winne, Mark. 2008. *Closing the Food Gap: Resetting the Table in the Land of Plenty.* Boston, MA: Beacon Press.

Wrangham, Richard R. 2009. *Catching Fire: How Cooking Made Us Human.* New York: Basic Books.

CHAPTER **2**

Identifying and Using Indicators to Assess Program Effectiveness

Food Intake, Biomarkers, and Nutritional Evaluation

Alyson Young and Meredith Marten

Introduction

Accurate information about dietary determinants and behaviors of people in specific populations is necessary for nutrition policy and effective nutrition intervention programs. The utility of an evaluation depends on its ability to provide reliable, reproducible, and timely information for making the needed decisions. Program evaluations fall into two general categories: (1) evaluations to improve an ongoing program and (2) evaluations to assess the impact of a program. Ongoing program evaluations are commonly referred to as "formative evaluations," while the impact assessments are called "summative evaluations" (see Sahn, Lockwood, and Scrimshaw 1984; Habicht, Pelto, and Lapp 2009; and Rossi and Freeman 1999 for guides to developing evaluation strategies). Whether data is being used for improvement or impact assessment, monitoring and evaluation requires appropriate indicators for the establishment of population baselines for the characteristic under consideration as well as follow-up evaluation. The indicators identified in this chapter can be used for both estimating population baselines and assessing the impact of nutritional interventions (examples of nutritional program effectiveness assessments include Berti et al. 2004; Penny et al., 2005; Gibson 2011; Gunaratna et al. 2010; and Masset et al. 2012).

Selecting an Indicator

Since the field of nutrition epidemiology emerged as a recognized domain in the 1980s, research into methods of dietary exposure assessment and the application of these techniques to population-based research has become a prolific area of investigation. As a result, a variety of methods are in use to measure diet in cohort, cross-sectional, and intervention studies, where the aim is to assess contemporaneous diet (Bingham 1987; Cameron and van Staveren 1988; Gibson 2005; Willett 2012; Margetts and Nelson 1997; McNutt, Zimmerman, and Hull 2008; Preedy, Hunter and Patel 2014). Methods generally involve either collation of observations from a number of separate investigations, for example records, checklists or 24-hour recalls; or attempts to obtain average intake by asking about the usual frequency of food consumption, as in the diet history and food-frequency questionnaire. All methods of dietary assessment require some estimate of the weight of food consumed, and to determine nutrient or other food component intake, either an appropriate description for use with food tables or an aliquot for chemical analysis is necessary. The investigator should keep several considerations in mind when choosing an indicator for assessment:

- *Scale of analysis:* Byers (1998) notes that the measures that are useful for monitoring and surveillance at the population level are often quite different from those that are useful for assessing the diet or nutritional status of individuals. Researchers therefore need to keep in mind the final scale of analysis and determine whether a selected indicator will provide information that is relevant to the goals of monitoring and evaluation.
- *Cost:* The researcher needs to consider the cost of each indicator in terms of both monetary budgets and human capacity. Calculation of costs should consider collection equipment and personnel, transport and storage costs (including data storage and archiving), laboratory fees or assay costs, data analysis, and any necessary training.
- *Ease/frequency of monitoring strategies:* It is important to balance the frequency of data collection for indicators with the relative ease of data collection/participant burden. Detailed indicators such as biomarker data and observed weighted food records can yield detailed and highly accurate data, but can also entail considerable time investments on the part of participants and researchers.
- *Triangulating methods:* Each indicator used for monitoring program effectiveness has strengths and shortcomings. Triangulation (using more than one indicator to assess a particular outcome variable) is often a good way to overcome shortfalls in particular research methods or provide context for the results of a specific indicator. This approach has been particularly fruitful with regard to dietary intake and diversity, where issues of recall bias may influence study results (regarding triangulation and using biomarkers to offset measurement error, see Johns and Eyzaguirre 2007; Keogh, White, and Rodwell 2013; Saracci 1997; Freedman et al. 2010).

Specific Methods for Assessing Program Effectiveness

Dietary Diversity and Food Intake

Dietary diversity is identified as the number of either unique foods or food groups consumed by an individual or household during a given period of time. The most common methods for estimating dietary intake are food diaries or surveys of food consumption, observed weighed food records, and weighed food records. Dietary intake information is often used for assessing the adequacy of food supply, improving nutritional quality, setting targets for food production, monitoring progress toward production targets, and assessing food distribution within a population; it is also a basis for food regulations and guidelines developed for nutrition education.

Intake is normally measured by estimating current diet (prospective analyses) or past diet (retrospective analyses). Information on dietary intake and dietary diversity is collected using a range of methods. The majority center on identifying a dietary diversity score (DDS), food frequency score, or food consumption score (FCS). The DDS involves simple counts of food groups consumed over a certain reference period by an individual or a household. The FCS, measured at the household level, combines the measurement of dietary diversity, the frequency with which different foods are consumed, and the relative nutritional importance of various food groups. Measurement tools are widely available from several sources, including the CDC, FAO, and USAID (see the resources section at the end of this chapter for links to sites with survey instruments and guidelines for use).

Dietary recall

Collecting survey data about dietary intake is straightforward compared to biological indicators. Training field staff is not complicated and the questions are not especially intrusive or burdensome (Swindale and Bilinsky 2006). Furthermore, dietary recalls can be conducted face to face or by telephone or web-based multi-pass interviewing systems (Preedy, Hunter and Patel 2014). Personal digital assistants (PDAs) and handheld devices such as smartphones and tablets are also becoming a popular way to quickly and effectively collect dietary intake and other nutritional data. A number of companies produce software for different operating systems (Android, iOS, Windows) that are relatively inexpensive to purchase while providing basic nutritional analyses and data recording capabilities. There are some limitations to digital data collection however—handheld devices can be expensive, often entail additional training for respondents and investigators, and require regular charging and data download/backup to function effectively (see Fowles and Gentry 2008; McClung et al. 2009 for a discussion of the feasibility and accuracy of PDAs in dietary assessment).

It should be noted that recall bias can also be an issue with food diaries and dietary intake interviews (see Brown 2006; Illner et al. 2010; Kipnis et al. 2002;

Kirkpatrick et al. 2014; and Poslusna et al. 2009 regarding bias in dietary report instruments), so information on food consumption should be collected using the previous 24-hour period as a reference period and efforts should be made to validate survey responses (such as combination with weighed food records). When using the 24-hour recall method, the interviewer should first determine whether the previous 24-hour period was "typical" for that individual or household. If it was a special occasion, such as a funeral or feast, or if most household members were absent, another day should be selected for the interview (Swindale and Bilinsky 2006).

Weighed food record / Observed weighed food records
These methods require that all food and drink (including dietary supplements) consumed during a specified period are weighed and recorded along with detailed information on the methods of food preparation by either the participant (basic weighed food record) or a trained observer (observed weighed food record). The recorded data are converted to daily calorie and nutrient intake using food composition tables (see the list of resources for specific tables). Weighed food records are less prone to issues of recall bias because they are based on either actual or usual intakes of individuals. However, they are more time-consuming and expensive than dietary recall methods because they require estimation and accurate measurement of all food that has been consumed.

Biomarkers

A biomarker is clinically defined as a biological characteristic that can be objectively measured and serves as an indicator of normal biological processes, pathogenic processes, or responses to therapeutic interventions. Biomarkers can be broadly characterized into three groups: those that measure physical or genetic traits (anthropometric indexes, metabolic gene polymorphisms), those that measure chemical or biochemical agents in the biological system (plasma retinol, iron, zinc), and those that assess a measureable physiologic function (test of night vision, cognitive assessment) or future clinical risk (BDWG 2001; Potischman 2003). Biomarkers are most commonly used to assess dietary exposure, composition, and sufficiency regarding antioxidants, vitamins, minerals, and micronutrients; fatty acids; plant polysaccharides and phytochemicals; and food contaminants.

Biomarkers' contributions to the overall goal of the evaluation can be roughly grouped into three categories: (1) measuring exposure (e.g., baseline information on dietary presence/absence or sufficiency/insufficiency, or on physiologic response to a clinical condition or intervention), (2) establishing relative nutrient status, or (3) estimating direct and indirect physiological effects of an item that has been consumed. Some of the more common biomarkers used in assessing program effectiveness include dietary fatty acid composition; vitamin A, iron, iodine, and zinc levels; and measures of energy expenditure and metabolic markers (e.g., doubly labeled water, 24-hour nitrogen, and 24-hour urine potassium) (see Bingham 2002; Kant 2010; Spencer 2008 et al.; Yetley and Johnson 2011 for examples of dietary biomarkers and bioactive compounds).

When choosing an indicator, it is important for the researcher to understand how the biomarker relates to both dietary intake and the chronology of exposure. This includes whether the biomarker will be used to evaluate long-term nutritional status, recent dietary intake, effectiveness of dietary manipulation, or the efficacy of an intervention. For example, effective biomarkers for assessing program effectiveness should have (1) well-defined criteria for application at individual and population levels, (2) standardized methodologies, (3) evidence-based cutoffs to distinguish between "normal" status and varying degrees of deficiency or excess, (4) responsiveness to interventions that aim to improve status and prevent deficiency of a particular nutrient. Ultimately, the most effective biomarkers will act to guide resource allocation decisions and identify strategies for effective investment (see Raiten et al. 2011 on selection of biomarkers for program evaluation). Consideration should include the logistics of specimen collection and processing, including the type of specimen that needs to be collected for analyses (e.g., plasma, serum, bloodspots), the collection method (e.g., capillary sample, venipuncture, urine), proper storage and handling (e.g., finding out whether dilution, aliquoting, or hemolysate preparation is needed, or whether samples are sensitive to light, temperature, or oxygen). It is also important to identify whether analyses will be conducted in the field or a local laboratory, or else shipped out for analysis, and whether transportation of samples requires any special documentation or handling (Bingham 2002; Blanck et al. 2003; Jenab et al. 2009).

Nutrition Analysis

Nutrition analysis, or the process of determining the nutritional content of foods and food products, can be performed according to various certified methods (see Nollet 2004 for an overview of analytic methods). Nutritional analyses are commonly used to establish values for food labeling on menus and nutrition fact labels (IOM 2000, 2005). Program effectiveness evaluations can use nutritional analysis in conjunction with dietary intake measures to determine exact nutrient and energy composition of individual and household diets and estimate exposure to contaminants, phytochemicals, and the like. Nutritional analysis can be conducted by directly measuring food through chemical analysis in a laboratory or by comparing dietary ingredients to a database of known foods to estimate nutritional content.

Laboratory analysis, that is, chemical analysis of nutrient composition, becomes important when evaluation requires detailed information on food composition (e.g., fluctuations in nutrient composition and availability due to changes in agricultural production strategies or food processing practices). For example, aspects of cooking methods (e.g., times, temperatures) and processing (trimming meats, peeling fruits/vegetables, etc.) influence concentrations and oxidation states of food constituents such as vitamins, fatty acids, dietary fiber, starch, sugars, and cholesterol. Therefore, assays should be planned for those nutrients fundamental to the experimental hypothesis as well as nutrients known or suspected to influence outcome variables. Additional assays may be required to obtain reference points necessary for the nutrient parameters (e.g., if total fat will be calculated as a percent of total energy, total energy must be assayed in addition to total fat) (see Foote 1990; Holden 1995; and Phillips and Stewart 1999 regarding chemical analysis and laboratories specializing in nutrient analysis).

Commonly used reference databases for nutritional analyses include the USDA National Nutrient Database for Standard Reference and the Nutrition Analysis Tool (University of Illinois, Food Science and Human Nutrition Program). Also, a number of companies produce diet analysis software that allows users to calculate nutrient intake by comparing foods to proprietary databases. Online databases and desktop software can be lower-cost solutions to laboratory analyses when nutritional analysis is limited to basic calorie estimation and micronutrient analysis. It is important, however, that the researcher establish that the databases utilize nationally or internationally accepted reference standards, and know whether values are obtained from direct assays or imputed from "similar foods" or raw materials that constitute the foods (see Ahuja et al. 2013; Pennington et al. 2007; Leighton et al. 2013; Schakel, Sievert, and Buzzard 1988 regarding nutrient analysis protocols, reference standards, and food nutrient database design). Links to select databases are included in the resources section at the end of this chapter.

Turnkey nutrition analysis services, provided by a number of companies, offer inclusive nutritional analysis packages ranging from complete analysis of recipes based on ingredient lists, cooking methods, and serving sizes to full-scale data collection, storage, and analysis of population-level diet and activity data (see Falomir et al. 2012; Koenig et al. 2004).

As is the case with the other methods described in this chapter, decisions on selecting the appropriate method of nutrition analysis depend on the scale and specificity of information required. Laboratory analyses are best suited to projects that require detailed dietary monitoring, such as researching subtle changes in nutrient levels of foods, analyzing novel food sources, or studying nutrients not commonly reported on standardized food labels. Reference databases, in contrast, are more suitable for basic calculations of relative nutrient intake. Several questions should be considered when choosing a method for nutritional analysis: (1) What are the key nutrients in the study, and how much variability is expected in the levels of nutrients in foods that make up the diet? (2) Are exact nutrient levels important? (3) If differences among diets are vital, how far apart are the nutrient levels that are being studied? Finally, (4) what is the scope and quality of available food composition data for key nutrients?

Selecting a Laboratory for Biomarker or Nutritional Analysis

In addition to identifying the costs and time required for analyses, the investigator should confirm that the chosen laboratory (1) shows analytical performance sufficient to accomplish the goal of the evaluation, (2) meets acceptable precision and bias requirements, including calibration processes that are traceable to nationally or internationally accepted reference materials, (3) uses statistical quality control charts to maintain accuracy among runs, and (4) uses meticulous and reproducible sample handling procedures (e.g., precise measurement of critical volumes, avoidance of carry-over contamination). Countless national and international laboratories can conduct biomarker and nutritional analyses, but there is no central list of available services. Investigators can identify local facilities through web searches and contacts with nearby research universities and/or local cooperative extension agents (see Blanck et al. 2003; Sauberlich 1999; Petersen 1996; Phillips and Stewart 1999 for further guidelines and criteria for selecting a laboratory for specimen analysis.)

Measurement Error and Reporting

There are ways of adjusting the effects of imperfect diet measurement in dietary assessments and food frequency data (see Murray 1998; Marshall 2003; Willett 2012 for standards in statistical analyses for nutritional epidemiology). For example, a measure of effect can be adjusted if a description of the type and degree of mismeasurement is available. If it is known that dietary exposure is over-reported by a certain percentage among controls and under-reported by a different percentage among cases, it is possible to control for the association of exposure and case status in the absence of measurement error. As Marshall (2003) notes, however, this adjustment is sensitive to imprecision in the assessment of the nature and extent of the measurement error. Modest imprecision in the estimation of measurement error can lead to significant fluctuations in adjusted relative risk estimates.

In terms of biomarker data and chemical analysis, measurement error is generally classified as either preanalytical or analytical (laboratory) error. Preanalytical error includes both biological and sampling errors, whereas analytical error focuses on the laboratory environment and includes method, instrument, reagent, and/or matrix effects (see Potischman 2003; White 1997; Marshall 2003 regarding analytical error). Common sources of laboratory variability include errors in specimen collection and storage and/or errors during specimen analysis (e.g., from differences in reagents, instruments, and interfering substances). Any errors in measurement or analysis should be included in the reporting of the results to aid interpretation of findings and comparison with other studies.

Alyson Young is Assistant Professor in the Department of Anthropology at the University of Florida. She received her PhD in Anthropology from the University of Arizona in 2008. Her research focuses on stress and environmental risk, human-animal health systems, and the socioecology of maternal and child nutrition in African communities.

Meredith Marten is Assistant Professor of Anthropology at the University of West Florida. She received her MPH in International Health and Development from Tulane University in 2008 and her PhD in Anthropology from the University of Florida in 2014. Her research focuses on the sustainability of NGO-driven HIV/AIDS care and treatment programs in Tanzania. She has worked on several other research projects in medical anthropology, including a survey of stress and mental health among Inuit populations in the Canadian Arctic.

Additional Resources

Food and Agriculture Organization (FAO)
- FAO Nutrition assessment: http://www.fao.org/ag/agn/nutrition/assessment_en.stm

National Cancer Institute
- NCI Diet History Questionnaire II: http://appliedresearch.cancer.gov/dhq2/
- NCI Dietary Assessment Calibration/Validation Register: http://appliedresearch.cancer.gov/cgi-bin/dacv/index.pl

Nutritional Analysis Tool (NAT v. 3): http://www.myfoodrecord.com/

UN-World Food Program (WFP)
- List of publications and policy on nutrition evaluation: http://www.wfp.org/policy-resources

USAID Food and Nutrition Technical Assistance (FANTA)
- Dietary diversity, food access, and provisioning: http://www.fantaproject.org/monitoring-and-evaluation

U.S. Centers for Disease Control and Prevention (CDC)
- CDC Nutrition Survey Toolkit: http://www.micronutrient.org/nutritiontoolkit/

U.S. Department of Agriculture (USDA)
- Dietary Supplement Ingredient Database: http://dietarysupplementdatabase.usda.nih.gov/
- Database for the flavonoid content of selected foods: http://www.ars.usda.gov/ba/bhnrc/ndl
- Healthy Eating Index: http://www.cnpp.usda.gov/HealthyEatingIndex.htm
- Nutrient Analysis Protocols: http://www.fns.usda.gov/tn/resources/NAP2.pdf
- SuperTracker: http://www.supertracker.usda.gov/default.aspx

U.S. Food and Drug Administration (FDA)
- Food resources: http://www.fda.gov/Food/

World Health Organization (WHO)
- Nutrition resources: http://www.who.int/nutrition/en/

References

Ahuja, Jaspreet KC, Alanna J. Moshfegh, Joanne M. Holden, and Ellen Harris. 2013. USDA Food and Nutrient Databases Provide the Infrastructure for Food and Nutrition Research, Policy, and Practice. *The Journal of Nutrition* 143(2): 241S–249S.

BDWG (Biomarkers Definitions Working Group). 2001. Biomarkers and Surrogate Endpoints: Preferred Definitions and Conceptual Framework. *Clinical Pharmacology and Therapeutics* 69: 89–95.

Berti, Peter R., Julia Krasevec, and Sian FitzGerald. 2004. A Review of the Effectiveness of Agriculture Interventions in Improving Nutrition Outcomes. *Public Health Nutrition* 7(05): 599–609.

Bingham, Sheila A. 2002. Biomarkers in Nutritional Epidemiology. *Public Health Nutrition* 5 (6a): 821–827.

———. 1987. The Dietary Assessment of Individuals: Methods, Accuracy, New Techniques and Recommendations. *Nutrition Abstracts and Reviews* 57: 705–742.

Blanck, Heidi Michels, Barbara A. Bowman, Gerald R. Cooper, Gary L. Myers, and Dayton T. Miller. 2003. Laboratory Issues: Use of Nutritional Biomarkers. *The Journal of Nutrition* 133(3): 888S–894S.

Brown, Damon. 2006. Do Food Frequency Questionnaires Have Too Many Limitations? *Journal of the American Dietetic Association* 106(10): 1541–1542.

Byers, Tim. 1998. Nutrition Monitoring and Surveillance. In, *Nutritional Epidemiology*, vol. 30, ed. W. Willet. New York: Oxford University Press.

Cameron, Margaret E., and Wija A. van Staveren, eds. 1988. *Manual on Methodology for Food Consumption Studies: Oxford Medical Publications*. New York: Oxford University Press.

Falomir, Zoe, María Arregui, Francisco Madueño, Dolores Corella, and Óscar Coltell. 2012. Automation of Food Questionnaires in Medical Studies: A State-of-the-Art Review and Future Prospects. *Computers in Biology and Medicine* 42(10): 964–974.

Foote, D. 1990. Food Composition Data and Clinical Dietetics. *Food Australia-Official Journal of CAFTA and AIFST* 42: S8–S9.

Fowles, Eileen R., and Breine Gentry. 2008. The Feasibility of Personal Digital Assistants (PDAs) to Collect Dietary Intake Data in Low-Income Pregnant Women. *Journal of Nutrition Education and Behavior* 40(6): 374–377.

Freedman, Laurence S., Victor Kipnis, Arthur Schatzkin, Nataša Tasevska, and Nancy Potischman. 2010. Can We Use Biomarkers in Combination with Self-Reports to Strengthen the Analysis of Nutritional Epidemiologic Studies? *Epidemiologic Perspectives & Innovations* 7(1): 1.

Gibson, Rosalind A. 2005. *Principals of Nutritional Assessment*. 2nd ed. New York: Oxford University Press.

Gibson, Rosalind S. 2011. Strategies for Preventing Multi-micronutrient Deficiencies: A Review of Experiences with Food-based Approaches in Developing Countries. In *Combat-*

ing *Micronutrient Deficiencies: Food-based Approaches,* ed. B. Thompson and L. Amoroso. Rome: FAO and CABI.

Gunaratna, Nilupa S., Hugo De Groote, Penelope Nestel, Kevin V. Pixley, and George P. McCabe. 2010. A Meta-Analysis of Community-Based Studies on Quality Protein Maize. *Food Policy* 35(3): 202–210.

Habicht, Jean-Pierre, Gretel H. Pelto, and Julia Lapp. 2009. *Methodologies to Evaluate the Impact of Large Scale Nutrition Programs.* Doing Impact Evaluation Series. Washington, DC: World Bank.

Holden, Joanne M. 1995. Food Sampling Strategies for Energy Intake Estimates. *The American Journal Of Clinical Nutrition* 62(5): 1151S–1157S.

Illner, A. K., U. Nöthlings, K. Wagner, H. Ward, and H. Boeing. 2010. The Assessment of Individual Usual Food Intake in Large-Scale Prospective Studies. *Annals of Nutrition and Metabolism* 56: 99–105.

IOM (Institute of Medicine). 2000. *Dietary Reference Intakes: Applications in Dietary Assessments.* Washington, DC: National Academies Press.

———. 2005. *Dietary Reference Intakes for Energy, Carbohydrate, Fiber, Fat, Fatty acids, Cholesterol, Protein, and Amino Acids.* Washington, DC: National Academies Press.

Jenab, Mazda, Nadia Slimani, Magda Bictash, Pietro Ferrari, and Sheila A. Bingham. 2009. Biomarkers in Nutritional Epidemiology: Applications, Needs and New Horizons. *Human Genetics* 125(5-6): 507–525.

Johns, Timothy, and Pablo B. Eyzaguirre. 2007. Biofortification, Biodiversity and Diet: A Search for Complementary Applications Against Poverty and Malnutrition. *Food Policy* 32(1): 1–24.

Kant, Ashima K. 2010. Dietary Patterns: Biomarkers and Chronic Disease Risk. CSCN-CSNS 2009 Conference Proceedings, from "Are Dietary Patterns the Best Way to Make Nutrition Recommendations for Chronic Disease Prevention?" *Applied Physiology, Nutrition, and Metabolism* 35(2): 199–206.

Keogh, Ruth H., Ian R. White, and Shiela A. Rodwell. 2013. Using Surrogate Biomarkers to Improve Measurement Error Models in Nutritional Epidemiology. *Statistics in Medicine* 32(22): 3838–3861.

Kipnis, Victor, Douglas Midthune, Laurence Freedman, Sheila Bingham, Nicholas E. Day, Elio Riboli, Pietro Ferrari, and Raymond J. Carroll. 2002. Bias in Dietary-Report Instruments and its Implications for Nutritional Epidemiology. *Public Health Nutrition* 5(6a): 915–923.

Kirkpatrick, Sharon I., Jill Reedy, Eboneé N. Butler, Kevin W. Dodd, Amy F. Subar, Frances E. Thompson, and Robin A. McKinnon. 2014. Dietary Assessment in Food Environment Research: A Systematic Review. *American Journal of Preventive Medicine* 46(1): 94–102.

Koenig, Steven C., Cary Woolard, Guy Drew, Lauren Unger, Kevin Gillars, Dan Ewert, Laman Gray, and George Pantalos. 2004. Integrated Data Acquisition System for Medical Device Testing and Physiology Research in Compliance with Good Laboratory Practices. *Biomedical Instrumentation & Technology* 38(3): 229–240.

Leighton, Jessica, Kathleen M. Koehler, Claudine Kavanaugh, and Kasey Heintz. 2013. Nutrient Databases: Critical Tools for Policy Development. *Procedia Food Science* 2: 187–194.

Margetts, Barrie M., and Michael Nelson. 1997. *Design Concepts in Nutritional Epidemiology.* Oxford Medical Publications. 2nd ed. Oxford: Oxford University Press.

Marshall, James R. 2003. Methodologic and Statistical Considerations Regarding Use of Bio-markers of Nutritional Exposure and Status in Epidemiology. *The Journal of Nutrition* 133: 881S–887S.

Masset, Edoardo, Lawrence Haddad, Alexander Cornelius, and Jairo Isaza-Castro. 2012. Effectiveness of Agricultural Interventions that Aim to Improve Nutritional Status of Children: Systematic Review. *BMJ* 344: d8222.

McClung, Holly L., Lori D. Sigrist, Tracey J. Smith, J. Philip Karl, Jennifer C. Rood, Andrew J. Young, and Gaston P. Bathalon. 2009. Monitoring Energy Intake: A Hand-Held Personal Digital Assistant Provides Accuracy Comparable to Written Records. *Journal of the American Dietetic Association* 109 (7): 1241–1245.

McNutt, Suzanne, Thea P. Zimmerman, and Stephen G. Hull. 2008. Development of Food Composition Databases for Food Frequency Questionnaires (FFQ). *Journal of Food Composition and Analysis* 21: S20–S26.

Murray, David M. 1998. *Design and Analysis of Group-Randomized Trials.* Vol. 29. Oxford University Press, USA.

Nollet, Leo. 2004. *Handbook of Food Analysis: Physical Characterization and Nutrient Analysis.* New York: CRC Press.

Penny, Mary E., Hilary M. Creed-Kanashiro, Rebecca C. Robert, M. Rocio Narro, Laura E. Caulfield, and Robert E. Black. 2005. Effectiveness of an Educational Intervention Delivered Through the Health Services to Improve Nutrition in Young Children: A Cluster-Randomised Controlled Trial. *The Lancet* 365(9474): 1863–1872.

Pennington, Jean AT, Phyllis J. Stumbo, Suzanne P. Murphy, Suzanne W. McNutt, Alison L. Eldridge, Beverly J. McCabe-Sellers, and Catherine A. Chenard. 2007. Food Composition Data: The Foundation of Dietetic Practice and Research. *Journal of the American Dietetic Association* 107(12): 2105–2113.

Petersen, Per Hyltoft, Carmen Ricos, Dietmar Stockl, Jean Claude Libeer, Henk Baadenhui-jsen, Callum Fraser, and Linda Thienpont. 1996. Proposed Guidelines for the Internal Quality Control of Analytical Results in the Medical Laboratory. *European Journal of Clinical Chemistry and Clinical Biochemistry* 34(12): 983–1000.

Phillips, K. M., and K. K. Stewart. 1999. Validating Diet Composition by Chemical Analysis. *Well-Controlled Diet Studies in Humans: A Practical Guide to Design and Management.* Chicago, Ill.: American Dietetic Association, 336–367.

Poslusna, Kamila, Jiri Ruprich, Jeanne HM de Vries, Marie Jakubikova, and Pieter van't Veer. 2009. Misreporting of Energy and Micronutrient Intake Estimated by Food Records and 24 Hour Recalls, Control and Adjustment Methods in Practice. *British Journal of Nutrition* 101 (S2): S73–S85.

Potischman, Nancy. 2003. Biologic and Methodologic Issues for Nutritional Biomarkers. *The Journal of Nutrition* 133(3): 875S–880S.

Preedy, Victor R., Lan-Anh Hunter, and Vinood B. Patel. 2014. *Diet Quality.* Humana Press.

Raiten, Daniel J., Sorrel Namasté, Bernard Brabin, Gerald Combs, Mary R. L'Abbe, Emorn Wasantwisut, Ian Darnton-Hill. 2011. Executive Summary: Biomarkers of Nutrition for Development; Building a Consensus. *American Journal of Clinical Nutrition* 94: 633S–650S.

Rossi, Peter H., Howard E. Freeman. 1999. *Evaluation: A Systematic Approach.* 6th ed. Thousand Oaks, CA, and London: Sage.

Sahn, David E., Richard Lockwood, and Nevin S. Scrimshaw, eds. 1984. *Methods for the Evaluation of the Impact of Food and Nutrition Programmes.* Tokyo: United Nations University.

Saracci, R. 1997. Comparing measurements of biomarkers with other measurements of exposure. *IARC Scientific Publication* 142: 303–312.

Sauberlich, Howerde E. 1999. Introduction. In *Laboratory Tests for the Assessment of Nutritional Status,* ed. I. Wolinsky. 2nd ed. Boca Raton: CRC Press, 3–8.

Schakel, S.F., Y. A. Sievert, and I. M. Buzzard. 1988. Sources of Data for Developing and Maintaining a Nutrient Database. *Journal of the American Dietetic Association* 88: 1268–1271.

Spencer, Jeremy PE, Manal M. Abd El Mohsen, Ann-Marie Minihane, and John C. Mathers. 2008. Biomarkers of the Intake of Dietary Polyphenols: Strengths, Limitations and Application in Nutrition Research. *British Journal of Nutrition* 99(1): 12–22.

Swindale, Anne, and Paula Bilinsky. 2006. *Household Dietary Diversity Score (HDDS) for Measurement of Household Food Access: Indicator Guide* (v.2). Washington, DC: FHI 360/FANTA.

White, E. 1997. Effects of Biomarker Measurement Error on Epidemiological Studies. *IARC Scientific Publication* 142: 73–93.

Willett, Walter C. 2012. *Nutritional Epidemiology.* Monographs in Epidemiology and Biostatistics. 3rd ed. New York: Oxford University Press.

Yetley, Elizabeth A., and Clifford L. Johnson. 2011. Folate and Vitamin B-12 Biomarkers in NHANES: History of Their Measurement and Use. *The American Journal of Clinical Nutrition* 94 (1): 322S–331S.

CHAPTER 3

Focused Ethnographic Studies for Food and Nutrition Planning and Program Development

Gretel H. Pelto

Introduction

The long history of application of anthropological theories and methods in research activities related to public health nutrition dates back more than a century. Applied anthropological research on food and nutrition covers a wide spectrum of topics and issues. Collectively, the body of research that has been generated through applied anthropological studies on food and nutrition reflects the flexibility and diversity of anthropological sciences. They have been used to inform policy development, support the design and implementation of interventions, and evaluate programs. One of the most historically notable examples of applied nutritional anthropology is the work of the Committee on Food Habits, chaired by Margaret Mead, which was established in 1943 to provide guidance to the U.S. government during World War II. Ethnography played a central role within the broad scope of anthropological approaches in nutrition.

This chapter is devoted to a specific methodology—the Focused Ethnographic Study (FES) approach—that uses mixed methods and draws on several qualitative and quantitative techniques to address food and nutrition questions. The chapter emphasizes a specific FES: the Focused Ethnographic Study for Infant and Young Child Feeding. This is a tool developed under the auspices of the Global Alliance for Improved Nutrition, which also supported its application in several sites (see, e.g., Pelto et al. 2013).

In general, whether for nutrition or other areas of health, the goal of a FES is to obtain information on conditions and behaviors in a population that are important for decisions, including (1) identifying potential interventions; (2) planning interventions that are appropriate for local conditions; (3) identifying potential bottlenecks that are likely to affect the success of an intervention; (4) designing and developing communication strategies and content, especially for behavior change communication (BCC); (5) determining whether a proposed intervention is likely to be feasible or effective in a given environment, and/or (6) informing the design and content of program evaluations.

Characteristics of a FES Approach

What's in a Name?

We coined the label "focused ethnographic studies" in the early 1990s to emphasize three features of the methodology:

1. It is focused on a specific set of questions or issues for which data and insights are required, and which can be addressed within a relatively short period of research.
2. It is a systematic study grounded in a strong theoretical framework.
3. It preserves the strengths of ethnographic techniques for data collection and analysis.

Focus and Time Challenges

Since the inception of research efforts undertaken to bring anthropology to bear in nutrition (and other public health arenas) a critical challenge has been reducing the time it takes to conduct ethnographic studies. Classic anthropological research models of holistic, in-depth studies often require many months (sometimes a year or more), even when they are limited to the domain of food. This length for a study, no matter how valuable and insightful the results are, is almost never feasible for applied research. Apart from the financial costs of long-term research, agencies, programs, and policymakers are not in a position to wait around for anthropologists to conduct a holistic study. Moreover, they rarely see the value of a broad, holistic overview when they need answers to specific questions. On the other hand, anthropologists often feel that policy and program professionals frame questions too narrowly and therefore miss critically important information and insights that are fundamental to effective decisions. Thus, designing an ethnography study faces two related challenges:

1. Defining the questions with sufficient breadth and clarity to cover the most important topics; and
2. Conducting the research efficiently and in a timely fashion, without losing the strengths of holistic ethnography.

How does one narrow the vast arena of potentially important food-related issues in a sociocultural investigation to something that is manageable? In setting up their studies in the early 1940s, Mead and her colleagues in the Committee on Food Habits addressed this challenge by identifying specific areas for investigation. They articulated the need for a "standardized form of study of diet patterns in terms of their physiological, sensory, chemical, nutritional and cultural characters" (Mead 1943). From the perspective of the second decade of the twenty-first century, these categories are dauntingly massive and broad, but the basic intent is clear. The goal was to narrow the research to a manageable set of topics.

A full discussion about the challenge of "question definition" is beyond the scope of this chapter. It involves negotiation with the people with whom and for whom the study is conducted. It requires flexibility to modify, expand, and contract questions, both during planning and during the conduct of the study. It also requires examination and re-examination of the theoretical underpinnings of the study, including modifications that need to be considered in relation to emerging insights from data as the research progresses.

For a program that is already defined, the questions addressed by a FES may fall under the rubric of "formative research." In this case the delivery platform is already decided, the policy is well defined, and the delivery structure is essentially in place. Information needs include data to support message development, materials and aide-memoire, and frontline worker training. These information needs are associated with behavior change communication (BCC). When the intervention is broadened to include other types of social interventions, the goal is to support "social and behavioral communication (SBCC). It should be noted that FES is not synonymous with formative research, and that other research methodologies also need to be utilized during the period of formative research when the program is being developed.

The decades since the 1940s have witnessed continuing efforts, particularly by anthropologists, to develop ethnographic research approaches that are compatible with the time and other constraints imposed in most situations in which ethnographic research is sought. Pertti J. Pelto has recently reviewed these in his book on applied ethnography in a chapter titled "Qualitative Research Guidelines: RAP, PRA, RRA, FES and Others" (Pelto 2013).

We do not use the word rapid in the title of a "focused ethnographic study," although speed is, de facto, an important characteristic of research undertaken for program planning and policy development. We were concerned to avoid equating the approach with the connotations of another phrase in common usage—the idea of "quick and dirty" research.

The importance of a manual to guide an FES study

To support the conduct of the research in a systematic and timely fashion, Mead's Committee on Food Habits created the *Manual for the Study of Food Habits*

(1945), an important feature of their work. The *Manual* helped with the time challenge by establishing a basic methodology for data collection and analysis so investigators did not have to start from scratch each time a study was undertaken in a new location or on a different social group. Equally important, it provided a template to direct investigators' attention to the features of the "dietary patterns" the Committee felt were essential to understand. Thirdly, it facilitated a reporting structure that could be used to derive interpretations and policy recommendations. Finally, another benefit of creating the *Manual* was that it made it possible to compare results across studies.

In the ensuing decades, manuals have become a common feature of instruments that are designed to bring anthropological perspectives to bear in intervention-related research. The creation of a manual for the focused ethnographic study of infant and young child feeding is an example. In addition to providing specific and detailed guidance about data collection, analysis, and preparation of the report, it also provides an opportunity to discuss the theoretical underpinnings of the study, including the rationale for the methods.

Theoretical Grounding

The dictionary definition of ethnography as "the scientific description of the customs of individual peoples and cultures" (New Oxford American Dictionary) and the Encyclopedia Britannica definition, "descriptive study of a particular human society or the process of making such a study," reflect the difficulty of characterizing the types of research that are included under the rubric "ethnography." Nowadays ethnography is employed in many disciplines—sociology, psychology, education, anthropology, and so on—and is used to study many different things besides "customs" or a "human society." Many if not most scientists and applied investigators regard ethnography as fundamentally a methodological approach. Historically, however, ethnography was situated in anthropology and reflected a set of theoretical propositions about how societies work. "Focused ethnographic studies," for their part, are explicitly embedded in and designed from an explicit theoretical framework. Together with program-generated questions, the theoretical framework is part of the foundation on which decisions about a focus are made.

Combining emic and etic perspectives

The concepts of "emic" and "etic" are central to ethnographic studies, whether the research is directed to description or hypothesis testing. The term emic, which is derived from the linguistic concept of "phonemic" or culturally meaningful units of language, refers to the insider's perspective, reflecting the implicit and explicit knowledge frameworks of the people who are being studied. In contrast, etic, derived from the word "phonetic," refers to concepts that are defined by the observer and come from the implicit and explicit knowledge frameworks of the investigators. Ethnographers seek to discover and describe emic concepts, particularly as they are coded in words and connotations in the local language (labels, names, phrases.) At the same time, they also have to employ etic concepts, not least because these are crucial for "translating" emic insights and interpretations into knowledge that can be shared and utilized by those who are not members of the culture. Unfortunately, scientists who are attempting to study behaviors and beliefs often fail to recognize the danger of imposing their own concepts and therefore may structure questions in a fashion that implies a particular definition or interpretation that is not that of the respondent. The consequent answers are distortions of the cognitive or cultural reality that the investigators are trying to study and understand. Cultural domain analysis (see below) is one of the techniques that can be used to reduce this danger.

Etic categories and perspectives are also clearly essential for studies addressed to identifying and finding solutions to health and nutrition problems. Nutritional investigations must be able to assess, for example, whether there are specific problems in reported dietary practices and behaviors. However, in naming the approach discussed here (i.e., focused ethnographic study) the terms "assessment" or "appraisal" were not used—even though this is a significant goal or purpose of these investigative endeavors—due to a wish to preserve an emphasis on the dual characteristics of the methodology, which involves examining both emic and etic perspectives within the scope of the study. The researchers' sense was that the concepts of assessment and appraisal typically evoke or connote etic constructs, whereas ethnography encompasses attention to both emic and etic elements.

The word "study" was included in the title to emphasize that this is a research activity, even at the risk of its being labeled an academic exercise. In nutrition and public health, evidence-gathering activities related to biological conditions are seen as scientific endeavors that give the results an imprimatur of authority, whereas the results of parallel efforts on social parameters are often dismissed as "common sense" or confirming "the obvious." The word study also implies a theoretical framework, even when it does not involve an emphasis on testing a predetermined hypothesis.

Pelto (2013) also emphasizes the scientific validity of research conducted with the aid of tools and guidelines. In the conclusion of his chapter on "Qualitative Research Guidelines," he writes:

> The research results based on guidelines are not weaker in validity, reliability or overall credibility than the products of more academic, expanded research. Rather the projects of the various RAP, PRA, RRA and FES styles of research are simply more focused in specific areas—for example, descriptions of local conditions and environments—and less concerned about generalizability and contribution to general theory. (Ibid.: 279)

Methodology: Preserving the Strengths of Ethnographic Techniques

A focused ethnographic study is a mixed-methods approach, in which techniques are drawn from multiple disciplines and reflect different disciplinary approaches. It applies both "qualitative" and "quantitative" approaches to data collection and analysis. Applied, program-oriented research commonly distinguishes between "survey research" and "ethnography." (See discussion below.) As a descriptor of a research style, "ethnography" has come to be synonymous with qualitative research. However, small-scale survey research has historically been part of ethnographic research (Bennett and Thais 1967), and ethnographic research techniques are not limited to the collection of data that can only be analyzed with qualitative methods. As Strauss (1987) observed in his influential book *Qualitative Analysis for Social Scientists*, the distinction between qualitative and quantitative approaches lies in "how data are treated analytically," rather than in the types of data that are amassed to examine an issue.

Methodologically, the FES relies heavily on interviewing respondents with "guiding questions" intended to initiate a dialogue on issues and areas of concern, which are captured orally as narrative. Thematic analysis, a qualitative analysis technique, is used to analyze the "text" created by the narratives. Additionally, the approach also uses standard dietary intake procedures, and demographic and socioeconomic information is collected via several types of questioning procedures employed in many social science disciplines.

The FES approach draws significantly on cognitive mapping techniques. The basic techniques of cultural domain analysis were described by Weller and Romney (1988), and the use of formal ethnographic methods, including cognitive mapping techniques and their use in ethnographic research, was explicated by Pelto and Pelto (1976) and Bernard (2011). Applied anthropologists have made extensive use of cognitive mapping techniques as a methodological approach that facilitates the application of ethnographic techniques in rapid assessment/formative research (Gittelsohn et al. 1998; Schensul and LeCompte 2013. Two recent methodological discussions in applied ethnography (Borgatti and Halgin 2012; Pelto 2013) have outlined their utility and presented guidance on their execution. These types of data collection techniques include free listing, pile sorting, rating, and ranking. In addition to cognitive mapping or cultural domain analysis, the FES methodology may include social mapping (e.g., to identify sources of food acquisition). FES studies have also employed structured observations and structured visual assessments in clinical settings, or observation using videos (Blum et al. 1997).

Shifting from data collection techniques to the structure of a FES, an important feature of the approach is its modular construction. Organizing data collection into short modules, each directed at a specific issue (e.g., beliefs about disease etiology, sources of medical care, dietary intake during illness), adds greatly to the flexibility of the tool, making it possible to modify the number of respondents for any given issue, to modify the flow of interviews and to easily add, subtract, or modify specific focal issues so that data collection can be fine-tuned to differences within a population and across populations, as well as different intervention purposes.

Another essential feature of the FES methodology is that the field research is typically conducted in phases. Phase 1 uses classical anthropological interviewing of key informants and community observations, including mapping of key locations (e.g., health centers, food stores, drugstores. The results from Phase 1 are analyzed and used to fine-tune the data-collection modules for Phase 2. Phase 2, which is conducted with a small representative sample that is designed to confirm and expand the provisional picture that has emerged from the key informants, consists of in-depth interviews using a variety of methods to obtain data. The data are then subjected to qualitative and quantitative analysis. Usually the study is designed to be conducted by trained investigators in a period of 10–16 weeks.

Differences between FES and survey research

FES differs from survey research in several ways. Survey research often uses only one mode of data collection, that is, a verbal or written exchange in which questions are presented to a respondent, who is asked to answer with a minimum number of words—frequently yes or no, or agree or disagree (or a somewhat more nuanced option of three or five gradations)—or by supplying specific data in the form of a number, a time, or a sentence. Variations on the approach may include asking respondents to choose from a set of options that are read out or visually presented. A classic survey is pre-coded; either respondents select the pre-code themselves or the interviewers make the coding decisions during the interview. Exceptionally, the investigators use open-ended questions and the coding takes place after the interview.

In contrast, as discussed above, FES studies use a mix of data collection and analysis techniques ranging from survey-type questions to guided questions designed to produce "narrative" as a more extended response that is orally captured and provides the material for text analysis. In survey research the investigators pre-code questionnaires that are based on a set of assumptions about how people will answer. Ethnographic methods attempt to reveal realities from an emic or insider's perspective. Ethnographic techniques also permit the discovery of conditions, values, and behaviors that the investigators did not foresee.

Another difference between a survey and an FES is that the former usually involves large sample sizes because the investigators want to describe the distribution of characteristics (e.g., mean and standard deviation or quartiles) within a population. In ethnography the goal is to describe the typical or usual behaviors, conditions, values, and beliefs in the population. In many situations, decisions need not rely on the statistical precision of a large survey. The FES is based on small samples that are intensively interviewed, and participants' representativeness is assessed beforehand through careful sampling and then through "saturation"—the technical term for the situation in which no new information or insights are obtained with further interviews. (Given 2008). In qualitative research, saturation is often achieved with samples of 30–35 respondents.

FES in Action

The First FES Instrument: A FES for Acute Respiratory Infections

The first formally named focused ethnographic study tool to address defined program needs was developed at the World Health Organization (WHO) for the Programme for the Control of Acute Respiratory Infections (ARI Programme) (Gove and Pelto 1993; Hudelson 1994). Based on a large body of clinical and epidemiological research, the ARI Programme had already created generic recommendations for health-service procedures and household management of ARI. These guidelines included patient assessment procedures, treatment guidelines, and generic messages to use in communicating with families about how to manage ARI illness. The goal was to institute these guidelines worldwide, and many types of materials—training manuals, training courses, treatment charts and patient counseling materials—were needed to achieve the goal of reducing mortality from ARI, the number one killer of children at the time the WHO program was established. The program's leadership recognized that to achieve its goals, it was essential to adapt the guidelines to meet local conditions. The FES was the vehicle for meeting that implementation challenge.

The FES study for the ARI Programme was designed to cover the following issues:

1. Peoples' beliefs about ARI in children, including their causes and treatments;
2. Identification of the factors that facilitate or constrain the seeking of treatment;
3. Description of household management of children with ARI;
4. Identification of caregivers' expectations about treatment;
5. Identification of other cultural characteristics and conditions likely to influence household responses to accessing the ARI Programme and accepting the recommendations; and
6. Identification of the language that caregivers use to refer to ARI signs, symptoms, and illnesses, as well as treatments. (Adapted from Gove and Pelto 1993: 411)

The WHO FES for ARI was translated into French and Spanish and applied in more than twenty-five countries. After the development of the ARI FES, a study manual was also created for the WHO Diarrheal Disease Control program. It too was translated into French and Spanish and applied in a number of countries. However, in the mid-1990s, driven by donor policies, the emphasis in child health programs began to shift from so-called "vertical" (disease-specific) programs to "integrated management of childhood illness." Consequently applied research on specific childhood infectious diseases was no longer part of the WHO strategy to support national programs' efforts to adapt generic management guidelines for individual country uses.

A FES Directed to a Nutrition Problem

The first effort to create a FES for a nutrition issue was undertaken by the International Union of Nutritional Sciences, Committee II-6, Nutrition and Anthropology. With the support of the United Nations University, the committee developed a manual to study Vitamin A and identify and support potential food-based approaches to address vitamin A deficiency (Blum et al. 1997). The fundamental purpose was to "provide essential information for program planning aimed at increasing consumption of vitamin A–rich food among populations at risk for deficiency" (ibid.: 3). Like the focused ethnographic studies for acute respiratory infection and diarrheal disease control, the manual was addressed to a set of predefined goals, namely:

1. Identify significant sources of preformed vitamin A and carotene-rich food in the context of the local food system;
2. Describe patterns of food consumption, especially for vitamin A–containing food, particularly with respect to infants, young children, and women of reproductive age;
3. Identify cultural beliefs that influence food choice and consumption patterns;
4. Identify cultural, ecological, and socioeconomic factors that constrain or facilitate consumption of vitamin A; and
5. Describe the community explanations and understandings of vitamin A–deficiency diseases and symptoms.

With UNU support, the manual was applied in six countries. The results were published as a monograph by the International Nutrition Foundation (Kuhnlein and Pelto 1997). This tool is in the public domain and is available online in Google Books. The vitamin A FES served as a starting point for a study in Nepal (Dickerson et al. 2008) in which the focus of interest included other micronutrients in addition to vitamin A.

FES for Infant and Young Child Feeding

The GAIN-supported FES was initially developed to address a specific, non-programmatic, narrowly defined question: whether a fortified, but not instant, cereal would be an appropriate intervention in urban Ghana (Pelto and Armar-Klemesu, 2011). The study concluded that unless the new product was an instant cereal it would be unacceptable to families and uncompetitive with alternatives already available in the environment. Between 2009 and 2013, modifications were developed to expand the potential to examine other questions. For example, a study in five locations in Afghanistan was an exploratory effort to identify potential new interventions; in South Africa, rural and urban sites were studied to identify the potential for home fortification interventions (Pelto et al. 2013). In Kenya, the focus was explicitly on agriculture-related interventions, but the research also identified other potential interventions to address the multiple issues affecting nutrition that caregivers contend with in feeding infants and young children (Hotz, C. et al. 2015). In this research the ethnography was complemented with another innovative research approach (Ferguson et al. 2006), which was developed to assess the potential of any local dietary system to meet the nutritional needs of specific categories of the population (http://www.fantaproject .org/tools/optifood). Further FES studies have been undertaken in Ethiopia and Bangladesh, each designed to address specific program planning and development challenges.

The theoretical underpinning of the FES for Infant and Young Child Feeding derives from cultural-ecological theory. The basic model for nutrition, first described by Jerome, Pelto, and Kandel (1980), was refined for the FES (see Figure 3.1). As described in the FES manual (Pelto et al. 2014), the cultural-ecological model on which the FES is based contains five components, each of which encompasses multiple factors. There is strong empirical evidence to support each component's role in affecting nutritional status in populations. This evidence comes from nutritional epidemiology, program evaluations, and program experiences. For example, the component labeled "social organization" includes, at the household level, such fundamental aspects as household income; household expenditures for food, housing, clothing, and other necessities; the earning potential of household members; and household living conditions. It also includes socio-demographic features (e.g., household size and composition) and the health status and educational attainment of household members. From the perspective of infant and young child (IYC) feeding, another critical aspect of social organization concerns how the household is organized to care for its dependent members. This includes the allocation of responsibilities for child care in relation to allocation of time to other activities, including food acquisition. Thus, many of the important determinants of IYC feeding are contained within this one component.

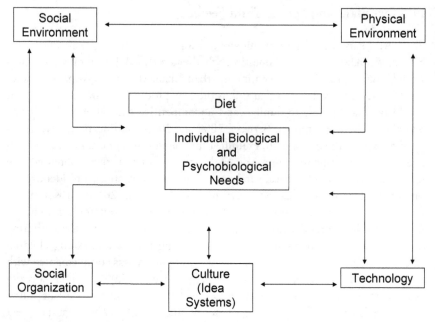

Figure 3.1. An Ecological Model of Food and Nutrition
Source: Redrawn with modifications from Jerome et al. (1980).

Proceeding to the component "technology," factors affecting IYC nutrition cover the range of tools, techniques, and equipment involved in the production, distribution, preparation, and consumption of food, including the presence of refrigeration and other storage facilities, the quality of water available to the household, the ease or difficulty of preparing heated foods, the ease or difficulty of maintaining a sanitary environment, and so on.

At the household level, the "culture" component encompasses all the ideas—knowledge, beliefs, values, perceptions, and motivations—that affect and relate to the acquisition, preparation, and consumption of food. Special emphasis should be placed on mothers. However, it is important to remember that when it comes to IYC feeding and care, the mother is almost never the only player, as grandmothers, fathers, and other household members are also involved in direct childcare. Moreover, the cultural knowledge, beliefs, and perceptions of fathers, grandparents, other children, and other relatives inside and outside the household are often influential in IYC feeding.

The last two components of the general theoretical model—"physical environment" and "social environment"—concern the sources from which households acquire foods and other resources that affect nutrition. In urban areas most food is acquired in the social environment, where various types of markets, stores, street vendors, and restaurants offer foods and food supplies for purchase. In rural areas, where many households grow at least part of their own food, some aspects of food acquisition depend on characteristics of the physical environment such as climate, water resources, soil characteristics, transportation networks, and other features that establish the conditions for food production. However, even in rural areas the social environment is important in food acquisition. The relative importance of the physical and social environments are matters of degree, which illustrates a basic feature of the model, namely that all the components affect IYC feeding in all societies, though their relative importance may vary. Also, all the components of the model are interrelated.

The cultural-ecological model provides the general theoretical framework. Theories and research drawn from nutritional epidemiology and the expanding body of empirical research on the factors that are associated with nutritional status and feeding behavior provide more specific guidance about what to study. However, even in a long-term ethnographic study, it would be very difficult to include all of the factors in each of the components that have been shown to affect infant and young child feeding. Consequently, every application of the tool needs to begin with a reexamination of the potential factors in order to select those likely to be most important in relation to the questions the study is directed to. As described in the next section, the modular structure of the tool and the ease with which questions and procedures can be modified and new modules added (or deleted) is a central feature of the FES as a tool for applied research.

Structure of the FES for Infant and Young Child Feeding

The original version of the FES on infants and young children (Pelto et al. 2014)—*Focused Ethnographic Study of Infant and Young Child Feeding 6–23 Months: Behaviors, Beliefs, Contexts and Environments: Manual on Conducting the Study, Analyzing the Results and Writing the Report* (http://www.gainhealth .org)—contains four protocols. There are two protocols for household behaviors (one for key informants and one for caregiver-respondents) and two protocols for obtaining data on local marketing conditions.

For household behaviors, the Phase I protocol for interviewing key informants consists of seven modules exploring (1) foods for IYC, (2) food preparation and feeding practices, (3) sources of food acquisition and food expenditures, (4) types of caregiving challenges faced by parents of IYC, (5) food and nutrition-specific problems of IYC, (6) health and food perceptions, and (7) perceptions about micronutrient supplements and fortification of infant foods.

For Phase II, examination of household behaviors, the basic structure of interviewers with caregiver-respondents contains eight modules applied to interview caregivers of a child between 6 and 24 months of age. These modules are designed to provide data and insights about a range of issues, including: (1) demographic and socio-economic characteristics, (2) a 24-hour recall for the index child, (3) food preparation and feeding behavior, (4) perceptions about cultural dimensions related to health and food; (5) perceptions about factors that influence IYC feeding, (6) perceptions about micronutrient supplements and fortification of infant foods, (7) estimated weekly food expenditure, and (8) food and feeding-related problems, challenges, and solutions.

The sample design requires filling caregiver-respondent categories based on subgroups of the 6–24-month age range, as well as ensuring that there is a range of socioeconomic subgroups within the larger category of poor and disadvantaged families.

Of the two protocols directed to an examination of local marketing characteristics, one is used with formal economic-sector entrepreneurs, and the other is directed to informal economic–sector sellers (e.g., street vendors or people who sell from their home). In these protocols different modules are used to obtain data on inventory, selling strategies, sources of products, and questions that are aimed at understanding sellers' views about their motivations and plans, and their perceptions about the population in which they operate.

In addition to the four core protocols, additional protocols have been developed to meet context-specific needs. For example, in urban communities it is important to examine how IYC are fed in daycare centers and crèches. In rural populations, particularly among families who are engaged in agriculture, a module on the effects of seasonality and seasonally related food insecurity is essential. New modules are currently being developed and applied to understand how families respond to and use new techniques for home fortification to address nutritional deficiencies.

Using the FES on IYC Feeding in Various Research Contexts

The FES is intended to be a flexible tool that can be utilized together with other types of research, depending on the contexts and purposes for which the study is undertaken. In virtually all circumstances, a descriptive study alone is insufficient to meet the information needs for planning and implementing a nutrition intervention. Here are some examples of the types of other studies with which FES research can be combined:

1. When it is important to document nutritional status in a population and describe the proportions who are at risk of sub-optimal outcomes (e.g., stunting, obesity, micronutrient deficiencies), nutritional surveys are essential.

2. When it is important to assess whether the local food system *could* meet nutritional needs in the population if everyone was in a position to make adequate use of current resources, the innovative Optifoods analysis tool is invaluable.

3. When a potential nutrition intervention has already been tested for biological efficacy, and a policy decision has been made to introduce it in a population, the next steps, after or concurrent with an FES study, could involve a number of different research activities, depending on the nature of the intervention. These activities may include:

   i. Research to determine the best methods for adapting the new behaviors and new products to local cultural and social conditions, for which the TIPS methodology is particularly strong (Dickin, Griffiths, and Piwoz 1997; for examples of its application see also Dickin and Seim 2015; Paul et al. 2008).

   ii. Research to determine the acceptability of a new product from an organoleptic perspective.

   iii. Research to identify the most appropriate program platforms for implementing a delivery program, which are an essential part of developing the program theory (Roberfroid et al. 2007) that provides a basis for establishing an explicit program impact pathway (Kim et al. 2011; Neufeld et al. 2013).

   iv. Research to test and refine messages intended to support behavior change interventions to improve nutrition..

   v. Market research to determine best approaches to promoting new interventions through private-sector initiatives.

The examples listed above are illustrative and not intended as a definitive inventory of how FES studies could be used in combination with other research activities to improve nutrition in geographically or socially defined populations. Focused ethnography can also be conducted as a stand-alone effort for purposes of exploratory research to describe a situation and identify potential interventions, or to inform decision makers about the appropriateness or feasibility of a contemplated intervention.

Gretel Pelto is a Graduate Professor in the Division of Nutritional Sciences at Cornell University in Ithaca, New York. She received her BA in sociology and MA and PhD in anthropology from the University of Minnesota. She is internationally recognized for her work on bridging the interface between academic research and actions to improve nutrition and public health in communities. The interaction between theory and practice brings social science methods, particularly those of ethnography, to bear on nutrition and child health research, with an emphasis on infant and young child nutrition. She has written and edited four books on the field, as well as numerous articles on theoretical and empirical issues, often addressed to the academic nutrition community. In 2007 she received the Malinowski Award from the Society for Applied Anthropology, which is given "to an outstanding social scientist in recognition of efforts to understand and serve the needs of the world's societies and who has actively pursued the goal of solving human problems using the concepts and tools of social science." She was a founding editor of the journals *Medical Anthropology* and *Reviews in Anthropology*, which were established to further the quality of published academic anthropological research. To provide a forum for nutritional anthropology she worked with colleagues within the Society for Medical Anthropology to establish a group that is now an independent organization (The Society for Food and Nutrition) operating under the umbrella of the American Anthropological Association. She currently serves on the editorial board of several nutrition and health journals.

Online Resources

Vitamin A Manual:
 http://books.google.com/books?id=1V8vCL19PMkC&printsec=frontcover&dq=
 Community+Assessment+of+Natural+Food+Sources+of+Vitamin+A+-+Guidelines+-
 for+a+Ethnographic+Protocol
Optifoods Manual:
 http://www.fantaproject.org/tools/optifood
FES Manual and protocols:
 http://www.gainhealth.org/
 http://www.hftag.org/resource-search/page/2/?search_query=FES&wpas=1

References

Bernard, H. Russell. 2011. *Research Methods In Anthropology: Qualitative And Quantitative Approaches.* 5th ed. Latham, MD: Altamira Press.

Bennett, John W and Gerald Thais. 1967. Survey Research and Sociocultural Anthropology. In *Survey Research in the Social Sciences,* ed. CY Glock, 269–314. New York: Russell Sage Foundation.

Blum Lauren, Perrti J. Pelto, Gretel H Pelto, and Harriet V. Kuhnlein. 1997. *Community Assessment of Natural Food Sources of Vitamin A: Guidelines for an Ethnographic Protocol.* Boston: International Nutrition Foundation for Developing Countries.

Borgatti, Stephen P, and Douglas S. Halgin. 2012. Elicitation Techniques For Cultural Domain Analysis. In *Specialized Ethnographic Methods: A Mixed Methods Approach,* ed. Jean J. Schensul and Margaret D. LeCompte, pp: 80–116. Lanham, MD: Altamira Press.

Committee on Food Habits. 1945. *Manual for the Study of Food Habits.* Washington, DC: National Research Council, National Academy of Sciences.

Dickin, Katherine L, Marcia Griffiths, and Ellen Piwoz. 1997. *Designing By Dialogue: A Program Planners' Guide To Consultative Research For Improving Young Child Feeding.* Washington, DC: Academy for Educational Development.

Dickin, Katherine L. and Gretchen Seim. 2015. Adapting The Trials Of Improved Practices (Tips) Approach To Explore The Acceptability And Feasibility Of Nutrition And Parenting Recommendations: What Works For Low-Income Families?. *Maternal & Child Nutrition* 11.4: 897–914.

Dickerson T, Fernandez D., Topgyal, Samen, A., Gelek, Nyima, Pelto G, Craig S. and Dye T. 2008. From Butter Tea To Pepsi®: A Rapid Appraisal Of Food Preferences, Procurement Sources And Dietary Diversity In A Contemporary Tibetan Township. *Ecology of Food and Nutrition* 47(3): 229–253.

Ferguson, Elaine L., Nicole Darmon, Umi Fahmida, Suci Fitriyanti, Timothy B. Harper, and Inguruwatte M. Premachandra. Design of optimal food-based complementary feeding recommendations and identification of key "problem nutrients" using goal programming. *The Journal of Nutrition* 136, no. 9 (2006): 2399–2404.

Gittelsohn Joel, Pertti J. Pelto, Margaret E. Bentley, K Bhattacharyya and J.L Jensen JL. 1998. *Rapid Assessment Procedures (RAP): Ethnographic Methods to Investigate Women's Health.* Boston: International Nutrition Foundation.

Given, Lisa M., ed. 2008. *The Sage Encyclopedia of Qualitative Research Methods.* Thousand Oaks, CA: Sage.

Gove, Sandy and Gretel H. Pelto. 1993. Focused Ethnographic Studies In The WHO Programme For The Control Of Acute Respiratory Infections. *Medical Anthropology,* 15(4), 409–424.

Hotz, Christine, Gretel H. Pelto, G., Margaret Armar-Klemesu, Elaine F. Ferguson, Peter Chege, and Enock Musinguzi (2015) Constraints And Opportunities For Implementing Nutrition-Specific, Agricultural And Market-Based Approaches To Improve Nutrient Intake Adequacy Among Infants And Young Children In Two Regions Of Rural Kenya. *Maternal & Child Nutrition,* 11(S3), 39–54.

Hudelson, Patricia M. 1994. The Management of Acute Respiratory Infections in Honduras. *Medical Anthropology* 15(4): 435–446.

Jerome, Norge W., Gretel H. Pelto, and Randy F. Kandel. 1980. An Ecological Approach To Nutritional Anthropology. In Norge W. Jerome, Randy F. Kandel and Gretel H. Pelto, eds *Nutritional Anthropology: Contemporary Approaches to Diet and Culture,* 13–45. Pleasantville, NY: Redgrave.

Kim, Sunny, Jean-Pierre Habicht, Purnima Menon, and Rebecca J. Stoltzfus. 2011. *How Do Programs Work To Improve Child Nutrition? Program Impact Pathways Of Three Nongovernmental Organization Intervention Projects In The Peruvian Highlands.* Washington, DC: International Food Policy Research Institute.

Kuhnlein, Harriet V. and Gretel H. Pelto. 1997. *Culture, Environment, and Food to Prevent Vitamin A Deficiency.* Boston: International Nutrition Foundation for Developing Countries (INFDC).

Mead, Margaret. 1943. The Committee On Food Habits. *Psychological Bulletin* 40(4): 290–293.

Neufeld, Lynnette M., Jalal Chowdary, Juan-Pablo Peña-Rosas, David Tovey, Chessa K. Lutter, Rebecca J. Stoltzfus, and Jean-Pierre Habicht. 2013. The WHO Evidence-Informed Guideline Development Process and Implications for Vitamin and Mineral Research Priorities: Symposium Rationale And Summary. *Advances in Nutrition: An International Review Journal* 4(5): 557–559.

Paul, Keriann H., Katherine L. Dickin, Nadra S. Ali, Eva C. Monterrosa, and Rebecca J. Stoltzfus. 2008. Soy-and rice-based processed complementary food increases nutrient intakes in infants and is equally acceptable with or without added milk powder. *The Journal of Nutrition* 138, 10 (2008): 1963–1968.

Pelto Gretel H., and Margaret Armar-Klemesu. 2011. Balancing Nurturance, Cost and Time: Complementary Feeding in Accra, Ghana. *Maternal and Child Nutrition* 7 (Suppl. s3): 66–81.

Pelto, Gretel H., Margaret Armar Klemesu, and Faith M. Thuita. 2014. Focused Ethnographic Study Of Infant And Young Child Feeding 6–23 Months: Behaviors, Beliefs, Contexts And Environments. Manual On Conducting The Study, Analyzing The Results And Writing The Report. www.hftag.org/assets/downloads/hftag/1.%20FES%20Manual%20 v1%20Feb%202014.pdf. Accessed 13 November 2016

Pelto, Gretel H., Margaret Armar-Klemesu, Jonathan Siekmann, and Dominic Schofield. The Focused Ethnographic Study 'Assessing The Behavioral And Local Market Environment for Improving The Diets Of Infants and Young Children 6 To 23 Months Old'and Its Use in Three Countries. *Maternal & Child Nutrition* 9, no. S1 (2013): 35–46.

Pelto, Gretel H. and Sandy Gove. 1992. Developing A Focused Ethnographic Study For The WHO Acute Respiratory Infection Control Programme. In *Rapid Assessment Procedures: Qualitative Methodologies for Planning and Evaluation of Health Related Programmes*, ed. N. S. Scrimshaw and G. R. Gleason, 215–226. Boston, MA: International Nutrition Foundation for Developing Countries.

Pelto, Pertti J. 2013. *Applied Ethnography: Guidelines for Field Research*. Walnut Creek, CA: Left Coast Press.

Pelto, Pertti J. and Gretel H. Pelto. 1976. *Anthropological Research: The Structure of Inquiry.* New York: Cambridge University Press.

Roberfroid, Dominique, Gretel H. Pelto and Patrick Kolstern. 2007. Plot and See! : Maternal Comprehension Of Growth Charts Worldwide. *Tropical Medicine and International Health* 12: 1074–1086.

Schensul, Jean J. and Margaret D. LeCompte, eds. 2013. *Specialized Ethnographic Methods: A Mixed Methods Approach.* Ethnographer's Toolkit 4. Lanham, MD: Altamira Press.

Strauss Anselm L. 1987. *Qualitative Analysis for Social Scientists.* New York: Cambridge University Press.

Weller, Sue C. and A. Kimball Romney. 1988. *Systematic Data Collection.* Newbury Park, CA: Sage.

CHAPTER 4

Methods for Community Health Involvement

David A. Himmelgreen, Sara Arias-Steele,
and Nancy Romero-Daza

Introduction

In both anthropology and public health, there is growing recognition of the importance of community participation and local knowledge in the development, implementation, and evaluation of health promotion and disease prevention programs, including nutrition education and nutritional interventions. Different terms are used to describe the setting and the degree to which community members are involved in the research endeavor. These terms include community-based research, community action research, participatory action research, and participatory rural appraisal. Unlike traditional research, where the researcher comes up with the research questions, defines the population to study, and carries out the data collection, analysis, and interpretation, community participatory research projects adopt a bottom-up approach that actively involves community participants in the research process. Here, community members become part of the research team, and in doing so are engaged and empowered to identify the problem(s), develop the research plan, assist in data collection and analysis, and use the results to find solutions that are relevant and more likely to be adopted by the larger community. There is evidence that the use of community participatory research increases the likelihood of development plans that are successful and sustainable (Goh et al. 2009; World Bank 2012c).

Community Action Research and Community-Based Research

Community action research (CAR) is defined as an alternative research method that uses the community as the unit of analysis. This approach forges research alliances with relevant stakeholders in the community to explore and develop solutions to local problems, but does not always require community participation throughout all stages of the research process (Ozanne and Anderson 2010). In contrast, community-based research (CBR) is defined as a collaborative approach that involves all partners in the research process (community members, key informants, and experts) so that investigators work side-by-side with local residents to define questions, methods, and routes of information dissemination (allowing for inclusion of community members on the research team and researchers' engagement in the community) (Israel et al. 2005). In this chapter, community-based research is used as an umbrella term that also covers community-based participatory research (CBPR), with its emphasis on equitable participation of all parties in decision making (Minkler and Wallerstein 2003). It should be noted however, that earlier iterations of CBR were more loosely defined and emphasized the locale of research (in local communities) without necessarily involving full participation of community stakeholders (e.g., key informants, local residents, community organizations). Today, because CBR involves collaboration between researchers and local community members, a set of principles has been developed to guide this approach and minimize the shifting powers of knowledge between the two groups in order to maintain a collaborative balance. According to Israel and colleagues (2005: 7–9), CBR approaches are based on the following central tenets:

1. Recognition of the community as the unit of identity;
2. Building on the community's strengths and resources;
3. Facilitation of collaborative partnerships throughout the research process;
4. Integration of knowledge and action for the benefit of all partners;
5. Promotion of co-learning and empowerment that attends to social inequalities;
6. Adoption of an iterative process;
7. Addressing of health (issues) from both positive (physical, social, and mental well-being) and ecological (family, social network, community, society) perspectives;
8. Dissemination of findings and knowledge gained to all partners.

Participatory Action Research and Participatory Rural Appraisal

Participatory action research (PAR) employs a range of methods to be used principally in the gathering of qualitative data (Davis 2001). Like CAR and CBR, the methodology of data collection privileges local knowledge and participant observation while still maintaining a solid theoretical foundation that informs action. The use of research methods, including interviews, surveys, focus groups, and asset mapping groups, is ideally guided by the local community, thereby increasing self-reliance, empowerment, and the development of more effective strategies for addressing problems at the local level. In addition, PAR can potentially include semi-quantitative and quantitative methods, for example, nutritional assessment (e.g., anthropometry, dietary intake, biochemical indicators, and clinical observations). While community members can guide this process, external parties such as NGOs, university researchers, and consultants can provide their expertise to carry out the research and disseminate the findings, and to develop and evaluate programs.

Participatory rural appraisal (PRA) is done in rural settings and employs methodology from the fields of agricultural research, rural development (Sikor 1994), anthropology, and rural sociology (Chambers 1994a, 1994b). PRA requires that community members participate actively in data collection and analysis, brainstorming of various solutions, implementation of programs, dissemination of information to the wider community (e.g., through workshops, brochures, and even social media), and local community members' training for carrying out programming (hopefully in a sustainable way) (Chambers 1994a, 1994b). PRA also involves community members in establishing social and political strategies for long-term engagement with external organizations and the local community, and for eventual program re-evaluation (Sikor 1994; Bhandari 2003; Shamsuddin et al. 2007). PRA is often confused with rapid rural appraisal (RRA), another approach that uses strictly outside resources and staff to both assess and implement solutions within a very limited time frame (Chambers 1994b).

PAR and PRA employ methodological and analytical techniques from the same tool kit, including social mapping, semi-structured interviews, activity profiles, seasonal calendars, charts (e.g., pie and bar), mobility diagrams, matrix ranking, preference ranking and scoring, system analysis diagrams, and focus groups (Shamsuddin et al. 2007; Olawepo 2008).

Qualitative Methods Used in CBR, CAR, PAR, and PRA

Despite minor differences among these community participatory approaches, they all seek to bring about change in community health, health-care, and agricultural systems, programs or policies through an applied approach that changes the traditional roles of the researcher and the participants. They also share a focus on the acquisition of qualitative data, although this does not preclude the collection of quantitative data when appropriate. Many of the methods used in these participatory approaches are derived from anthropology and other social sciences. It should be noted, however, that differences in communities, participants, and settings mean these methods cannot be universally applied, and that modification is often required to make them culturally appropriate. These methods include the following, as discussed by Israel and colleagues (2005: 6–11):

1. Interviews (structured, semi-structured, unstructured)
2. Focus groups (group discussions led by a facilitator and note taker)
3. Observation (unobtrusive and direct) and participant observation

4. Surveys
5. Document retrieval (primary and secondary books, files, reports, news articles, maps)
6. Audio-visual methods (e.g., photovoice or photojournal)
7. Electronic media retrieval (e.g., Governmental & NGO websites, blogs)

In addition, Bhandari (2003) offers additional methods and strategies for PRA, some of which can also be used in the other three research approaches:

8. Analytical games (e.g., priority lists)
9. Oral histories (e.g., stories)
10. Diagrams (e.g., maps, flow diagrams, timelines)
11. Workshops (e.g., knowledge dissemination, methods trainings)

Challenges in Using These Methods

Although the use of these methods has proved beneficial for the overall goal of fostering true collaboration between researchers and communities, their implementation also poses some challenges that could impact the overall quality of the research process and the outcomes. For instance, in settings characterized by marked gender biases, it is often difficult to get females to take part in community participatory research activities. Similar difficulties affecting the involvement of women and other community members occur in places where there is economic and power inequality, racism, and ethnic prejudices (Leurs 1996; Chambers 1994a). Conversely, it is often challenging to recruit males into these studies because of their work schedules, the timing of the research activities, and perhaps their general unwillingness to share thoughts with members of, or from outside of, the community. Another challenge is getting adequate representation of community experiences and perspectives from a variety of key informants, community leaders, and others, without giving unfair weight to any one specific group. Additionally, since some of these methods are narrowly focused on a particular topic or theme, the data may miss key interconnected elements, for example, the bidirectional relationship between food insecurity and stress often manifested as anxiety and depression. Hence, it is critically important to use multiple methods and to triangulate the findings in order to construct a clearer picture of the problem or issue at hand. Finally, time constraints and research costs can make for hasty training and implementation of research, at least in the eyes of the community members. This may result in community apprehension, or worse, the production of misleading findings. These challenges and others must be considered when conducting CBR, CAR, PAR, and PRA.

Tables 4.1 and 4.2 provide more detailed information on these methods, including their pros and cons and key literature and case study citations. Com-

Table 4.1. Community Action Research and Community-Based Research Methods

Methods	Type of Data	Pros	Cons and Cautions	Key Literature and Examples
Interviews (structured/semi-structured/unstructured)	Qualitative	Both predetermined and new questions arise in initial data gathering stage. Interview key informants, community members, and stakeholders to learn from local knowledge.	Maintain optimal ignorance (ignore responses not related to topic of questioning). Refocus questions back to topics at hand. Not all local knowledge is applicable; training community on a new skill/methodology may be required.	Israel et al. 2005; Bhandari 2003; Ozanne and Anderson 2010
Focus Groups (groups of individuals asked about their thoughts, feelings, and perceptions about a given topic; freedom to discuss ideas openly, facilitated by one or two individuals)	Qualitative	Participation of community stakeholders May use a community member as facilitator	Level of community facilitators'/key informants' accountability to community needs being assessed can vary. Beware of gender biases (participants should include women) and power inequalities (participants should be representative community members, including marginalized individuals).	Leurs 1996; Chambers 1994a; Israel et al. 2005; Ozanne and Anderson 2010 Example: Muroki et al. 1997, in which women were asked about their thoughts on weaning food ingredients, preparation, and perceptions of baby's weight progression using a gruel.
Observation (unobtrusive or participant)	Qualitative	Simple way of collecting preliminary data	During observation, jot down questions concerning your findings to discuss with locals in interviews.	Ozanne and Anderson 2010; Bhandari 2003
Survey (short list of questions concerning a topic of interest, e.g., community perceptions of a program's effectiveness in resolving a problem or of the level of performance of staff)	Qualitative/Quantitative	Allows for the collection of both types of data sets from larger samples Very quick to distribute Succinct questions asked Best used after development of initial exploratory analysis questions for getting community consensus, or for evaluating a project's progress	Some questions may be left unanswered or a specific issue may be ignored because it is not addressed in the survey questions. Less effective in initial exploratory assessment than interviews	Bhandari 2003; Ozanne and Anderson 2010 Example: Carroll-Scott et al. (2012), who found surveys useful in evaluating the efficacy of a "train-the-trainer" health assessment course with community staff.

(continued)

Methods	Type of Data	Pros	Cons and Cautions	Key Literature and Examples
Documents (secondary sources: e.g., books, files, reports, news articles, maps, literature reviews of peer-reviewed and gray literature)	Qualitative/ Quantitative	Provide necessary background information for initial exploratory questions on potential problems.	Be open to different interpretations and information from the community. Present outside sources of information to community only if this facilitates solution strategies.	Israel et al. 2005; Bhandari 2003; Leurs 1996 Example: Bhandari (2003), who recommends literature review of documents in the form of media reports, books, and maps to assess the potential problems and accessibility of the community one seeks to work in.
Audio-visual Materials *Photovoice* (training community members to take pictures of their community and provide narrative about the issue/problem being represented) *Photojournal* (a collection of photos with very brief narration of what is being pictured.)	Qualitative	Useful tools for helping community members identify issues/problems in the community Photovoice is useful for involving marginalized groups. Participants often prefer using their own smartphones for capturing photos/videos, which means less equipment to purchase.	Individuals in a community may have differing interpretations. Photos should be discussed with community to reach a general consensus in identifying the problem. Special attention to the ethics of visual data collection is necessary.	Israel et al. 2005 Example: Wang (1999), who used photovoice methods to assess health status of rural women in China, an extremely marginalized group. The women were able to photograph the lack of sanitation and educational opportunities for women in the countryside, which influenced policy change in the region.
Electronic Media (any type of electronic source, e.g., online news articles, media broadcasts, short infomercials, or online advertisement video. These can also include filmed observations of the conditions/problems of interest. Usually a valid source/citation indicates where information is found/gathered.	Qualitative	Effective in disseminating information (spreading awareness / marketing strategy)	Beware of biased views, making sure data presented is accurate and not sensationalized.	Israel et al. 2005 Example: Reininger et al. (2010), who used focus groups to evaluate marketing strategies for obesity awareness in Mexican-Americans. Results led to the use of morning shows featuring more role models, increasing coverage on the news, and more Spanish-language promoters in the media.

Methods	Type of Data	Pros	Cons and Cautions	Key Literature and Examples
Social Media: Use of digital technology (smartphones, cell phone applications or "apps,"), texting observation, media sharing technology (Facebook, Twitter, blogs, online forums)	Qualitative	Effective in both disseminating information (spreading awareness / marketing strategy) and gathering information from the community Appealing to younger participants with the use of "apps" and for those with smart phones, requiring minimal equipment and instant access to information	Beware of biased views, making sure data presented is accurate and not sensationalized. Beware of privacy issues, particularly with the use of online social media platforms (Twitter, Facebook, blogs and online forums). Make sure all information is anonymized, as even Internet screen names can be traced to personal information. Define what community is being studied (for network mapping, see Smith et al. 2014) as a geographical community or an online community (which may not include individuals who reside in the region of study). Presents special challenges for the informed consent process and for preservation of anonymity (e.g., if messages from community interest groups are posted, then there is a risk a post can be traced back to a particular individual, compromising anonymity)	Munson et al. 2013; Antypas and Wangberg 2014; Smith et al. 2014; Gruzd and Haythornthwaite 2013 Example: Munson et al. 2013 provide insight on the utility and challenges of social media use in promoting health intervention plans

Table 4.2.   Participatory Action Research and Participatory Rural Appraisal

Methods	Types of Data	Pros	Cons and Cautions	Key Literature and Examples
Analytical Game (find out a group's list of priorities, performances, ranking, scoring, or stratification)	Qualitative/ Quantitative	Community priorities and performances can be ranked, scored, or stratified. Makes statistical analyses of qualitative data easier	This preliminary data-gathering tool should include women, elders, and marginalized people—not just key informants.	Leur 1996; Chambers 1994; Bhandari 2003
Oral Histories (stories and portraits: a description of situations, local history, trend analysis)	Qualitative	Collects stories, portraits, trend analysis and useful local knowledge	All data sources must be triangulated (e.g., local stakeholders and secondary sources). If new methodology is to be taught to farmers, local knowledge and misgivings must be kept in mind.	Israel et al. 2005; Bhandari 2003; Leurs 1996
Diagrams (maps, aerial photos, transects, seasonal calendars, Venn diagrams, flow diagrams, historical profiles, ethnohistory, time lines)	Qualitative/ Quantitative	Provides visual comprehensive representation of data from rural, remote, and/or illiterate communities	In illiterate populations, illustrations must be comprehensive enough to be understood without written instructions, allowing for faster dissemination of information.	Bhandari 2003 Example: Muroki et al. 1997, in which nutrient-rich weaning foods were developed based on regional recipes
Workshops (gatherings of community members and researchers to present findings or teach a new skills/methodology to the community	Qualitative	Locals and outside researchers disseminate information, training, and demonstrations for the community to evaluate.	Location, accessibility and frequency of these workshops may present challenges when training community members in methodology.	Example: In Harris et al. (2001), priming seeds (presoaking seeds before planting) in rural Zimbabwe and India yielded faster results than the traditional "dry seed" planting method.

Methods	Types of Data	Pros	Cons and Cautions	Key Literature and Examples
Interviews (structured/ semi-structured/unstructured)	Qualitative	Most effective method of data collection for developing questions and clarifying observations Key informants should set up interviews with key community members.	Key informants may not allow interviews with women or marginalized individuals due to cultural customs or prejudices. Whether the inclusion of these marginalized individuals supersedes insulting the key informant must be determined on a case-by-case basis.	Bhandari 2003
Observation (structured, unstructured, wandering). The latter involves walking or vehicle tours, depending on the setting, and allows for an assessment of the physical and social landscape of a community.	Qualitative	Rural research may often require wandering to obtain adequate data.	Observations not discussed with local individuals can be misinterpreted. Most effective when done under the guidance of locals serving as "tour guides."	Bhandari 2003; Israel et al. 2005

Note: Some of these methods can also be used in CAR and CBR.

ments are also offered on areas where special caution may be needed during the implementation of these methods.

Thinking Through the Use of These Methods

Considering that Participatory Rural Appraisal is done in rural and usually agricultural settings, which can present some unique challenges, this approach will be discussed first, followed by a discussion of Community-Based Research, Community Action Research, and Participatory Action Research.

Participatory Rural Appraisal Guidelines, Steps, and Evaluation

Devandra (2007) offers guidelines for undertaking PRA, starting with a consideration of the accessibility (both cultural and geographical) of the region of study. This initial assessment should be followed by contact with local authorities and community leaders; clarification of the goals and objectives of the research; a request for formal introduction of the external research team to the community; establishment of liaisons with community elders, leaders, and/or experts; arrangement of meetings with community members, including those often overlooked by local leaders (e.g., women, youth); conduct of exploratory research; and then initiation of PRA-related activities.

Before researchers commence with primary data collection, secondary sources should be reviewed and incorporated into the research plan. The research team (local community and external members) should be divided into subgroups, each with a leader, to carry out different components of the project. The piloting of instruments such as surveys and interview guides should be reviewed by key informants and then tweaked to make them culturally appropriate. Thereafter, initial or exploratory data collection can begin. As part of this process, other methods—for example, observation and participant observation, asset mapping and other types of mapping, focus groups, and checklists—can be employed. Evaluation of procedures and techniques along with data analysis should take place throughout the study in order to refine, modify, and even experiment with techniques as needed in order to answer the research question(s) (Devandra 2007). For example, community members' understanding of survey and interview questions may differ from what the research team intended. Flexibility is the key to the success of community participatory research approaches such as PRA.

Various analytical techniques (e.g., descriptive statistics, non-parametric and parametric statistics, and—for some data—content analysis and cultural domain analysis) are used to summarize the study findings and for comparative purposes. These findings can then be confirmed and cross-checked with community members, and weighted according to their relative importance (based on feedback or follow-up research). Diagrams and charts are useful in summarizing and presenting the main findings for review by the community. Education and literacy levels should be taken into account when presenting the findings. Community members who did not participate in the research should be included in workshops or presentations where the findings are discussed. It may be necessary to conduct additional research to answer new questions that arise from the data. This will likely involve current participants in addition to new ones. Depending on the goals of the study, the findings can be used to develop programming and interventions.

CAR, CBR, and PAR Guidelines, Steps, Evaluation, and Action

Although many of the methods, steps, and analyses for PRA are similar to those for CAR, CBR, and PAR, there are also some differences. In particular, the latter community participatory approaches are usually conducted in urban, peri-urban, and exurban settings where agriculture is not the primary economic activity and where the pace of life is faster and lifestyles may be more complicated.

Various authors have offered guidelines for carrying out CAR, CBR, and PAR projects, and for addressing the challenges faced during their implementation (Ozanne and Anderson; Israel et al. 2005; De Koning and Martin 1996; and Minkler and Wallerstein 2003). In general, three stages of action strategies have been defined: Stage 1 focuses on developing partnerships and identifying needs and resources, Stage 2 prepares for ongoing research, drawing on dialogue, reflection, and analysis, and Stage 3 focuses on action and evaluation.

Stage 1: Developing partnerships and identifying needs and resources
The first stage of an action strategy should address establishing rapport, demonstrating the benefits of the study and actions that follow for the community, and entering into collaboration with diverse community members (e.g., community organizers, teachers, parents, and children). Interviews, focus groups, and other qualitative methods should be used to develop relevant research questions (or revisions). Finally, policies and procedures regarding ethical issues related to research with human subjects (e.g., confidentiality), the ownership of data, and the dissemination of findings need to be agreed upon during the initial stages of collaboration.

Stage 2: Ongoing Research: Dialogue, Reflection and Analysis
It is critically important that the local experts and at-large community members be involved in the ongoing research. In addition to taking active roles in designing research instruments and collecting data, they can also be instrumental with research logistics. For example, community leaders and community-based organizations can be of considerable help in dealing with challenges such as partici-

pant recruitment and misunderstandings that might arise between the research team and the non-participating community. Conflict in particular needs to be addressed immediately and resolution sought with the guidance of trusted members of the community. In addition, research updates and even early findings should be disseminated via presentations and workshops during the ongoing research. Early dissemination of research cements trust between researchers and community members, provides opportunities for additional input from various stakeholders, and fosters engagement from wider local audiences not directly involved in the research collaboration.

Stage 3: Action and Evaluation

Upon completion of the study, it is imperative to disseminate results fast, in a manner that is accessible to all interested stakeholders. Importantly, the community and those members that participated in the development of the project and the data collection and its analysis must be publicly recognized and given appropriate credit for their contributions. This will lay the foundation for community accountability and ownership and the success of any future actions such as programs or interventions.

Case Studies on Community Participatory Research

Despite the many challenges in implementing participatory research projects, there are successful examples of CBR, CAR, PAR, and PRA. The following two descriptions of case studies address nutritional anthropology and public health nutrition problems in Peru and Lesotho. These cases highlight both the successes and challenges encountered in carrying out this type of research.

Globalization, Shifting Diets, and Health in Peru (Contributed by Allison Cantor, MA, MPH/PhD student, University of South Florida)

Globalization processes are dramatically affecting the diets and health of people worldwide. Some of these effects, like increased food availability and dietary diversity, are positive; others—such as reduction of locally grown food (dietary delocalization) and higher consumption of energy-dense foods high in fat and sugar—are negative. Dietary delocalization, along with other lifestyle changes (e.g., reduced physical activity) contributes to the rise in chronic non-communicable diseases, including heart disease, type 2 diabetes, and obesity. In low-income countries, such as Peru, these changes are occurring alongside undernutrition and micro-nutrient deficiencies (e.g., iron-deficiency anemia) (Eckhardt 2008).

In 2012, Allison Cantor (a graduate student in anthropology and public health) and several other students conducted a community participatory study to assess maternal nutrition status and knowledge in three rural highland communities in Peru. The goal of this study was to identify community-relevant channels through which nutritional health could be promoted.

Although the study communities were increasingly participating in the market economy of this highland region, many households still practiced subsistence agriculture and participated in animal husbandry, raising pigs, guinea pigs, chickens, and sheep. However, development and tourism in the area have altered the diets and food habits of these communities via introduction of non-local food items. To assess maternal nutritional status and identify the best channels by which to promote nutritional health in the region, the researchers made use of the following methods: participatory action research (PAR) workshops, 24-hour food recalls, demographic surveys, administration of a food security scale, anthropometry, asset mapping, participatory community walk-throughs, and participant observation. In view of the focus of this chapter, the discussion will be limited to the community participatory methods and findings. For more information on the other methods used in this study see Cantor et al. (2012).

A PAR workshop involving 25 local residents was conducted in each of three study communities (for a total of 75 participants). The workshop protocol was developed in collaboration with the Center for Social Well-Being, a local community partner, and was modeled after other validated protocols that had previously been used to examine the health of Andean women (Hammer, Monasterios, and Tsuyuki 2004). As such, the PAR workshops emphasized an open and collaborative process between the women of these communities and the student researchers. Together, the two groups were co-collaborators and co-learners (Calisaya 2004; Minkler and Wallerstein 2003).

The workshops consisted of group interactions focused on elucidating community perspectives and practices regarding nutrition during pregnancy and the postnatal period. These activities included community resource mapping, food journals, group problem-solving, and healthy-recipe exchanges. Workshops were conducted in both Spanish and Quechua, the local language, with the aid of a trained, local community member who helped facilitate both cultural and linguistic fluidity.

The PAR workshops provided insight into community perceptions about nutrition during and after pregnancy, especially in regard to culturally-based food taboos, relevant changes to accessing nutrition resources, and understandings of "healthy" versus "unhealthy" foods. For example, recurring themes identified in all three communities included (1) "hot" and "cold" foods and their impact on pregnancy and postpartum health; (2) a focus on protein consumption during pregnancy; (3) a common concern about shifts in agricultural practices that are increasing the use of chemical fertilizers and pesticide; and (4) an experienced tension between continued subsistence farming and the demands of wage labor to make ends meet (The et al. unpublished).

The participants produced both text-based and pictorial data. This was critically important because it facilitated the inclusion of literate, partly literate, and nonliterate women alike in the study. Moreover, these data were included in the community deliverable, a nutritional pamphlet containing local recipes, which also featured healthy or traditional ingredients, mother-to-mother messages, and activities for applying the information contained in the pamphlet. The production of drawings during these workshops was particularly helpful, as it addressed the varying literacy of the communities by including visual aids, particularly with recipes.

The pamphlets were distributed to the participating communities, local health centers, community partners, and other interested stakeholders. After three months, an output evaluation followed, seeking to identify strengths and weaknesses of the materials. Based on the results of the evaluation, the pamphlet was revised to include more mother-to-mother messages and higher quality drawings, and to reduce the text and adapt some terms for the sake of community relevance. The second version of the deliverable was then distributed to all relevant stakeholders.

Ultimately, the community-based participatory nature of this research helped to elucidate both the local perspective on nutrition during and after pregnancy, and the lived experience of global-local food shifts and their impacts on daily life. Further, the emphasis on participation helped to validate local women's knowledge via the printing and dissemination of the data produced during the workshops. The Center for Social Well-Being has indicated that participants demonstrated increased confidence in their own nutritional knowledge as well as increased engagement in local food efforts (Isabella Chan, personal communication, 2 August 2013).

The Global Food Crisis, Urban Food Gardens, and Food Insecurity in Lesotho (Contributed by Charlotte A. Noble, MA, MPH, PhD student, University of South Florida)

In the aftermath of the 2008 global food crisis, it was recognized that increasing food prices were making urban households in developing countries more vulnerable to food insecurity than previously believed (Ruel et al. 2010; Stanford 2008; Himmelgreen, Romero Daza, and Noble 2012). Programs attempting to address this vulnerability included the implementation of an urban garden project in two districts in Lesotho, Southern Africa. In 2009, Charlotte Noble, a graduate student in anthropology and public health, conducted thesis research examining food security status, food acquisition, and community members' participation in and perceptions of one of the urban garden programs (Noble 2010). This project had in large part been designed by an international NGO, but local residents were involved in training, construction of raised bed gardens, and evaluation of the initiative.

The Household Food Insecurity Access Scale (HFIAS) was used to measure food security status, while the Household Dietary Diversity Score (HDDS) was used to measure the breadth of the diet among the participating households. Both these survey instruments were very easy to administer once they were adapted, typically taking less than ten minutes, which allowed Noble to spend most of her time with community members talking about barriers and benefits to participation in the urban garden program. Community and stakeholder participation was vital to the adaptation and translation of the surveys (see Coates, Swindale, and Bilinsky 2007 and Swindale and Bilinsky 2006 for guidance on adapting these instruments).

The HFIAS required modification beyond mere translation of the instrument, in order to adapt the survey to local contexts. This involved discussions with key stakeholders whose help was sought to elucidate culturally appropriate definitions of concepts such as "household" and "preferred foods." This was done in individual and group settings and included people at many different levels of a local organization involved in the project (e.g., food security staff, professional office staff, clerical and cleaning office staff, and interns). These individuals were interviewed to obtain meaningful, local understandings of important concepts. This was followed up with group meetings to discuss nuances in wording and find consensus regarding the terms used in the HFIAS. Thereafter, pilot testing of the HFIAS commenced using cognitive interview guides with community members to make sure that the "translations" in the instrument made sense.

The HDDS required similar adaptation in that local items needed to be added to the list of food and food groups in the instrument. For example, *papa* (stiff maize porridge) was added to the cereal group, and local plants such as *sepaile* and *rapa* were added to green vegetables. Examples of locally representative foods were reviewed with the same participants to create a culturally appropriate dietary diversity survey. Without the involvement of the community stakeholders, these instruments would not have been successfully adapted.

Noble's results showed that households in the urban garden project were more likely to be food secure and had higher dietary diversity than those that did not participate in the project. However, because the study was cross-sectional, it could not be determined if participation in the project caused this difference, or if households already experiencing these issues had self-selected themselves as participants. The main barrier to participation was lack of awareness of the project. However, one interesting point that emerged from speaking with community members about awareness of the program was that they lacked a clear understanding of who was or was not a member of the community for whom the program was intended. For example, recent arrivals (there is considerable rural-to-urban migration in Lesotho) did not know whether they could participate in the program, or if the program was intended exclusively for long-term residents. This underscores the need to provide clear, detailed information to local community members, and to ensure all sectors of the target community have adequate participation in the intended programs. Doing this effectively requires the active involvement of local stakeholders who are familiar with the nuanced nature of group identity and formation.

Conclusions

Ideally, community participatory initiatives should engage community stakeholders as active participants in all aspects of research, from identification of research questions, conceptualization of ideas, creation of research protocols, collection and analysis of data, and translation of research into applications, to the evaluation of such programming. In reality, however, such levels of participation are often hard to achieve, despite our best intentions. For example, the normal day-to-day activities of local stakeholders (e.g., employment, family obligations) may preclude their full participation. Similarly, local stakeholders may lose motivation or interest, especially when the research project spans a long time from start to finish. Nevertheless, committed efforts to participatory research are becoming more common in anthropology in general and in nutritional anthropology specifically.

Communities' active participation in the design, implementation, and evaluation of research projects has proven highly beneficial at several different levels. First, it increases the cultural appropriateness of our research endeavors by ensuring that our approaches and protocols are responsive to and respectful of the cultural, economic, social, and political realities of the communities with whom we work. Second, it enhances the potential effectiveness and sustainability of programming that derives from such research, fostering a sense of ownership among local stakeholders. Finally, and more importantly, it acknowledges the value of community stakeholders' experiential knowledge as an essential complement to the academic expertise researchers bring to the table. This validation of other types of knowledge contributes to the creation of meaningful partnerships between academics and community members, thus increasing the likelihood that our collaborative research endeavors will have a tangible impact outside of academia.

David A. Himmelgreen, PhD, is Professor and Chair of Anthropology at the University of South Florida. He specializes in biocultural and nutritional anthropology with a focus on food insecurity, nutritional health in the context of migration and the global market economy, growth and development, and the rise of diet-related chronic diseases. Himmelgreen has conducted research in Costa Rica, the United States, Lesotho, India, and Puerto Rico. With NSF funding, he is currently examining food choices and decision making in low-income U.S.

households at risk of food insecurity. Himmelgreen co-directs the Globalization and Community Health Field School in Costa Rica, which trains undergraduate students in anthropology, public health, and engineering to conduct community health research and program development. Himmelgreen has published over eighty academic papers, edited volumes, book chapters, and book reviews.

Sara Arias-Steele, M.S., is a doctoral student in the Department of Applied Anthropology at the University of South Florida. Her research applies a biocultural approach to the role of adolescent agency and body image perception in eating habits and physical activity among Latinos in Tampa Bay. She attended the Globalization and Community Health Field School in 2013 in Monteverde, Costa Rica, and co-authored a book chapter on the use of community-based participatory research methods to address food insecurity in Monteverde using an experimental keyhole garden. She was also the Health Project Coordinator for a CBPR health-assessment project in Wimauma, Florida, with the Hispanic Services Council of Tampa Bay. She has been a student lecturer for introductory biological anthropology courses at USF since 2012.

Nancy Romero-Daza, PhD, is Professor of Anthropology at the University of South Florida. Romero-Daza is a medical anthropologist specializing in HIV/AIDS research and intervention, health disparities, the political economy of health, and the social determinants of health. Her research interests include the impact of labor migration on the spread of HIV/AIDS in Lesotho; HIV risk among injection drug users, crack users, and sex workers in the United States; the impact of tourism on the spread of HIV and other STIs in Costa Rica; and the syndemic interaction among poverty, food insecurity, and HIV risk. Along with David Himmelgreen, she has received funding from the National Science Foundation to conduct research on the impact of globalization and the changing economy of nutritional health in Costa Rica and to train undergraduate students to conduct community-based research combining anthropology and engineering in Costa Rica. She is also a co-investigator in SHARE (Syndemic HIV AIDS Research Education) Haiti, which, funded by the National Institutes of Health, provides Haitian medical and social scientists with training in the use of syndemic theory to conduct community-based HIV research.

References

Antypas, Konstantinos, and Slije C. Wangberg. 2014. Combining Users' Needs with Health Behavior Models in Designing an Internet- and Mobile-Based Intervention for Physical Activity in Cardiac Rehabilitation. *Journal of Medical Internet Research Protocols* 3(1): e4.

Bhandari, Bishnu B. 2003. *Participatory Rural Appraisal (PRA)*. Kamiyamaguchi, Japan. Institute for Global Environmental Strategies.

Calisaya, Emilia. 2004. *Voces de Mujeres de Ancash: Género y Salud Reproductiva.* Lima, Peru. Movimiento Manuela Ramos.

Cantor, Allison, Isabella Chan, Curtis DeVetter, and Kristina Baines. 2012. From the Chacra to the Tienda: Examining Food Insecurity and Nutrition in Rural Peru. Unpublished manuscript.

Carroll-Scott, Amy, Peggy Toy, Roberta Wyn, Jazmine Zane, and Steven P. Wallace. 2012. Results from the Data & Democracy Initiative to Enhance Community-Based Organization Data and Research Capacity. *American Journal of Public Health* [serial online] 102(7): 1384–1391. Available from MEDLINE, Ipswich, MA. Accessed 29 January 2013.

Chambers, Robert. 1994a. Participatory Rural Appraisal (PRA): Challenges, Potentials and Paradigm. *World Development* 22(10): 1437–1454.

Chambers, Robert. 1994b. The Origins and Practice of Participatory Rural Appraisal. *World Development* 22(7): 953–969.

Chan, Isabella, Allison Cantor, Curtis Devetter, and Kristina Baines. 2012. "Debemos Alimentarnos Como Antes con las Cosas de la Chacra": Understanding Shifts in Maternal Diets in Rural Peru through Participatory Action Research (PAR). Unpublished manuscript.

Coates, Jennifer, Anne Swindale, and Paula Bilinsky. 2007. *Household Food Insecurity Access Scale (HFIAS) for Measurement of Household Food Access: Indicator Guide,* vol. 3. Washington, DC: Food and Nutrition Technical Assistance Project, Academy for Educational Development.

De Koning, Korrie, and Marion Martin, eds. 1996. *Participatory Research in Health: Issues and Experiences.* London: Zed Books.

Davis, A. S. C. 2001. Participatory Rural Appraisal: Rural Travel and Transport Program. http://www.transport-links.org/rtkb/english/Module%205%5C5_6a%20Participatory% 20Rural%20Appraisal.pdf. Accessed 3 June 2014.

Devandra, Canagasaby. 2007. Constraint Analysis to Improve Integrated Dairy Production Systems in Developing Countries: The Importance of Participatory Rural Appraisal. *Tropical Animal Health and Production* 39(8): 549–556.

Eckhardt C. L., L. E. Torheim, E. Monterrubio, S. Barquera, and M. T. Ruel. 2008. The Overlap Of Overweight And Anaemia Among Women In Three Countries Undergoing The Nutrition Transition. *European Journal of Clinical Nutrition* 62(2): 238–246.

Goh, Ying-Ying, Laura M. Bogart, Bessie Ko Sipple-Asher, Kimberly Uyeda, Jennifer Hawes-Dawson, Josephina Olarita-Dhungana, Gery W. Ryan, and Mark A. Schuster. 2009. Using Community-Based Participatory Research to Identify Potential Interventions to Overcome Barriers to Adolescents' Healthy Eating and Physical Activity. *Journal of Behavioral Medicine* [serial online] 32(5): 491–502. Available from Academic Search Premier, Ipswich, MA. Accessed 29 January 2013.

Gruzd, Anatoliy, and Caroline Haythornthwaite. 2013. Enabling Community Through Social Media. *Journal of Medical Internet Research* 15(10): e248.

Hammer, Patricia J., Carmen Monasterios, and Kiyomi Tsuyuki. 2004. *Guia de Autodiagnóstico Comunitario de Investigación Participativa Comunitaria de las Necesidades Frente a Problemas en la 1ra Mitad del Embarazo. Manual Para Facilitadores [A Guide to Community Self-Assessment for the Conduct of Community Participatory Research on Problems During the First Half of Pregnancy. Facilitators' Manual].* La Paz, Bolivia: Programa PAC Bolivia.

Harris. A, A. K. Pathan, P. Gothkar, A. Joshi, W. Chivasa, and P. Nyamudeza. 2001. On-Farm

Seed Priming: Using Participatory Methods to Revive and Refine a Key Technology. *Agricultural Systems* 69: 151–164.

Himmelgreen, David A., Nancy Romero-Daza, and Charlotte Noble. 2013. Anthropological Perspectives on the Global Food Crisis. In *Nutritional Anthropology*, ed. D. Dufour, 120–127. New York: Oxford University Press.

Israel, Barbara A., Eugenia Eng, Amy J. Schulz, and Edith A. Parker. 2005. Introduction to Methods in Community-Based Participatory Research for Health. In *Methods in Community-Based Participatory Research for Health*, ed Barbara A. Israel, Eugenia Eng, Amy J. Schulz, and Edith A. Parker, 3–26. San Francisco: Jossey-Bass.

Leurs, Robert. 1996. Current Challenges Facing Participatory Rural Appraisal. *Public Administration and Development* 16(1): 57–72.

Minkler, Meredith, and Nina Wallerstein, eds. 2003. *Community-Based Participatory Research for Health*. San Francisco: Jossey-Bass.

Munson, Sean A., Hasan Cavusoglu, Larry Frisch, and Sidney Fels. 2013. Sociotechnical Challenges and Progress in Using Social Media for Health. *Journal of Medical Internet Research* 15(10): e226.

Muroki, Nelson M., Gabriel K. Maritim, Edward G. Karuri, Hilary K. Tolong, Jasper K. Imungi, Wambui Kogi-Makau, Suzanne Maman, Eloise Carter, and Audrey N. Maretzki. 1997. Involving Rural Kenyan Women in the Development of Nutritionally Improved Weaning Foods: Nutribusiness Strategy. Society for Nutrition Education *Journal of Nutrition Education and Behavior* 29: 335–342.

Noble, Charlotte Ann. 2010. Small Plots, Big Hopes: Factors Associated with Participation in an Urban Garden Project in Lesotho. Thesis, Department of Anthropology, University of South Florida, Tampa.

Olawepo, Raphael Abiodun. 2008. Using Participatory Rural Appraisal to Explore Coastal Fishing in Badagry Villages, Nigeria. *Environmentalist* 28: 108–122.

Ozanne, Julie L., and Laurel Anderson. 2010. Community Action Research. *Journal of Public Policy and Marketing* 29(1): 123–137.

Reininger, Belinda M., Cristina S. Barroso, Lisa Mitchell-Bennett, Ethel Cantu, Maria E. Fernandez, Dora Alicia Gonzalez, Marge Chavez, Diamantina Freeberg, and Alfred McAlister. 2010. Process Evaluation and Participatory Methods in an Obesity-Prevention Media Campaign for Mexican Americans. *Health Promotion Practice* 11(3): 347–357.

Ruel, Marie T., James L. Garrett, Corinna Hawkes, and Marc J. Cohen. 2010. The Food, Fuel, and Financial Crises Affect the Urban and Rural Poor Disproportionately: A Review of the Evidence. *Journal of Nutrition* 140(1): 170S–176S.

Shamsuddin, Mohammed., Monjurul Alam, Mokbul Hossein, William Goodger, Farida Yaesmin Bari, Tomiz Uddin Ahmed, and A. H. M. S. I. Khan. 2007. Participatory Rural Appraisal to Identify Needs and Prospects of Market-Oriented Dairy Industries in Bangladesh. *Tropical Animal Health and Production* 39(8): 567–581.

Sikor, Thomas O. 1994. Participatory Methods and Empowerment in Rural Development: Lessons From Two Experimental Workshops With a Chilean NGO. *Agriculture and Human Values* 11(2–3): 151–158.

Smith, Marc A., Lee Rainie, Ben Shneiderman and Itai Himelboim. 2014. Mapping Twitter Topic Networks: from Polarized Crowds to Community Clusters. Available from Pew Research Internet Project, Washington, DC. http://www.pewinternet.org/2014/02/20/map

ping-twitter-topic-networks-from-polarized-crowds-to-community-clusters/. Accessed 3 June 2014.

Stanford, L. 2008. Globalized Food Systems: The View from Below. *Anthropology News* 49(7): 7–10.

Swindale, Anne, and Paula Bilinsky. 2006. *Household Dietary Diversity Score (HDDS) for Measurement of Household Food Access: Indicator Guide, Version 2.* Food and Nutrition Technical Assistance Project, Academy for Educational Development, Washington, DC.

Wang, Caroline C. 1999. Photovoice: A Participatory Action Research Strategy Applied to Women's Health. *Journal of Women's Health* 8(2): 185–192.

Additional Resources

Astrade, Laurent, Céline Lutoff, Rachid Nedjai, Céline Philippe, Delphine Loison, and Sandrine Bottollier-Depois. 2007. Periurbanisation and Natural Hazards. *Journal of Alpine Research* 95(2): 19–28.

Colecraft, Esi, Grace S. Marquis, Richmond Aryeetey, Owuraku Sakyi-Dawson, Anna Lartey, Benjamin Ahunu, Emmanuel Canacoo, Lorna M. Butler, Manju B. Reddy, Helen H. Jensen, and Elisabeth Huff-Lonergan. 2006. Constraints on the Use of Animal Source Foods for Young Children in Ghana: A Participatory Rapid Appraisal Approach. *Ecology of Food and Nutrition* 45(5): 351–377.

Coreil, Jeannine, ed. 2009. *Social and Behavioral Foundations of Public Health.* New York: Sage.

Henning, J., A. Khin, T. Hla, and J. Meers. 2006. Husbandry and Trade of Indigenous Chickens in Myanmar: Results of a Participatory Rural Appraisal in the Yangon and the Mandalay Divisions. *Tropical Animal Health and Production* 38(7–8): 611–618.

Manijeh Ali and Hélène F. Delisle. 1999. A Participatory Approach to Assessing Malawi Villagers' Perception of Their Own Food Security. *Ecology of Food and Nutrition* 38(2): 101–121.

World Bank. 2012a. *Central African Republic: Food Crisis Response Project.* Washington, DC: World Bank. http://documents.worldbank.org/curated/en/2012/12/17154513/central-african-republic-food-crisis-response-project-central-african-republic-food-crisis-response-project. Accessed 5 June 2014.

World Bank. 2012b. *Global Food Crisis Response Program: Progress and Lessons Learned.* Washington, DC: World Bank. http://documents.worldbank.org/curated/en/2012/11/17036849/global-food-crisis-response-program-progress-lessons-learned. Accessed 5 June 2014.

World Bank. 2012c. *Mauritania: Community-Based Rural Development Project.* Washington, DC: World Bank. http://documents.worldbank.org/curated/en/2012/06/16601345/mauritania-community-based-rural-development-project. Accessed 5 June 2014.

Wong, Susan. 2012. What Have Been the Impacts of World Bank Community-Driven Development Programs? CDD *Impact Evaluation Review and Operational and Research Implications.* Washington, DC: World Bank. http://documents.worldbank.org/curated/en/2012/03/16374801/impacts-world-bank-community-driven-development-programs-cdd-impact-evaluation-review-operational-research-implications. Accessed 5 June 2014.

CHAPTER **5**

Understanding Famine and Severe Food Emergencies

Miriam S. Chaiken

Everyone has the right to a standard of living adequate for the health and well-being of himself and of his family, including food, clothing, housing and medical care and necessary social services, and the right to security in the event of unemployment, sickness, disability, widowhood, old age or other lack of livelihood in circumstances beyond his control.

—United Nations Declaration for Human Rights, Article 25 (1948)

Every gun that is made, every warship launched, every rocket fired, signifies in the final sense a theft from those who hunger and are not fed, those who are cold and are not clothed.

—President Dwight D. Eisenhower

Introduction

Hunger and famine are not new problems. Throughout history plagues, droughts, crop failures, wars and other calamities have resulted in hunger and even starvation on mass scales. The Old Testament is rife with dire tales of plagues and pests, and in more recent eras we can recall the siege of Stalingrad, the starvation of untold numbers of Chinese following Mao's revolution, or the widespread famine in eastern and southern Africa in the early twentieth century, which caused untold suffering and misery (Vaughn 1987). But these tragedies largely became known long after they had wreaked havoc on the populations that suffered—in other words, they were largely invisible to others while they were taking place. In the early 1980s this pattern of invisible famines was interrupted and famine became visible, tangible, visceral, and global, in part because of the work of a courageous

Kenyan photographer named Mohammed Amin (Mohammed *Mo* Amin n.d.). Amin traveled to the hellholes that were refugee camps in Ethiopia and Kenya as the Horn of Africa Famine began to ravage the populations of Somalia, Ethiopia, Kenya, and Uganda. With his camera he captured and shared haunting images of gaunt children cradled by emaciated parents. Famine now had a face. These images were splashed across the global media, and for the first time there was not only global awareness, but global empathy and determination to address this problem. With the Live Aid concerts that resulted from this movement, people from around the world used the beauty of art and music to raise money and awareness to fight the horror and ugliness of famine.

Long- and Short-Term Consequences of Food Emergencies

The crisis that Amin uncovered was a tragedy not only for those who died from the famine, but also for the survivors, who for the rest of their lives are haunted by the long-term consequences of this type of stress. A great deal of research has documented the effects of chronic and acute undernutrition on children. Children experiencing a sudden and severe food shortage often exhibit wasting, characterized by extremely lean children with gaunt faces and knobby joints. Wasting is measured by comparing children's mid-upper arm circumference (MUAC) with a referent for healthy children of the same age. This type of screening is becoming increasingly popular, as MUAC measurements are easy to collect, even with minimally trained staff, and are fairly reliable predictors of risk of mortality (Walters, Sibson, and McGrath 2012; Young and Jaspars 2009). In instances where food has been chronically in short supply or inadequate in quality, children typically exhibit stunting, or low height for age and weight for height. In both stunting and wasting, children compensate for the inadequacy of their diet, first by curtailing activity, and then by growing more slowly, which ultimately results in impairment of physiological and neuromotor response. These stresses can cause measurable deficits in proper growth. They also diminish intellectual and cognitive development, reduce activity and motor skills, impair immune responses, and ultimately lead to significantly higher risk of death due to inability to combat infections and illnesses (Black, Morris, and Bryce 2003; Diaz-Briquets, Cheyney, and Germano 1992; Pelletier 1999; Pelto et al. 1991; Kurz and Johnson-Welch 2001; Quisumbing 2003; Pelto and Backstrand 2003). The consequences of extreme hunger are indeed tragic and debilitating when they are manifested in refugee camps, war zones, or sites of natural disasters, but it is important to also focus on the long term, recognizing that impairments appearing in children in times of stress result in life-long limitations. In order to ensure adequate quality of life decades later, it is critical that these nutritional stresses be mitigated as much as possible in early childhood (Pelletier 1999; Scrimshaw 1991).

New Approaches: Famine Early Warning Systems

Since Mohammed Amin's work raised global awareness of famine, important innovations have emerged, yet many challenges remain. Today there are many organizations that work to improve access to food, predict food shortfalls, educate people about better nutrition, and address hunger where it is documented.

One of the first innovations in understanding and addressing food emergencies was the creation of the first Famine Early Warning System Network (FEWS 2013). Funded by USAID, the FEWS Network uses satellite imagery, remote sensing, agroclimatic data, and other sources to monitor the conditions in twenty-five target countries located mostly in sub-Saharan Africa. Since its inception immediately following the Horn of Africa Famine in 1985, the FEWS Network has monitored agricultural production to determine where shortfalls in production may be occurring, in order to prepare timely responses. The system is predicated on the assumption that famines rarely occur overnight (except in cases of massive natural disasters); rather, most food emergencies evolve over many weeks or months as food access fails to reach appropriate levels. Using images of vegetative cover, rainfall data, and other information gained remotely, the FEWS Network can predict which areas are experiencing stress, crisis, emergency, and catastrophe, so that other agencies that address this vulnerability can respond in a timely fashion. In recent years the FEWS Network has begun supplementing its periodic reports of food status with livelihood analyses that delve more deeply into the local issues that affect food access (market pricing, food production patterns, income opportunities) so that more disaggregated responses are possible (FEWS 2013). As the impact of global climate change becomes more significant, so too will the urgency of monitoring systems (Verdin et al. 2005).

The impact of the FEWS has been positive, but the approach continues to have significant limitations. First, only twenty-five vulnerable countries are monitored, and many of them share boundaries with countries facing challenges that, though equally compelling, are not of the same level of strategic interest to the U.S. government (e.g., Kenya, Tanzania, Rwanda, Burundi, and Zambia are monitored, but not neighboring DR Congo). Second, data tend to be presented on a national level, or at best provincial, whereas there may be complex local-level variations in production systems, microclimate, socioeconomic inequality, infrastructure, market access, and other variables that influence whether a given community is more or less vulnerable than the national data suggest. This macro-level view masks a great deal of local-level variation.

Finally, the objective of the FEWS Network is to understand emerging food emergencies and to share that data widely, but—as we have seen far too often—knowledge of a food emergency does not necessarily equate to sustained action to address it by the governments, policy makers, and organizations that have the potential to resolve the problems.

Following on the successful model of the FEWS Network, other regional and local-level early warning systems have been developed to understand the climatic factors that influence food production and access. For example, the Permanent Interstate Committee for Drought Control in the Sahel (CILSS), which is the technical arm of the Economic Community of West African States (ECOWAS), works with the assistance of the UN Food and Agriculture Organization (FAO) to ensure that its members are never surprised by changing weather or market conditions that can affect their national food security. In this age of rapid climate change, the work of CILSS assists in monitoring levels of food (especially cereal) production, while other efforts to control erosion, evaluate plant drought-tolerance, and protect plants are helping to build resilience in areas vulnerable to chronic drought (FAO 2013a).

Humanitarian Organizations and the Problem of Silos

One logistical challenge, which perhaps is not apparent to those on the sidelines of the struggle to end hunger, is presented by the mutually exclusive domains of responsibility that constrain many agencies' activities in this battle. In most cases of widespread hunger and famine, we also find war and conflict. This instability results in a situation that compromises food production, distribution, and access (Messer 1998). Ultimately, the final solution to famine must couple meaningful and sustained economic development with peaceful nation-building. Ironically, though, the organizations delivering humanitarian aid and emergency relief rarely undertake such activities. The "silos" in humanitarian organizations have often been remarked on: while one division may focus on promoting economic development, the same organization maintains a wholly separate division to address famine and emergency response. Often these divisions have separate staff, mandates, programs, and ultimately separate sources of funding that effectively reinforce these artificial distinctions. Practitioners in the field have called for decades for a bridge to link short-term relief to development activities for the long term, but this has seldom been achieved in practice (Chaiken, Deconinck, and Degefie 2006).

Today a wide array of organizations, large and small, address famine and hunger as their mission. Table 5.1 identifies some of these organizations, but this list is far from exhaustive. Some larger organizations, such as Save the Children and World Vision, are really federations of international organizations; thus for example there is a Save the Children UK as well as parallel agencies in each of the Scandinavian countries (called Redd Barna). Most of these organizations receive funding from multiple sources—governments, private donors, religious organizations—and different components of their programming may have different funding streams.

Table 5.1. Examples of Organizations that Address Famine and Food Emergencies

Type of Organization	Name	Description & Specific Mandate
Multilateral and UN	UNICEF www.unicef.org	To improve the lives and welfare of children under 5 years of age, and to promote child survival, gender-equitable access to education, and freedom from abuse.
	Food and Agriculture Organization (FAO) www.fao.org	To improve nutrition, increase agricultural productivity, raise the standard of living in rural populations and contribute to global economic growth.
	World Food Programme (WFP) www.wfp.org	WFP uses food aid to support economic and social development; to meet refugee and other emergency food needs, and provide the associated logistics support; and to promote world food security in accordance with the recommendations of the United Nations and FAO.
	World Health Organization www.who.org	WHO provides leadership on global health matters, shaping the health research agenda, setting norms and standards (including for nutritional status), articulating evidence-based policy options, providing technical support to countries, and monitoring and assessing health trends.
Donor Governments	USAID www.usaid.gov	USAID invests in ideas that work to improve the lives of millions of men, women and children by investing in agricultural productivity so countries can feed their people; combating maternal and child mortality and deadly diseases like HIV, malaria, and tuberculosis; providing life-saving assistance in the wake of disaster; promoting democracy, human rights, and good governance around the world; fostering private-sector development and sustainable economic growth; helping communities adapt to a changing environment; and elevating the role of women and girls throughout all our work.
	Danida http://um.dk/en/danida-en/ about-danida/	Denmark's development cooperation aims to reduce poverty by promoting human rights and economic growth. It is focused on some of the poorest countries in the world.
Nonsectarian Humanitarian NGOs	Save the Children/*Redd Barna* www.savethechildren.org	Save the Children seeks to create lasting change in the lives of children in need. It works with other organizations, governments, nonprofits, and a variety of local partners while maintaining its own independence without political agenda or religious orientation. When disaster strikes around the world, Save the Children is there to save lives with food, medical care, and education, and remains to help communities rebuild through long-term recovery programs.
	Valid International http://www.validinternational .org/demo/index.php	An Irish NGO that pioneered the use of ready-to-use therapeutic foods for community-based therapeutic care.

(continued)

Type of Organization	Name	Description & Specific Mandate
Faith-Based NGOs	World Vision www.worldvision.org	World Vision is a Christian humanitarian organization dedicated to working with children, families, and their communities worldwide to reach their full potential by tackling the causes of poverty and injustice.
	Samaritan's Purse http://www.samaritanspurse.org	Samaritan's Purse is a nondenominational evangelical Christian organization providing spiritual and physical aid to hurting people around the world. Since 1970, Samaritan's Purse has helped meet needs of people who are victims of war, poverty, natural disasters, disease, and famine.
	Mazon: Jewish Response to Hunger http://mazon.org/about-us/	To provide for those who are hungry regardless of background and to raise awareness in the Jewish community of the problem of hunger and the obligation of service and charity.
Corporate and Philanthropic	Bill and Melinda Gates Foundation www.gatesfoundation.org	Grant-making supports relief efforts in response to rapid-onset natural disasters such as cyclones and earthquakes, slow-onset crises such as famine and drought, and acute complex emergencies such as those related to political unrest and violence.
	Land O'Lakes http://www.idd.landolakes.com	Uses experience of American agribusiness and co-ops to lift many of the world's most vulnerable people out of poverty and enable them to achieve food security and self-reliance. These households may be vulnerable due to weather-related shocks (i.e., droughts or floods) or conflict, lack of access to productive assets or market opportunities, or the impacts of poor health and nutrition, particularly among pregnant and lactating women, and children under age two.

Useful Resources for Understanding Problems and Responses

All the organizations that engage in humanitarian response have websites with useful resources for understanding both the work they do and the issues they address. Up-to-date data on food emergencies and vulnerability are often more readily available through these websites than from national government sources.

In addition to the websites and publications of the many governments and NGOs that address the issue of famine, the extremely useful resources readily available to interested scholars include two important publications—*State of the World's Children* (UNICEF), and *State of the World's Mothers* (Save the Children)—that annually update the data on nutritional status, access to services, mortality, and other measures of quality of life for the entire world. UNICEF's annual report typically takes an important challenge facing the children of the world—such as disabilities, or equal access to primary education—and includes a well researched and thorough examination of this topic (UNICEF 2013). The report also annually summarizes the rates of stunting, wasting, undernutrition, access to Vitamin A supplementation, use of iodized salt, breastfeeding frequencies, and mortality data for children in all countries that are member nations of the United Nations. Though these national-level data likely belie localized variation, this annual report remains one of the most useful documents for understanding the impacts of food insecurity and hunger on children. Released annually on Mother's Day, Save the Children's *State of the World's Mothers* provides a similarly comprehensive annual report that focuses on the status of women, prenatal care, newborn mortality, and the status of women (Save the Children 2013).

Two essential organizations that generate research and data on global food issues are the Food and Agriculture Technical Assistance Project (FANTA) and the International Food Policy Research Institute (IFPRI). FANTA, which is funded by USAID, brings together a collection of academic, humanitarian, and policy-oriented institutions to improve the health and well-being of vulnerable groups. FANTA provides technical support in the areas of maternal and child health and nutrition in both development and emergency contexts (FANTA 2013). FANTA's staff collaborate with in-country NGOs addressing hunger in eighteen target countries, largely in sub-Saharan Africa, to bring state-of-the-art knowledge and approaches to bear in addressing food insecurity and food emergencies. FANTA also produces a wide range of databases, training materials, and policy papers about hunger, household resource allocation, community-based management of malnutrition, HIV/AIDS, and related topics. FANTA has been a leader in identifying strategies to systematically measure household food insecurity, and these methodologies are now the standard for use across the humanitarian assistance community (Ballard et al. 2011).

IFPRI is one of fifteen organizations that comprise the Consultative Group on International Agricultural Research (CGIAR System), and within this consortium it is the only organization specifically focused on nutrition rather than food production and agricultural technologies. IFPRI collaborates with the commodity-oriented CGIAR centers to ensure that nutritional goals are integrated into the work of the agricultural research, and has the goal of seeing an end to hunger globally. IFPRI's strives to help achieve the Millennium Development Goals (MDGs), its core goals being to ensure that every person has secure access to safe food that is sufficient to sustain a healthy and productive life, and to disseminate food-policy guidelines based on sound science and transparent collaboration and decision making. IFPRI has produced a wide range of critical publications that frame food policy and food aid decisions today, notably the annual Hunger Index (IFPRI 2013).

The UN Food and Agriculture Organization (FAO) synthesizes a wealth of data on food production, productivity, demographics, land use patterns, environmental issues, employment, and food security through its statistical division (FAOSTAT). Its publications build on work obtained via FEWSNet, include in-depth information on productive systems and food access, and specifically address the issue of hunger and food insecurity (FAO 2013b).

The UN-sponsored Integrated Regional Information Networks (IRIN) disseminates information on current humanitarian aid and emergency activities (IRIN 2013). This news outlet covers activities in seventy countries as well as the work of both UN agencies (FAO, WFP, UNICEF) and many NGOs working in the area of humanitarian assistance.

Humanitarian Response is a clearinghouse and data repository for humanitarian organizations and their website summarizes data on current resource availability, shocks or challenges to health and well-being, demographic profiles of refugees and internally displaced persons, and resource needs for both individual countries and regions. Comprehensive information is available through this source, but it also creates "dashboards": user-friendly summaries of each area's profile of strengths and needs (Humanitarian Response 2013).

The Household Economy Approach and Cost of the Diet website is another central web-based repository of reports from regions throughout the world. Organizations like NGOs can opt to share the results of their studies and gray literature on a variety of issues related to food access, distribution, production, livelihood zones, vulnerability, and related topics. As noted above, these on-the-ground assessments, often conducted by NGOs, are frequently the most accurate and timely sources of information on food emergencies and humanitarian response. Though theoretically global in scope, they relatively seldom include reports from the Caribbean or South and Southeast Asia, but there is a rich repository of reports for Africa, especially Sahelian regions (HEA 2013).

Contemporary Strategies to Address Food Emergencies

The Sphere Project was initiated in the late 1990s to establish a baseline for best practices for humanitarian aid and to promote information sharing between organizations. Sphere has brought together representatives of NGOs, donor nations, and UN agencies to establish parameters for delivering humanitarian aid, and to ensure minimum thresholds for acceptable response and impact. The Sphere work revolves around the following core values:

- the right to life with dignity,
- the right to receive humanitarian assistance,
- the right to protection and security.

To comply with these core principles, all humanitarian aid should be delivered in a "people-centered humanitarian response" and be as participatory as possible, as quickly as possible. Sphere-compliant programming should be transparent and culturally sensitive, and the core values require that all humanitarian aid be delivered equitably, with no exclusions due to political orientation, religious beliefs, ethnicity, or other issues that were divisive in the past. The Sphere standards specify benchmarks for programs to achieve in areas of food security, infant and young child feeding, management of acute malnutrition and micronutrient insufficiencies, water and sanitation, and adequate shelter. All programming is evaluated relative to these Sphere-established standards for effective and appropriate humanitarian response (Sphere 2013).

A sequel to the Sphere Project has been the Global Nutrition Cluster, which is an umbrella for forty partner organizations that permits information sharing, identification of standard operating practices, and codification of best practices in food emergency settings. The Global Nutrition Cluster partners work together to identify and develop key activities to ensure that emergency response is predictable, timely, effective, and at scale. The Cluster has developed training materials, strategies for evaluation of supplementation, and feeding programs to ensure consistently positive impacts of intervention programs. Though the Cluster approach includes efforts in many areas related to nutrition, much of its main focus has been on promoting community-based strategies for management of malnutrition, as discussed below (Global Nutrition Cluster 2013).

The common thread that unites most contemporary efforts to prevent and address famine and food emergencies is the issue of resilience. Much of the work of the past decade has recognized that famine and food emergencies typically emerge slowly, and that individual actors respond to perceived constraints in resource availability in rational ways. In essence, specific coping behaviors can serve as early-warning indicators of famine (Chaiken et al. 2009; Chaiken, Dixon, and Herminio 2012; Companion 2008). Recently efforts have been made to develop systems for community-level monitoring of behaviors associated with growing food scarcity, in order to raise awareness of the emerging problems in time to forestall full-blown food emergencies. The flip side of monitoring signs of increasing vulnerability is identifying and strengthening sources of resilience (Thoric Cederstrom, personal communication 2013; Ina Schonberg, personal communication 2013). This emphasis builds on earlier approaches such as positive deviance (Zeitlin 1990), acknowledges the agency of people in poor communities, and is less focused on deficits than its forerunners were. Nonetheless, this approach may also be used to justify decreased foreign assistance as the focus shifts to identifying strengths within poor communities.

This new emphasis on resilience resulted in the near universal advocacy of community or home-based management of malnutrition, even in rather severe cases. Home management of malnutrition is often termed community-based therapeutic care or community-based management of acute malnutrition, and the initiation of these strategies was made possible by the development of the first Ready-to-Use Therapeutic Foods (RUTF). The first of these RUTFs, a peanut butter–based paste packed with micronutrients called Plumpynut, was the brainchild of the French corporation Nutriset, in collaboration with pediatricians and nutritional researchers with the Irish NGO Valid International (Valid 2013). These RUTFs, which have been described as nothing short of miraculous for rehabilitating even very severely malnourished children, are far more effective than earlier strategies that relied on hospitalization in nutritional rehabilitation units (NRUs) and administration of the milk-based formulas F75 and F100, which had to be mixed with care and good hygiene. Unlike the care given in NRUs, the use of RUTFs can be handled in homes, does not rely on mixing and measuring, raises no concerns about use of unsafe water, empowers parents to address their children's health (rather than relying on "experts") and permits the child and parents to remain at home rather than abandoning household responsibilities to be present in a clinic or hospital. Not surprisingly, RUTF programs have shown far more positive compliance and follow-through than traditional treatment programs in NRUs (Collins 2001; Collins et al. 2005; Chaiken et al. 2006).

Recently there has been a move to develop locally produced RUTFs based on available food products in countries with high rates of undernutrition, rather than relying on imported products. Ultimately this will be more economically and logistically sustainable, and may boost local economies if there new markets emerge for quality food products such as peanuts and beans. Demand for RUTFs is likely to continue growing, especially in Africa, as it has become apparent that maintaining a positive nutritional status is an effective tool for prolonging the life and viability of people living with HIV/AIDS (Bennink 2012; Nyandiko et al. 2008; USAID 2005).

Other organizations, especially the U.S. Centers for Disease Control, have developed packets or sachets of micronutrient sprinkles intended to fortify foods normally consumed at home. These sprinkles can be added to children's foods to boost the nutritional value—though not the caloric value—and combat deficiencies of certain important micronutrients such as Vitamin A, iron, and zinc (Jefferds et al. 2010; Zlotkin 2009). As in the case of RUTFs, administering these sachets of sprinkles does not require careful measurement or parental literacy, and they are relatively cost-effective to distribute.

Research points increasingly to the importance of key micronutrients in ensuring robust immune response, ability to recover from illness, and optimal cognitive and mechanical performance (Allen 1995; Allen et al. 1991; Long et al. 2005; Murphy and Allen 2003; Neumann et al. 2003). Given the synergism between malnutrition and morbidity, addressing micronutrient deficiency is an important strategy (Pelletier 1999; Scrimshaw 1991). The negative side of both RUTF and sprinkles use is that they rely on supplementation rather than a diet-based approach to optimal nutrition, even though both approaches acknowledge that adequate access to nutritious foods remains a challenge in many regions that fall far short of true famine conditions.

To prevent problems associated with malnutrition, two other promoted strategies focus on improving the qualities of foods people, and especially small children, consume. The international Consultative Group on International Agricultural Research is comprised of more than a dozen centers around the globe that conduct research on key crops and agricultural systems. Initially established to address hunger in the early 1960s, CGIAR centers were responsible for the Green Revolution. Approaches that were integral to the Green Revolution strategies—especially the reliance on chemicals, machinery, and other inputs that proved to be beyond the means of the average farmer in a developing country—have been targets of much criticism. However, the newer strategies promoted by CGIAR centers and the research projects are part of the USAID-funded Collaborative Research Support Programs (CRSPs) focused on food crops that are widely consumed in developing countries. Specifically, several CGIAR Centers have developed Harvest Plus research programs, which seek to identify strains of commonly consumed subsistence crops that have higher micronutrient values, and then to replicate those varieties to enhance nutritional qualities. Examples of Harvest Plus programs include the development of varieties of orange-fleshed sweet potatoes that are very high in beta carotene (the biological precursor of Vitamin A) in Uganda, and high-iron bean varieties in Rwanda (Harvest Plus 2013).

Similarly, research supported through the CRSP projects has emphasized improving the bioavailability of some crops that are not readily digested, thus improving the consumer's ability to absorb key nutrients. For example, recently developed new bean varieties are more easily digested, especially by children, and are a relatively high-protein plant-sourced food (Mazur et al. 2011). These strategies to enhance crops' nutritional value or foods' bioavailability should not be confused with the controversial practice of genetic engineering of crops, as these strategies do not insert genetic information from other species, but rather use traditional plant breeding strategies to enhance desirable properties already found in some varieties. The rationale is that if the nutritional value of crops already commonly consumed by the global poor—grains, pulses, greens—can be improved, the nutritional status of these people will be improved as well. Much of this work is in its infancy, but it shows promise for introducing useful cultivars that do not require wholesale modifications of the agrarian systems.

Finally, a growing literature is validating the need for foods of animal origin in the diets of children. Animal-source foods (ASF), especially meat, have been demonstrated to significantly increase children's performance in school, improve their intellectual abilities, and maintain robust immune response (Murphy and Allen 2003; Neumann et al. 2003). In most cases of true famine, both available livestock and bushmeat sources are often depleted as people try to cope with food stress. Understanding the critical importance of ASF in children's diets suggests that relief efforts in food emergencies should explore means of providing access to ASF, not just grains and pulses as is the norm.

Conclusion

No discussion of the problem of famine, or of the strategies that can address such a crisis, would be complete without reiterating the link between famine and conflict. Ellen Messer (1998) poignantly documented this a decade ago while examining how, in times of war, food becomes not only a scarce commodity but also a tool of warfare and conflict itself. More recent work has reinforced our understanding of the destructive impacts of conflict in civil wars in western Africa, the ongoing struggles in Afghanistan, and in all places where people feel unsafe and flee their homes (Bolten 2013; Coulter 2009). The World Disasters Report indicated that in 2012, more than 43 million people left their homes as a consequence of conflict, and overall there were 73 million refugees or internally displaced persons worldwide—that is, one of every 100 people on the globe (IFRC 2013). This sobering statistic should serve as a reminder of the need to find ways to promote peace and tolerance so that good people can simply go about their lives making a living, caring for their children, and seeing a brighter future in a world free of famine.

Miriam S. Chaiken is a nutritional anthropologist who has worked extensively with NGOs in the global South to address issues of chronic food insecurity and child vulnerability. Her recent work in eastern and southern Africa has been to increase understanding of the conditions of vulnerability and resilience in regards to food shortage, and develop strategies to address these problems through community-based early warning systems. She is Distinguished Faculty in Anthropology at New Mexico State University, and Dean of NMSU's Conroy Honors College.

Acknowledgements

I would like to thank Thoric Cederstrom (Director, Sustainable Livelihoods Practice Area, Creative Associates International), Tina Lloren (FANTA Mozambique), Deborah Rubin (Director, Cultural Practice), and Ina Schonberg (Senior Advisor, University Research Inc.) for their insights and suggestions for this essay. Any errors or omissions remain the fault of the author alone.

References

Allen, Lindsay H. 1995. Malnutrition and Human Function: A Comparison of Conclusions from the INCAP and Nutrition CRSP Studies. *Journal of Nutrition* 125: 1119S–1126S.

Allen, Lindsay H., Anne K. Black, Jeffrey R. Backstrand, Gretel H. Pelto, Richard D. Ely, Elsa Molina, and Adolfo Chávez. 1991. An Analytical Approach for Exploring the Importance of Dietary Quality versus Quantity in the Growth of Mexican Children. *Food and Nutrition Bulletin* 13(2): 95–104.

Ballard, Terri, Jennifer Coates, Anne Swindale, and Megan Deitchler. 2011. *Household Hunger Scale: Indicator Definition and Measurement Guide.* Washington, DC: FANTA2 Bridge.

Bennink, Maurice. 2012. *Improving Nutritional Status and CD4 Counts in HIV-Infected Children through Nutritional Support. Work Plan and Budget FY 12.* Dry Grain Pulse CRSP. East Lansing: Michigan State University.

Black, Robert E., Saul S. Morris, and Jennifer Bryce. 2003. Where and Why Are 10 Million Children Dying Every Year? *The Lancet* 361(9376): 2226–2234.

Bolten, Catherine E. 2013. *I Did it to Save My Life: Love and Survival in Sierra Leone.* Berkeley: University of California Press.

Chaiken, Miriam S., Hedwig Deconinck, and Tedbabe Degefie. 2006. The Promise of a Community Based Approach to Managing Severe Malnutrition: A Case Study from Ethiopia. *Food and Nutrition Bulletin* 27(2): 95–104.

Chaiken, Miriam S., J. Richard Dixon, and Agy Herminio. 2012. Food Security and Safety Nets: NGOs in Northern Mozambique. *Bulletin of the Association of Concerned Africa Scholars* 88: 20–25.

Chaiken, MS, JR Dixon, C Powers, E Wetzler. 2009. Asking the Right Questions: Community-Based Strategies to Combat Hunger. *NAPA Bulletin* 32(1): 42–54.

Collins, Steven. 2001. Changing the Way We Address Severe Malnutrition during Famine. *The Lancet* 358(9280): 498–501.

Collins, Steven, Kate Sadler, Nicky Dent, Tanya Khara, Saul Guerrero, Mark Myatt, Montse Saboya, and Anne Walsh. 2005. *Key Issues in the Success of Community-Based Management of Severe Malnutrition.* Technical Paper. Valid International.

Companion, Michèle. 2008. The Underutilization of Street Markets as a Source of Food Security Indicators in Famine Early Warning Systems: A Case Study of Ethiopia. *Disasters* 32(3): 399–415.

Coulter, Chris. 2009. *Bush Wives and Girl Soldiers: Women's Lives through War and Peace in Sierra Leone.* Ithaca: Cornell University Press.

Diaz-Briquets, Charles C. Cheyney, and Susan Germano. 1992. *Nutrition CRSP Feasibility and Planning Activity.* Arlington, VA: Casals & Associates.

FANTA. 2013. *Food and Nutrition Technical Assistance Program.* Publications Catalog. http://www.fantaproject.org/index.shtml. Accessed 3 November 2016.

FAO (Food and Agriculture Organization). 2013a. Permanent Interstate Committee for Drought Control in the Sahel. http://www.fao.org/in-action/sahelian-and-west-african-governments-avoid-surprises-thanks-to-seasonal-monitoring/en/. Accessed 28 July 2013.

FAO. 2013b. Food and Agriculture Data. Statistical Division of the Food and Agriculture Organization. http://faostat.fao.org/beta/en/#home. Accessed 3 November 2016.

FEWS (Famine Early Warning System). n.d. Famine Early Warning System. www.fews.net. Accessed 28 July 2013.

Global Nutrition Cluster. n.d. *Global Nutrition Cluster.* Nutritioncluster.net. Accessed 3 November 2016

Harvest Plus. n.d. Harvest Plus. CGIAR. http://www.harvestplus.org/. Accessed 27 July 2013.

HEA. 2013. Household Economy Approach, and Cost of the Diet. http://www.heawebsite.org. Accessed 27 July 2013.

Humanitarian Response. 2013. Humanitarian Response. http://assessments.humanitarianresponse.info. Accessed 27 July 2013.

IFPRI. 2013. The International Food Policy Research Institute. www.ifpri.org. Accessed 27 July 2013.

IFRC. 2013. *World Disasters Report.* International Federation of Red Cross and Red Crescent Societies. http://www.ifrc.org/en/publications-and-reports/world-disasters-report-2012/. Accessed 27 July 2013.

IRIN. 2013. Integrated Regional Information Networks. http://www.irinnews.org/. Accessed 27 July 2013.

Jefferds, Maria Elena D., Lorraine Ogange, Mercy Owuor, Kari Cruz, Bobbie Person, Alfredo Obure, Parminder Suchdeve, and Laird J. Ruth. 2010. Formative Research Exploring Acceptability, Utilization, and Promotion in Order to Develop a Micronutrient Powder (Sprinkles) Intervention among Luo Families in Western Kenya. *Food and Nutrition Bulletin* 31(Suppl. 2): 179–185.

Kurz, Kathleen M. and Charlotte Johnson-Welch. 2001. Enhancing Women's Contributions to Improving Family Food Consumption and Nutrition. In *Long-Term Food-Based Approaches Toward Eliminating Vitamin A Deficiency in Africa.* Special issue, *Food and Nutrition Bulletin* 22(4): 443–453.

Long, Jennifer K., Constance Gewa, Nimrod O. Bwibo, Lindsay Allen, Suzanne Murphy, and Charlotte Neumann. 2005. Anemia in Rural Kenyan Children: Role of Malaria, Infection and Poor Diet Quality and Meat Intake. *GL CRSP Research Brief* 05–01-CNP.

Mazur, Robert, Henry Kizito Musoke, Dorothy Nakimbugwe, and Michael Ugen. 2011. Enhancing Nutritional Value and Marketability of Beans through Research and Strengthening Key Value-Chain Stakeholders in Uganda. *2020 Conference Note* 1. Washington, DC: IFPRI.

Messer, Ellen. 1998. Conflict as a Cause of Hunger. In *Who's Hungry? And How Do We Know? Food Shortage, Poverty, and Deprivation,* ed. L. Derose, E. Messer, and S. Millman, 164–180. Tokyo: United Nations University Press.

Mohammed *Mo* Amin: 1943–1996. n.d. Mohamed Amin Foundation. http://www.moforce.com/moamin.html. Accessed 27 July 2013.

Murphy, Suzanne P., and Lindsay H. Allen. 2003. Nutritional Importance of Animal Source Foods. *Journal of Nutrition* 133(11): 39325–39355.

Neumann, Charlotte G., Nimrod O. Bwibo, Suzanne P. Murphy, Marian Sigman, Shannon Whaley, Lindsay H. Allen, Donald Guthrie, Robert E. Weiss, and Montague W. Demment. 2003. Animal Source Foods Improve Dietary Quality, Micronutrient Status, Growth and Cognition Function in Kenyan School Children: Background, Study Design, and Baseline Findings. *Journal of Nutrition* 133(11): 39415–39495.

Nyandiko, Winstone, Abraham Siika, Judith Ernst, Grace Ettyang, Charlotte Neumann, and Constantin Yiannoutsos. 2008. The Academic Model Providing Access to Healthcare (AMPATH) in Kenya. *GL CRSP Research Brief* 08–0.

Pelletier, David L. 1999. Nutritional Status: The Master Key to Child Survival. In *Scaling Up, Scaling Down: Overcoming Malnutrition in Developing Countries*, ed. Thomas J. Marchione, 23–40. Amsterdam: Gordon and Breach.

Pelto, Gretel H., and Jeffrey R. Backstrand. 2003. Interrelationships between Power-Related and Belief-Related Factors Determine Nutrition in Populations. In *Symposium on Beliefs, Power, and the State of Nutrition: Integrating Social Science Perspectives in Nutrition Interventions*, supplement. *Journal of Nutrition* 133: 297S–300S.

Pelto, Gretel H., Jocelyn Urgello, Lindsay H. Allen, Adolfo Chavez, Homero Martinez, Luzmaria Meneses, Constance Capacchione, and Jeffrey Backstrand. 1991. Household Size, Food Intake and Anthropometric Status of School-Age Children in a Highland Mexican Area. *Social Science and Medicine* 33(10): 1135–1140.

Quisumbing, Agnes R. 2003. *Household Decisions, Gender, and Development: A Synthesis of Recent Research*. Washington, DC: International Food Policy Research Institute and Johns Hopkins University Press.

Save the Children. 2013. *State of the World's Mothers*. www.savethechildrenweb.org/SOWM-2013. Accessed 27 July 2013.

Scrimshaw, Nevin. 1991. Iron Deficiency. *Scientific American* (October): 46–52.

Sphere. 2013. http://www.spherehandbook.org/. Accessed 27 July 2013.

UNICEF. 2013. *State of the World's Children*. http://www.unicef.org/sowc2013/statistics.html. Accessed 27 July 2013.

USAID. 2005. *Global Horticulture Assessment*. Davis, CA: University of California.

Valid. 2013. Valid International. http://www.validinternational.org. Accessed 27 July 2013.

Vaughn, Megan. 1987. *The Story of an African Famine*. Cambridge: Cambridge University Press.

Verdin, J., Funk, C., Senay, G., & Choularton, R. (2005). Climate science and famine early warning. *Philosophical Transactions of the Royal Society of London B: Biological Sciences, 360*(1463), 2155–2168.

Walters, Tamsin, Victoria Sibson, and Marie McGrath. 2012. Mid Upper Arm Circumference and Weight-for-Height Z-score as indicators of Severe Acute Malnutrition: A Consultation of Operational Agencies and Academic Specialists to Understand the Evidence, Identify Knowledge Gaps and Inform Operational Guidance. Final Review Paper. *Field Exchange: Emergency Nutrition Network*, Save the Children UK, Action Contra Faim, and UNHCR.

Young, Helen, and Susanne Jaspars. 2009. *Review of Nutrition and Mortality Indicators for the Integrated Food Security Phase Classification (IPC): Reference Levels and Decision Making*. Inter-agency Standing Committee Nutrition Cluster.

Zeitlin, Marian. 1990. *Positive Deviance in Child Nutrition*. Tokyo: United Nations University Press.

Zlotkin, Stanley. 2009. *Overview of Efficacy, Effectiveness and Safety of Micronutrient Powders (MNPs)*. Sprinkles Global Health Initiative.

CHAPTER 6

Food Activism
Researching Engagement, Engaging Research
Joan Gross

Introduction: Scale, Focus and Mode

Foodways, like language, are practices that we assimilate in a largely unconscious manner. The broadest definition of food activism, then, is bringing food practices into consciousness with a goal of changing them. However, food activism becomes more interesting to anthropologists as it moves beyond the individual. Food activists work to improve the health of the environment in its role as food producer and the health of people in their role as food consumers. Efforts to change ways of eating often lead to analyzing the economic structures that have helped create our present practices and to militating for changes in political policies. Markowitz and Brett (2012) for example, take an advocacy stance in discussions of the importance of U.S. food policy for determining practice both within the United States and globally.

When choosing a topic to research within the broad field of food activism, you might think about the scale, focus, and mode of activism. Regarding scale, is one an activist if the site of the action is one's own body? What about one's household or one's circle of friends? Mobilizing for change rather than unconsciously accepting a given structure shows human agency, but should people be considered activists because they take the time to prepare fresh, local food for their families, decide to no longer eat factory-produced meat, or opt to stop using toxic chemicals on their farms? These people are repudiating the dominant system and taking power for themselves, bringing about change at the micro level. As Mintz (1985) has pointed out, food holds a privileged position because it connects inside and outside meanings. Nestle (2000) suggests something similar when she states that we must "vote with our forks," another way of saying that the personal is political and economic. Many food activists working at the community, regional, national, and international levels began by consciously changing the way they ate. So it seems that personally breaking with the status quo in some fashion often motivates people to scale up their activism.

Psychological methods are in order if one is interested in motivations for changing individual food practices, whereas statistical methods will suit a focus on large-scale shifts. Ethnography, with its cornerstone of participant observation, is a particularly rich way of studying how people organize to make changes in their communities (whether face-to-face or virtual) and will be our focus here. Bernard (2011) gives a thorough discussion of ethnographic methods, while Wolcott (2004) reminds us to be holistic but know when to resist the endless task of accumulating data and begin searching for underlying patterns, relationships, and meanings. A good place to start for examples of the ethnographic study of food activism is Counihan and Siniscalchi (2014), which presents fourteen case studies exploring food activism in different settings around the world from local, national, and transnational angles.

The complexity of the food system fosters myriad possible subjects that one can work to improve, from saving seeds to altering school lunch programs. Under the broad definition offered above, we might imagine a place and time when working families organize in order to have more fast-food outlets in their neighborhood, but food activism at this historical juncture has a distinctly anti-corporate bent. How are people fighting against such things as the privatization of water, mega feed lots, food deserts, monocultures of corn and soybeans, pesticide poisoning of agricultural laborers, the reduction of biodiversity, and the loss of food traditions? Food activist organizations tend to privilege changes in practices within the realm of production or consumption. For instance, some work to reduce the use of chemicals in agriculture; others work to increase access to healthy food for people with low incomes. These two poles often conflict with each other in wealthy countries, where organic produce raised on small farms by people paid a living wage generally costs more than produce cultivated with the use of various chemicals in large-scale monocultures planted and harvested mechanically by low-paid workers.

One way that food activists around the world (see especially Slow Food www.slowfood.com and Via Campesina viacampesina.org/en/) have attempted to solve this dilemma is by creating stronger connections between food producers and food consumers and trying to convince people that their consumption choices have an effect on both the health of the global environment and their own personal health. To counteract the detachment between eaters and the sources of their food in the global food system, food activists create opportunities to bring people into contact with the producers of food and to encourage direct sales. By cutting out or taking over operations that generally take place between production and consumption (cleaning, processing, packaging, marketing, selling), prices can be kept lower for the consumer and higher for producers who sell at retail rather than wholesale prices. As an added benefit, the buying and selling of food creates social ties in the community.

Cooperative and fair trade movements work along these lines on an international scale, and anthropologists are well set up to examine how the organizations behind specialty labels actually work (e.g., Jaffee 2007). De Neve et al.'s (2008) volume on ethnographies of fair trade, ethical consumption, and corporate responsibility contains several food system articles (Pratt, Luetchford, Berlan, Markowitz). Lavin (2012) and Guthman (2011) criticize local food movements for proposing market solutions to political problems.

When choosing a topic within food activism, besides scale and focus, we can talk about mode of action. How is the activism carried out? Some groups do mainly educational events, others fundraise for various projects that they may or may not be responsible for, and others work on a specific project. How groups organize themselves to increase capacity and membership is also a topic worthy of study. Direct action is distinct from indirect action. Graeber (2009) describes direct action as aiming to achieve goals through our own activity rather than through the actions of others. It repudiates the existing order and demonstrates that we have both the right and power to change the world by doing it. At the level of the individual and family, the mode is always direct, but indirect modes tend to dominate when the scale moves up to national and international levels. Most food activists participate in both kinds of activism. They might indirectly support national and global food sovereignty movements by subscribing to listservs, signing petitions, and sending donations, but in their communities they focus on direct actions like convincing neighbors to change their consumption habits, establishing new venues for direct sales, and so on. A time allocation chart of the kinds of food activist work done by affiliated members will give you a sense of where energy is being spent, by individuals and by the group as a whole. Chances are that the group you choose to study has relations with other groups, and you will spend some time sorting out the different angles of interacting food activist groups (Hassanein 2012).

You should get to know both the structural and the personal relations within the group you study, through document and website reviews, key informant interviews, and observation. Many food activist organizations are registered NGOs or nonprofit organizations and, depending on the country, must follow certain legal guidelines. The AAA Special Interest Group on NGOs and Nonprofits (http://ngo.americananthro.org/about-us/) is a good source of anthropologists working on these organizations. You may also choose to study food activist projects that grow out of organizations with much broader missions, such as religious institutions or even government agencies. Indigenous groups have a different sort of organization often based on elected tribal councils or councils of elders. Groups like Food Not Bombs come from a more anarchist perspective and lack such an organizational structure as do freegans and guerilla gardeners. Other groups of interest may be more ephemeral, such as a group of parents calling for changes in school lunches. Some groups have defined roles for their members; others are more amorphous. Either way, personalities and personal relations are important to understanding ways in which people interact with one another.

Get to know how your chosen subjects see themselves within a framework of social change. When it comes to nonprofits and NGOs, this information is usually available in mission statements and strategic plans, but it can change based on funding opportunities and new board and staff members. Mares and Alkon's (2011) outline of four food movement discourses (local food, community food security, food justice, and food sovereignty) provides a good tool for preliminary categorization of food activist organizations. The idea of "sovereignty," for instance, will likely be far more important in dealings with indigenous groups than it is in work with urban anti-hunger activists. A human rights framework might be more common in international organizations, whereas the health of children might be the major motivation in changing food accessibility in a local school.

Whatever the scale, focus, and mode of the group you choose to study, you and your research should be acceptable to that group. Food activism is a rich area for anthropological research, and the ethical mandate of "do no harm to those we study" is as relevant here as in any research project. When researching practices that might be deemed illegal, such as guerilla gardening, dumpster diving, or even sale of food made in noncertified kitchens, care must be taken to protect anonymity and confidentiality. When working internationally, make sure you have research clearance from the proper institutions abroad. Indigenous groups may have their own research review boards through which research clearance must be obtained. Be aware that the wishes of "the group" could differ from those of the individual members of that group. Some groups may be unconcerned about your particular research questions. Others will want a major role in defining your study, so that it advances the work of the group. Any research on human subjects should be passed through your institution's review board (IRB), which ensures that your project is compliant with the Code of Federal Regulations. Be aware, however, that best practices within community-based participatory research (CBPR) conflict with the traditional scientific model that has guided the formation of IRB practices. Rigid, predetermined protocols and issues of anonymity and data ownership perpetuate an expert-led system that much food activist research seeks to change. The mismatch between CBPR and standard IRB practice is discussed in Cross, Pickering and Hickey (2014), who suggest that IRBs develop a more participatory, flexible system to accommodate the move away from top-down research.

Gathering Background Information: Talking the Talk

As in any ethnographic research, research begins with background reading. A few key academic works on the North American food system include Allen (2004) and Hinrichs and Lyson (2009). Holt-Gimenez (2011) gives an overview of international food activism. Food First offers a panoply of books, reports, primers ("backgrounders"), and policy briefs on food activist topics, many of which are available online at http://foodfirst.org/publications/. Academic work showing how corporate influence on scientific production within and outside of universities and the subsequent government policy and extension activities contribute to unhealthy structures provides an important background for much food activism (e.g., Guthman 2012; Sherwood et al. 2013). Food activists are often inspired by books and movies produced for a popular, rather than an academic audience. You should ask the food activists you are working with what inspired them. Some popular inspirational books are by Rachel Carson (1962), Sandor Katz (2006), Frances Moore Lappé (1971), Michael Pollan (2006), Eric Schlosser (2001), and Vandana Shiva (2000). Movies about the problems of the global food system have become an industry unto themselves. Some examples are *Fast Food Nation, Food, Inc., Forks over Knives, The Future of Food, King Corn, Supersize Me,* and *Resistance.* Exposing yourself to these materials will help you build your vocabulary and become familiar with alternative ways of seeing the food system.

The kind of food activist groups that develop depend on the physical, historical, economic, and social environment in which they are found. The revitalization of food traditions would be a likely focus in New Orleans or within a Native American tribe, whereas mega–confined-animal feedlots might be a target for food activists in the upper Midwest. Poor sections of large cities might well generate organizations to increase local access to fresh food no matter where it comes from, while farming communities might work on providing more outlets for direct sales. Look into the economic history of the area and of any prior alternative movements. When a large food-related corporation provides a high percentage of jobs in the area (e.g., Striffler 2007), that fact will be an important component in organizing for change. Prominent grassroots organizing and other alternative movements in the area's history is also important and may even be a source of food activists (Belasco 2007). Check out local history organizations as well as unpublished theses and reports from local schools, colleges, and universities. Some organizations might allow you to examine their archives. Community Food Assessments have been done for many parts of the United States, and many of them are posted online, as are instructions on how to conduct one. Early guides (Pothukuchi et al. 2002; Cohen, Andrews, and Kantor 2002) were published by the Community Food Security Coalition and USDA. A more recent grassroots guide was prepared by Oregon Food Bank staff after assisting in the completion of fifteen community food assessments around the state (Oregon Food Bank and Masterson 2013).

Social considerations are always important, so be sure to collect demographic information on informants. Are activists predominantly of a particular socioeconomic class? Racial or ethnic group? Gender? Educational background? Bernard (2011) has good advice about the complexities of demographic information and ways to discern socioeconomic class beyond economic indicators. Are one group's interests promoted over the interests of less dominant groups? Research into the area of food justice or food democracy is bringing a lot of these issues to light. A conference held in 2012 called Food + Justice = Democracy came up with principles of food justice that are available at http://www.iatp.org/files/2013_02_08_FoodJusticePrinciples_v2_0.pdf. See Slocum (2007, 2011) for a discussion of whiteness in the alternative food movement in the United States and the collection *Cultivating Food Justice: Race, Class, and Sustainability* (Alkon and Agyeman 2011) for studies of institutional racism in the food system.

Depending on your prior experience and the topic you choose to research, your vocabulary will expand in the direction of both the subject of activism (e.g., farming, food preparation/preservation, healthful eating) and the mechanisms of activism or organization building. The latter might well include the legalities of nonprofit operation as well as various pathways to capacity-building. You cannot assume that words carry the same meaning in different places, especially when working internationally. For instance, "agroecology" in the United States has developed differently from "agroecología" in Latin America, and within the country of Ecuador the term is understood one way in the mountains and another way along the coast. Thus you must never take for granted that you know what a term means. Context and history determine meaning.

A big part of activism involves trying to get a larger public to see things the way your group does, so it is important to examine the choice of words and how certain meanings are promoted and others demoted. It is important to document discussions involving keywords like "organic" and "sustainable." Food activists work against highly professional corporate marketers who use vast sums of money in framing information to create profit for their companies, so the path is not easy.

Researching activism generally means attending multiple meetings, both formal and informal. Field notes should be taken after these meetings (on writing field notes see Emerson, Fretz, and Shaw 2011 and Bernard 2011: 291–300). Many of these meetings will also generate texts and other materials that are ripe for analysis. In addition to mission and vision statements and strategic plans, pay attention to discussions of logos and organization and project names. You might compare your field notes to meeting minutes in order to determine what sort of material is being recorded and what sort is left out. Other literature that could be analyzed includes public advertisements for events, guides for workshops, and correspondence (with proper permission). An ethnography of communication approach will lead you to pay attention to who is using what kind of language with whom, in what context, and for what purposes (Hymes 1974).

Beyond doing no harm, anthropological research can assist food activist movements by providing information that can help direct their work. Participatory action research is particularly helpful here because it transforms the subjects of the research into co-researchers who define the questions to be researched. The FEAST Organizing Manual compiled by the Oregon Food Bank staff (2016) gives very clear directions about how to get started doing community food activism.

Walking the Walk: Observant Participation

As in any ethnographic project, you are yourself an instrument, and your positionality affects the information you receive. Though doing a dispassionate study of food activism is a perfectly reasonable proposition, I focus here on the role of the "observant participant," which Costa Vargas (2008) differentiates from participant observation, the mainstay of anthropological fieldwork. Borrowing from Hale (2008), I see activist social science as helping us to understand inequality and oppression. Methodologically it is carried out with people who are themselves subject to these conditions, and the research is used to formulate strategies to transform the conditions. For more on decolonizing methodologies and action research, see Smith (1999), Cameron and Gibson (2005), Greenwood and Levin (2006), Reason and Bradbury-Huang (2007), and elsewhere in this volume.

You might develop into an activist researcher by first becoming an activist and later deciding to research the topic that drew you to activism, or you might decide to research food activism and then feel that you want to play a more activist role. Many people go back and forth, privileging one role and then the other. In some ways, the issues that arise for food activist anthropologists mirror issues brought up by native anthropologists. The stage of description from an etic standpoint is often overwhelmed by the emic view of the insider. Narayan (1993: 680) prefers that we pay attention to the range of hybrid personal and professional identities that we negotiate in our daily lives, rather than classifying anthropologists as being either inside or outside the societies they study. Her discussion of situated knowledges is relevant here, because instead of learning conceptual categories and then finding contexts in which to apply them, native anthropologists absorb analytic categories that rename and reframe what is already known. This describes the trajectory of activists who turn their researcher's gaze on activist work in which they are involved.

Your role outside of food activism helps determine how you are seen by other members of the group. Most activist groups are anxious to recruit new members to their ranks, but you may be regarded with suspicion if you belong to a group that has been involved in exploitation. Situations that might give rise to suspicion include being from a rich country and working in a poor country; being from a dominant socioeconomic or ethnic group when the food activists are from non-dominant groups; being affiliated with a university while working with a community group. In any of these situations you may also be seen as an asset, but not necessarily.

The role of land grant universities deserves some attention here. One might assume there would be a high degree of coherence between a land grant university and a local food movement due to shared interest in growing food, rural development, and health, yet this is not always the case. Food activists usually support alternative farming practices, whereas universities since the 1950s have been the main disseminators of the Green Revolution—a movement based on economies of scale and chemical inputs—and are now at the center of GMO research, which most food activists see as contradictory to food sovereignty. Universities today are beginning to support alternative approaches with new programs for small-scale and sustainable agriculture, but alternative farmers who listened to earlier extension agents still harbor suspicions.

You probably possess skills and access to materials and information that are useful to an organization, but you may also need to unlearn ways of interacting that you have assimilated in an academic setting. Often the palpable split that can emerge between "town and gown" is due to economic rather than educational differences. At times you will want to downplay your connection with the university; other times, the university's vast holdings and connections will be seen as an asset. This could be seen as performing "la perruque," the term used by Certeau (1984) to describe the practice of disguising one's own work as work for one's employer. For university instructors, the shift in university politics toward involving students in community activities through experiential or service learning has proved a useful loophole in providing supplies and services for food activist groups. This loophole allowed me, for example, to spend countless hours in my university office organizing community events and meetings in which students were involved. Many grassroots groups lack the phones, computers, photocopiers, and sound and projection equipment that universities may have in abundance. Universities can also provide rooms for meetings and film showings, especially those included in class syllabi.

One of the most useful roles of the activist instructor is to bring students into community activism. Certeau further defines "la perruque" as diverting time away from one's employer and toward activities that are "free, creative, and precisely not directed toward profit." This describes activist work, but it also describes what is best about education. As activist researchers in the university, we can find plenty of justification for involving students in activist projects as an integral part of their education. A special bonus for anthropologists, who often do research in faraway places in foreign languages, is that work with local food activist groups means you can involve students without worrying about the cost of going abroad and their lack of language skills. Students who are practiced in local food activism are better prepared to engage in such issues abroad. Aligning students' projects with the goals of the local organization sets them up for an activist future while providing desired information for the organization. Synergistic relationships may develop, bringing the best collaborative work in the organization back to the research team, and taking the analytical lens of the academy into the organization. In addition, this synergy can bring about more coherence in the lives of students who begin to see the links between their lives in and outside of the classroom.

Food activism is of great interest to students today, and one good place to start is at the university itself. Are students on campus food-secure? If not, what can be done about it? Where does the food purchased by the university come from? Is it organic? Was it produced by socially just methods? Students who become interested in these issues can join the national Real Food Challenge (www.realfood challenge.org), which brings university students together to build a "healthy, fair, and green" food economy, starting by organizing on their own campuses. Peggy Barlett (2011) lays out four components of campus sustainable-food projects in her survey of thirty colleges known as leaders in sustainability.

Costa Vargas (2008) points out that scholars benefit disproportionately from their involvement with grassroots organizations, in part by expanding their skills in new directions. I have already mentioned the acquisition of new vocabulary sets, but that is only one way communicative repertoires can expand. Things I learned by holding various offices in a food activist organization include writing grants for community projects and organizational capacity building, facilitating meetings, reading a budget, developing public relations materials, engaging people at various fairs, putting on large events, and hiring and supervising people according to AmeriCorps protocol. None of these had been part of my prior experience at the university, but they are skills that do translate in various ways into practices at the university. Being involved in local food activism also can help academicians find coherence in their own lives. It allows us to connect with the place and community where we live, even if we grew up far away.

Nevertheless, the activist scholar will probably feel the tension of being accountable to the two worlds Hale (2008) talks about. People engaged in fulfilling the academic publication requirements of a university job or degree program may feel they have little time to devote to activism. Hale suggests developing research that is both theoretical and meant to be put to use. He elaborates:

> The world is in considerable need of improvement, and improvement comes in large part by means of social movements, struggles, and campaigns to change public agendas, not merely by the provision of technical expertise to those al-

ready in power. Activist scholarship can help movements have more success improving the world. (2008: xxv)

Food is a privileged terrain for both exploring residual and emergent cultural formations that coexist with the hegemonic system. Engaged research on food activism is one way to help movements have more success improving the world.

Joan Gross (PhD, University of Texas 1985) is Professor of Anthropology at Oregon State University, where she helped start the Food in Culture and Social Justice program. She is a founding member of Ten Rivers Food Web and Slow Food-Corvallis. Her current research focuses on food sovereignty activism in Oregon and Ecuador.

References

Alkon, Alison, and Julian Agyeman. 2011. *Cultivating Food Justice: Race, Class, and Sustainability.* Boston: MIT Press.

Allen, Patricia. 2004. *Together at the Table: Sustainability and Sustenance in the American Agrifood System.* University Park: Pennsylvania State University Press.

Barlett, Peggy. 2011. Campus Sustainable Food Projects: Critique and Engagement. *American Anthropologist* 113(1): 101–115.

Belasco, Warren. 2007. *Appetite for Change: How the Counterculture took on the Food Industry.* Ithaca: Cornell University Press.

Bernard, H. Russell. 2011. *Research Methods in Anthropology: Qualitative and Quantitative Approaches.* 5th ed. New York: Altamira.

Cameron, Jenny, and Katherine Gibson. 2005. Participatory Action Research in a Poststructuralist Vein. *Geoforum* 36(3): 315–331.

Carson, Rachel. 1962. *Silent Spring.* Boston: Houghton Mifflin.

Certeau, Michel de. 1984. *The Practice of Everyday Life.* Berkeley: University of California Press.

Cohen, Barbara, Margaret Andrews, and Linda Scott Kantor. 2002. *Community Food Security Assessment Toolkit.* (E-FAN-02-013). http://www.ers.usda.gov/webdocs/publications/efan02013/15824_efan02013_1_.pdf . Accessed 1 November 2016.

Costa Vargas, João. 2008. Activist Scholarship: Limits and Possibilities in Time of Black Genocide. In *Engaging Contradictions: Theory, Politics, and Methods of Activist Scholarship,* ed. Charles Hale, 164–182. Berkeley: University of California Press.

Counihan, Carole, and Valeria Siniscalchi. 2014. *Food Activism: Agency, Democracy and Economy.* New York: Bloomsbury.

Cross, Jennifer, Kathleen Pickering, and Matthew Hickey. 2015. Community-Based Participatory Research, Ethics, and Institutional Review Boards: Untying a Gordian Knot. *Critical Sociology,* 41(7–8):1007–1026.

De Neve, Geert, Peter Luetchford, Jeffrey Pratt, and Donald C. Wood, eds. 2008. *Hidden Hands in the Market: Ethnographies of Fair Trade, Ethical Consumption, and Corporate Social Responsibility. Research in Economic Anthropology* 28. Bingley, U.K.: Emerald Group.

Emerson, Robert, Rachel Fretz, and Linda Shaw. 2011. *Writing Ethnographic Fieldnotes,* 2nd ed. Chicago: University of Chicago Press.

Graeber, David. 2009. *Direct Action: An Ethnography.* Oakland: AK Press.

Greenwood, Davydd, and Morten Levin. 2006. *Introduction to Action Research: Social Research for Social Change,* 2nd ed. Thousand Oaks, CA: Sage.

Guthman, Julie. 2011. *Weighing In: Obesity, Food Justice, and the Limits of Capitalism.* Berkeley: University of California Press.

Hale, Charles, ed. 2008. *Engaging Contradictions: Theory, Politics, and Methods of Activist Scholarship.* Berkeley: University of California Press.

Hassanein, Neva. 2012. Practicing Food Democracy: A Pragmatic Politics of Transformation. In *Taking Food Public: Redefining Foodways in a Changing World,* eds. Carole Counihan and Psyche Williams-Forson, 461–474. New York: Routledge.

Hinrichs, C. Clare, and Thomas A. Lyson, eds. 2009. *Remaking the North American Food System: Strategies for Sustainability.* Lincoln: University of Nebraska Press.

Holt-Gimenez, Eric, ed. 2011. *Food Movements Unite! Strategies to Transform Our Food Systems.* Oakland, CA: Food First Books.

Hymes, Dell. 1974. *Foundations in Sociolinguistics: An Ethnographic Approach.* Philadelphia: University of Pennsylvania Press.

Jaffee, Dan. 2007. *Brewing Justice: Fair Trade Coffee, Sustainability, and Survival.* Berkeley: University of California Press.

Katz, Sandor. 2006. *The Revolution Will Not be Microwaved: Inside America's Underground Food Movements.* White River Junction, VT: Chelsea Green.

Lappé, Frances Moore. 1971. *Diet for a Small Planet.* Boston: Ballantine.

Lavin, Chad. 2012. The Year of Eating Politically. In *Taking Food Public: Redefining Foodways in a Changing World,* eds. Carole Counihan and Psyche Williams-Forson, 576–591. New York: Routledge.

Mares, Theresa, and Alison Alkon. 2011. Mapping the Food Movement: Addressing Inequality and Neoliberalism. *Environment and Society: Advances in Research,* 2: 68–86.

Markowitz, Lisa, and John Brett, eds. 2012. *U.S. Food Policy: Anthropology and Advocacy in the Public Interest.* New York: Routledge.

Mintz, Sidney. 1985. *Sweetness and Power.* New York: Viking.

Narayan, Kirin. 1993. How Native Is a "Native" Anthropologist? *American Anthropologist N.S.* 95(3): 671–686.

Nestle, Marion. 2000. Ethical Dilemmas in Choosing a Healthful Diet: Vote with Your Fork! *Proceedings of the Nutrition Society* 59: 619–629.

Oregon Food Bank. 2016. *FEAST Organizing Manual.* Portland: Oregon Food Bank.

Oregon Food Bank and Spencer Masterson. 2013. *Conversations across the Food System: A Guide to Coordinating Grassroots Community Food Assessments.* Portland: Oregon Food Bank. https://assets.jhsph.edu/clf/mod_clfResource/doc/Conversations%20Across%20the%20Food%20System1stEdwebpdf.pdf

Pollan, Michael. 2006. *The Omnivore's Dilemma: A Natural History of Four Meals.* New York: Penguin.

Pothukuchi, Kami, Hugh Joseph, Hannah Burton, and Andy Fisher. 2002. *What's Cooking in Your Food System: A Guide to Community Food Assessment.* Venice, CA: Community Food Security Coalition.

Reason, Peter, and Hilary Bradbury-Huang, eds. 2007. *The SAGE Handbook of Action Research, Participative Inquiry and Practice.* 2nd ed. Thousand Oaks, CA: Sage.

Schlosser, Eric. 2001. *Fast Food Nation: The Dark Side of the All-American Meal.* New York: Houghton Mifflin.

Sherwood, Steve, Alberto Arce, Peter Berti, Ross Borja, Pedro Oyarzun, and Ellen Bekkering. 2013. Tackling the New Materialities: Modern Food and Counter-Movements in Ecuador. *Food Policy* 41(August): 1–10.

Shiva, Vandana. 2000. *Stolen Harvest.* Cambridge, MA: South End Press.

Slocum, Rachel. 2007. Whiteness, Space and Alternative Food Practice. *Geoforum* 38(3): 520–533.

———. 2011. Race in the Study of Food. *Progress in Human Geography* 35(3): 303–327.

Smith, Linda Tuhiwai. 1999. *Decolonizing Methodologies: Research and Indigenous Peoples.* London: Zed Books.

Striffler, Steve. 2007. *Chicken: The Dangerous Transformation of America's Favorite Food.* New Haven: Yale University Press.

Wolcott, Harry. 2004. *The Art of Fieldwork.* New York: Altamira.

CHAPTER 7

Food Praxis as Method

Penny Van Esterik

This chapter explores food activism as a means of knowing and learning about food systems. The relation between food activism and academic research is seldom examined. Rather, food activism and academic research are often kept conceptually and practically separate, although many academics in nutritional anthropology and food studies consider advocacy an important part of how they teach about and research food. Students often come to food studies with their own agendas and "causes," such as an interest in food allergies, veganism, community gardening, or fat activism. This creates a situation where neither student nor teacher can claim neutrality around food.

Scholar-activists pose a significant problem for research methodology because they blur boundaries between objective ethnographic research, food justice work, and political advocacy, and they do not, or cannot, feign objectivity in a field that respects replicable methods (cf. Freire 1970). Although the opposition between objective science and political subjectivity has been effectively challenged, students still need guidance on how to fit their advocacy into a research framework. Much of this critique comes from feminist theory (cf. Letherby 2003).

Does this mean that the experiences of food activists and those of their students are lost to the research process? No: these actors have a special but underutilized expertise that should be carefully integrated into research designs and included in discussions of interdisciplinary methodology in food studies. Otherwise we are missing an opportunity to understand how food systems change, and how we can change food systems.

Topics such as disordered eating, food banks, food safety, hunger, school lunch programs, food advertising, community gardens, urban agriculture, and obesity are both subjects of research and bases for food activism, evoking subjective and emotional responses from both researchers and activists. Food studies as a field spawns scholar-activists and activist-scholars. Perhaps because food is so deeply entrenched in our daily practices, the distancing encouraged in other domains of inquiry cannot be sustained in food studies. After all, we are of the same order as that which we study. To be precise, we eat. Because we are also eaters, we feel empathy for those people with problems that we as eaters understand. How can we research hunger, obesity, anorexia, food banks, or immigrant food practices and only present our findings in academic journals for dissemination to the handful of (non-)relatives who read those papers (three on average) without being drawn to praxis? It is hard work to distance ourselves from food and eating because affect and emotion are writ large in food studies research. As a result, researchers who uncover or recognize injustices in the food system are drawn to food activism. There is often no middle ground in food studies.

Food praxis is a way of knowing and learning about the food system by participating in actions to change and challenge that system. Praxis can be defined as direct action to change a situation (cf. Van Esterik 1986). However, advocacy gets a bad name because it is most closely associated with the confrontational style of disreputable lawyers who are not concerned with right or wrong, but with what is winnable. Food praxis takes place in all segments of the food system, including growing, purchasing, and consuming food. In activism and advocacy, our political alignment with groups struggling for specific changes becomes explicit. Food praxis often involves learning by doing, but the stakes are higher because we are more personally invested in the outcome. This fact raises important questions for research methodologies.

Do we as researchers and academics make full use of the lessons of food praxis that emerge during experiences like internships, practicums, service learning, community collaborations, or participating in special interest groups or action research projects? Do we fully integrate lessons learned from community outreach into our research designs? How do we engage with the "learn by doing" of food praxis so that it contributes to both theory and research methods? When do we act as citizen-activists, and when do we advocate as anthropologists? In short, how can food praxis be better integrated with other research methods? Providing "educational opportunities for students" is not enough if we are not able to make full use of the often painful lessons of praxis.

Practical Concerns

It is perhaps easiest to begin with practical suggestions to identify questions that may not be asked explicitly when researchers and students become volunteers or protestors. Even before a proposal or contract is submitted, teams should consider: What is collaboration? Who are the key players? How is power distributed among different stakeholders? Who "owns" the findings? Where is there potential conflict of interest? What are the power relations between community groups and privileged academics? What are the points of friction that might lead to serious disagreements? Perhaps the most practical point of all is money. Many academics seek grants for academic work and slide activist work around the edges, since grants make you frame questions in certain ways that may not benefit community development groups or fit with their political agendas.

For example, should food groups accept donations from the food industry? Many food corporations may have legitimate concerns about hunger in their communities. But they also attend to their public image, look for tax incentives, and need to demonstrate their corporate social responsibility. Groups for advocacy work around breastfeeding will not accept funding from baby food companies. But what about breast pump manufacturers who, while claiming that their products help women to breastfeed, may manufacture feeding bottles as well? What about soup manufacturers who provide their products to food banks for a tax break when the project is intended to teach people to make their own soups from scratch? Every project, and perhaps all individuals associated with a project, must choose battles carefully, deciding whom to stand with as allies, and whom to oppose and confront in order to maintain the integrity of the project. Even the alternative agro-food movement requires negotiating coalitions for food democracy (Hassanein 2003).

Methodological Considerations

Researchers of activist groups and food praxis use the same ethnographic, qualitative, and quantitative methods discussed elsewhere in this book. The following comments on methods are additional considerations that might need to be worked into the research design. What are some methodological considerations that need to be explored when we incorporate or take account of food activism in our research designs?

Ethics

The ethical complexities of participating in activist groups include consideration of the consequences of making activist strategies known to the public, or making them visible to the food industries that are being critiqued. Is informed consent and confidentiality possible or desired by all parties? How can we ensure confidentiality, when activists we work with insist on naming groups and identifying leaders? For example, groups that are given pseudonyms are unable to make use of research results in grant applications.

Communication

Whom do food activists share their knowledge with? A decision to publish in an academic journal may mean waiting two years for publication, but advocacy writing must be rapid—"just in time" to accomplish a goal—easily translated, and directed to the general public. What written materials do community groups need? Instead of a report, NGOs might make better use of a training manual or a procedures manual. Whose names and logos appear on published reports? A further complexity in communication concerns authorship, considering shared student collaboration and community partners. Academics might want to consider removing their names from reports if doing so gives community groups ownership. What use can the community make of the portfolios students are often asked to prepare during their placements?

Degrees of Engagement

Researchers may need to negotiate between participant *observation* and *participant* observation. Personal boundaries may make food activists question interns' sincerity or commitment. Are they willing to engage in nonviolent protest, for example, or do they prefer library work? Many academics avoid confrontation and would not be prepared to be arrested for picketing or boycott work. Others would be uncomfortable with the temporal frame expected of volunteer activists—fast immersion and a brief report, whereupon they disappear from the community and the social relations they formed. Should students and researchers start conversations they cannot finish?

Food activists will be particularly attentive to whether academics only *talk the talk* rather than *walk the walk*. They expect to see academics move beyond social critique to social action. Placements in jails, schools, and community gardens provide valuable experiences in understanding power relations. However, any disjuncture between personal eating habits and political rhetoric will be quite obvious.

Appropriation

Food activists have the opportunity to illuminate the efforts and stories of people working to change the industrial food system. But how do we express solidarity with them by retelling their stories without appropriating their stories?

Personal Response

All food researchers must learn skills around handling emotions, particularly empathy and anger. For example, they may well be faced with questions about food sharing in a context of hunger and food insecurity. Do you eat in the soup kitchen where you serve food? Do you bring food to a food insecure family when your gift influences the research inquiry? Praxis identifies—often in a painful manner—what personal skills a student might need to develop, including ways of improving communication, handling interpersonal conflict, and understanding the delicate relation between self as researcher and self as eater/feeder (cf. Van Esterik 2011).

Reflection

Many personal and theoretical lessons have been lost to the research process because they were not adequately described or linked to broader theoretical issues. Students may enjoy the food-related experience and even be able to describe it, but they may not be able to assess the meaning of that experience, or connect it to concepts such as power or privilege. The development of a structured reflection form for food-based practicums might draw attention to both personal and emotional experiences and the critical thinking necessary to integrate theory and practice following the food praxis experience. There is a useful literature on the art of practical reflection, particularly the work of Ash and Clayton (2009), who provide examples of how to design critical reflection exercises. They argue that reflection needs to be intentionally designed, including when and where the reflection takes place. Using the acronym DEAL (describe, examine, articulate learning), they outline a structured reflection form that goes far beyond "touchy-feely" introspection, journaling, and chat room discussions. Some of these guided questions might include how students and community members assess the effectiveness of food-based projects from their distinct perspectives. Useful resources include guides to service learning published in the *Michigan Journal of Community Service Learning* and reports from the Institute for Community Engaged Scholarship, University of Guelph, Ontario, Canada.

Incorporating food praxis into research projects, adding an activist component into research projects, or researching food activism raises important theoretical issues for nutritional anthropology and food studies. Food praxis clarifies many abstract theoretical concerns, such as intersectionality. The intersections of gender, class, and race and the ways they operate on food practices become more visible in activist projects. The slow food movement in North America and internationally brings out significant issues around class and gender (cf. Leitch 2013). The Tomasita project maps the journey of corporate tomatoes from a Mexican agribusiness to a supermarket and a fast food restaurant, demonstrating globalization from above (the corporate agenda) and globalization from below (low-paid women workers). Here the intersections include north-south and rural-urban asymmetries, as well as age and family status (Barndt 2002: 82–83). Activist work focused on meatpacking plants or sugar-based children's foods provide more examples of micro-macro linkages and the entanglements of the personal, institutional, and global in food studies.

Conclusion

Given these dilemmas, is it worth the trouble to incorporate food praxis into re-search designs? Yes. Margaret Mead, who links us back to a tradition of engaged anthropology in food studies, broached no facile compartmentalization into applied or engaged anthropology and ivory-tower theoretical anthropology. Since that time, the discipline has moved away from research in the public interest, returning only in the last decade to engaged or public anthropology. Elsewhere in the world, anthropologists have had more to say about subjects of interest to the public, and consequently have had more impact. For example, "The Norwegian public is open to anthropological comment" (Howell 2010: S269), unlike North American publics, who are more interested in the opinions of economists. In North America, we have ignored the complex yet ambiguous relation between anthropology and activism in the ethnographic encounter and in our teaching. How can we call for an engaged anthropology if we have developed neither a pedagogy for activist anthropology, nor explicit research methods on how to integrate food activism into our teaching and research?

Without more attention to food praxis as a method in food studies, the insights of ethnography seldom move beyond social criticism to social action, and even more rarely inform public policy. How would ethnographic accounts of food-based practice need to change to make them accessible and useful to policymakers? This might require new styles of writing and new ways to avoid the substantial time lag between research and academic publication, perhaps using social media. The food industry can make use of praxis results much faster than academics can, picking up on new language or fears about particular foods such as unpasteurized cheese or tainted meats. How can we avoid taking discussions of food security and food sovereignty, for example, to such a high level of abstraction that the links to local regimens where food policies are implemented are obscured? The abstraction necessary for some general policy considerations could deny practitioners and policymakers insight into how food systems work locally.

There can be no public anthropology, nor any applied food advocacy work, without some meta-narratives as standpoints to guide praxis. They can be quite simply a moral stand on the basis of a non-negotiable standard that says people are entitled to be free from hunger, with access to safe food. Without these moral stands, we fail in the broader public mission of helping to produce responsible, well-informed citizens. Being well educated about food is a good place to start.

Perhaps we fear the radical potential of food activism—its confrontational nature and the challenge it raises to the neoliberalism of late capitalism. Food praxis almost always offers a critique of the North American industrial food system, often without accompanying suggestions about how to begin the process of change or envision alternatives. This can be distressing for students. But when students and researchers are prepared to counter the resistance and backlash they may face, the methods of food praxis may inform not only a student assignment, but also a lifetime of examining how change occurs in food systems.

Penny Van Esterik is Professor Emerita of Anthropology, recently retired from York University, Toronto, where she taught nutritional anthropology, advocacy anthropology, and feminist theory, and worked primarily in Southeast Asia (Thailand and Lao PDR). Past books include *Beyond the Breast-Bottle Controversy* (on infant feeding in developing countries), *Materializing Thailand* (on cultural interpretations of gender in Thailand), *Taking Refuge: Lao Buddhists in North America* (on the reintroduction of Buddhism by Lao refugees to North America), and *Food and Culture: A Reader,* edited with Carole Counihan (currently being updated). She is a founding member of the World Alliance for Breastfeeding Action (WABA) and has been active in developing articles and advocacy materials on breastfeeding and women's work, breastfeeding and feminism, and contemporary challenges to infant feeding such as environmental contaminants and HIV/AIDS. In 2007, she received the Weaver-Tremblay award from the Canadian Anthropology Society (CASCA) for contributions to applied anthropology in Canada, and in 2013, the lifetime achievement award for feminist anthropology from the Women's Network of CASCA.

References

Ash, Sarah and Patti Clayton. 2009. Generating, Deepening and Documenting Learning: The Power of Critical Reflection in Applied Learning. *Journal of Applied Learning in Higher Education* 1(fall): 25–48.

Barndt, Deborah. 2002. Fruits of Injustice: Women in the Post-NAFTA Food System. *Canadian Woman Studies* 21–22(4): 1.

Freire, Paolo. 1970. *Pedagogy of the Oppressed.* New York: Continuum.

Hassanein, Neva. 2003. Practicing Food Democracy: A Pragmatic Politics Of Transformation. *Journal of Rural Studies* 19: 77–86.

Howell, Signe. 2010. Norwegian Academic Anthropologists in Public Spaces. *Current Anthropology* 51: S269–S277.

Leitch, Alison. 2013. Slow Food and the Politics of Virtuous Globalization. In *Food and Culture reader,* ed. C. Counihan and P. Van Esterik, 409–425 3rd ed. New York: Routledge.

Letherby, Gayle. 2003. *Feminist Theory and Practice.* Buckingham: Open University Press.

Van Esterik, Penny. 1986. Confronting Advocacy, Confronting Anthropology. In *Advocacy and Anthropology,* ed. R Paine. St. John's Newfoundland: Institute for Social and Economic Research, 59–77.

———. 2011. Revisiting Lao Food: Pain and Commensality. In *Food: Ethnographic Encounters,* ed. L. Coleman. London: Berg, 59–68.

Technology and Analysis

CHAPTER 8

Using Technology and Measurement Tools in Nutritional Anthropology of Food Studies

John Brett

The authors in this final section explore how technology has created new ways of exploring humankind's relationships with its food. In some ways these are "add-ons" to our traditional methods, giving us greater range and flexibility to do what we have always done: interview, watch, listen, and participate (Murthy 2008). In other ways they have revolutionized what we can do and how we go about it, allowing us to ask new questions and creating new ways to collaborate and share findings (Underberg and Zorn 2013). "Technology" has always been a part of anthropological research, from the early days of photography and moving picture recording (methods pioneered by Boas, Bateson, and Mead) and creation of sound recordings (Boas and others); to George Peter Murdoch's efforts to systematize ethnographies and create mechanically searchable databases (later computerized as the Human Relations Area Files); followed by the early days of personal computers and associated software that opened up new avenues of analysis, documentation, and dissemination of results; and then the early access to satellite imagery and Global Positioning Systems (GPS) and Geographic Information Systems (GIS) that permitted new ways of studying and displaying landforms and human relations to them. Following the logic of Moore's law (which loosely states that computing power doubles every two years), the unprecedented complexity and breadth of current technology allows us to ask new kinds of questions and investigate others in new and innovative ways.

The authors in this last section highlight several important established and emerging uses of technology in anthropology. Some of these (photovoice, statistics) are relatively straightforward and generally accessible to most scholars, whereas others (GIS, digital storytelling) require greater commitment and training but have the potential for great returns. Barry Brenton explores the multiple ways GIS and associated technologies are valuable in food- and diet-related studies. Understanding these relationships is critical because food is necessarily geographic and spatial in its production, distribution, and consumption. Geographic data are widely available, and relatively straightforward programs like Google Earth or ArcGIS Explorer allow entry on a not-too-steep learning curve. More advanced applications require advanced training and/or collaboration or support from those with that training.

Helen Vallianatos takes up the highly versatile and powerful method of photovoice as a tool in participatory research. Confirming the old saying "a picture is worth a thousand words," putting cameras (still and video) in the hands of our community collaborators opens up dynamic new avenues toward comprehending peoples' environments as they see them. In a similar vein, Marty Otañez employs the powerful technique of digital storytelling, in which participants learn both the skills needed to tell a short, compelling, generally autobiographical story, and the technical process of producing the video. Creating and telling their own stories can lead people to empowerment, advocacy, and unique opportunities for research. Kristen Borre and Jim Wilson together explore two aspects of the tremendous wealth of data available on the Internet that can serve as primary data for specific studies or as contextual or background information on habits, places, and trends. Most entities that collect, collate, or disseminate data do so primarily online, and many earlier collections are being digitized. Finally, Craig Hadley and Lesley Jo Weaver highlight several statistical techniques commonly used in the process of developing and refining a food security questionnaire for anthropological nutritional research.

Below is a list of some of the ways technology is being used in anthropology and a few thoughts on how they might be used in anthropological studies with food and humans. These ideas were drawn from a variety of webpages, books, articles, et cetera.

- As in much of computing, the "cloud" has the potential to revolutionize how anthropologists do their work. Because everything from specific computer programs (for word processing, spreadsheets, databases, statistical and qualitative data analysis, etc.) to data can be accessed remotely from any specific device, opportunities for collaboration with colleagues, students, and members of our research communities have increased and become more dynamic. Though doctoral students are expected to launch into their fieldwork relatively independently, undergraduates and masters-level students need closer mentoring. Ready access to field notes, diary entries, and emerging analyses permit detailed mentoring even when the faculty and student(s) are in different locations (see Powis 2013 for a detailed example).

Likewise, as our research is increasingly collaborative, involving the communities in which we do our work, opportunities for closer, more diverse engagement are emerging through widespread access to technology. All anthropologists fear the loss of their precious data, given that in most cases it is irreplaceable. Access to the Internet (when available) immensely enhances data storage, backup, and security with the availability of multiple password-protected sites on which data can be stored (e.g., Dropbox, Google Drive, Evernote). Cloud computing can also substantially reduce the cost of research, again broadening access. For example, proprietary stand-alone qualitative data analysis (QDA) software programs (e.g., Atlas-ti, NVivo, MaxQDA) cost from $500 to $1,000 (though often with steep discounts for students), whereas companies like Dedoose (www.dedoose.com) practice innovative pricing by charging a flat fee per month of use ($14 as of this writing). The charge is not incurred after the researcher has not used the service for a month or more, making powerful QDA software more affordable, especially for students and short-term projects. It is platform-independent, meaning that teams using different computer operating systems (e.g., Windows vs. Max OS) can collaborate seamlessly without the hassles of incompatible files. All data and analyses remain on these companies' servers "free of charge" even for researchers who are not actively accessing the online data analysis program.

- Instagram, Tumblr, Facebook, and other social media sites are increasingly used as sites of research (but are not discussed as such here) and as data collection and dissemination tools. Instagram can be used to create "visual field-notes" that document research places and processes (Wang 2012). The photos are automatically geotagged (geographically located with latitude and longitude), so through the metadata collected they can be easily incorporated into place-based ethnographic efforts. As photos and text can be simultaneously posted on Instagram, Tumblr, Facebook, and other social media sites, the possibility of what Wang (2012) calls "live field notes" emerges: our field notes and diary entries need no longer be hidden away in our notebooks and personal computers but can be shared, discussed, and augmented. "Engaged" and "public" anthropology are increasingly important trends in the field. Digital tools open up tremendous opportunities for co-creation of ethnographic texts, ethnohistory, life history, and other applications (see Wang 2012 for a longer discussion). An important caveat here is to recall the importance of ethical behavior and adherence to human subjects protocols. Sharing can be a wonderful and productive exercise, but we must ensure we in no way compromise those from whom we collect data.
- Skype and conferencing software (WebX, Adobe Connect, GoToMeeting, Zoom) likewise broaden the scope for collaboration, mentoring, conducting interviews, and sharing research results. With cell phone coverage pene-

trating ever further into even remote areas, the communication possibilities expand dramatically. Though international cell phone calls may be too expensive, cell phone modems are relatively inexpensive (e.g., $25–30 for 3–4 GB of data transmission) and provide access to a wide range of Internet-based communication technologies. "Unlocked" smart phones that permit the changing of SIM cards from one country to another can also provide mobile "hot spots" for access to the Internet.

- Cell phones and tablet computers allow for rapid collection and analysis of quantitative data. For small-scale studies, the data can be digitally collected and analyzed in the field to gain immediate understanding of a situation (e.g., food security monitoring) and open up new possibilities for follow-up. Mixed-method designs (quantitative-qualitative) are increasingly used to more robustly capture our research questions. The ability to rapidly analyze quantitative data could lead to more timely collection of qualitative contextual and explanatory data. Instead of returning to communities weeks or months after the quantitative data are collected, it could be possible to go back the following day or week while the issue at hand is still fresh in people's minds. For larger quantitative studies, it is possible to immediately upload quantitative data directly to a remote (and secure) database anywhere there is sufficient cell phone connectivity. This provides instant backup of irreplaceable data and limits the amount of (potentially) sensitive data on field equipment. For example, the REDCap secure server (http://redcapinfo.ucdenver.edu/) at the University of Colorado Denver provides remote, secure storage for quantitative data. In REDCap researchers can design surveys for which data are automatically uploaded from the field—that is, the questionnaire can reside on the field device, but the data do not.
- Digitization and posting of primary research data both preserves originals and makes them available to other scholars beyond the life of the original scholar. For ethnographic and archaeological data in particular, digital repositories of primary field data can open new avenues of historical and secondary data analysis (see http://opencontext.org/ as an example of the kind of project that becomes possible with these technologies). The same ethical considerations noted above apply here as well.
- Digital translators like Google Translate or Zeta iMtranslator (http://imtranslator.com/) can aid in ethnographic work when language skills are not (yet) up to speed. Even in cases where language abilities are strong, being able to quickly translate and then proofread text could have multiple benefits in field work.
- Speech-to-text can be a tremendous time-saver for field note dictation and text creation. Programs like Dragon speech recognition software (http://www.nuance.com/dragon/index.htm) can speed up the creation of field notes. Several options are possible. For example, instead of typing in handwrit-

ten field notes, one could read them in, whereupon the considerably faster speed of transcription can allow for much more detailed notes. Digitally recorded field notes can be used in two ways: speech recognition software can transcribe the recording into text in the usual way, or else field notes can be digitally recorded and then coded directly from the recording, again permitting much more detail in less time than typing (see below).

- Many qualitative data analysis programs (NVivo, Atlas ti, MAXQDA, Transana) can be used to code digital text, video, and images directly, bypassing the transcription phase entirely. The coding process remains the same, but the laborious transcription process is eliminated.
- Although it is an "old" digital technology, email is still an important tool for communication and collaboration because it permits rapid and thorough communication among researchers, students, and mentors. Moreover, in work with literate and digitally connected populations, it opens new paths of communication among researchers and participants for "fact checking," conducting interviews, and collaboration in Community Based Participatory Research projects.
- A host of programs and apps can be used to capture data. Many of us encounter and use text in our work. Until recently, accessing this material meant taking detailed notes. The advent of scanners and Optical Character Recognition (OCR) opened important new avenues for analyzing printed material. Digital cameras and OCR extend those possibilities into the field, where scanners and texts may not be available at the same time. Because it is digital, a digital picture can be submitted to OCR and converted into readable text that can then be managed like any other text-based research document (e.g., coding, content analysis). For example, scanning/photographing cookbooks, memoirs, and so forth and loading them into text analysis software makes huge amounts of historical data on food accessible.
- As more publishing moves online, our capacities for display of data and findings change and expand dramatically: we now are able to embed recordings and video clips, display dynamic change over time, portray findings innovatively, give voice to those who previously were voiceless in our work, and so on. We now have the ability to create "pictures" from data, whether we are displaying standard graphs, charts, and tables more creatively, or visualizing the contents of data in new ways, such as tag clouds. For example, a content analysis of cooking shows could reveal embedded commercial messages or biases that can then be displayed visually much more dynamically than in print.
- A host of tools, many of them relatively straightforward, allow us to layer social and cultural data over geographic data, again prompting new kinds of questions and new ways of portraying and explaining our findings. In a similar vein, the increasing power of computers has made deeper exploration

of relationships among people, places and things possible through network analysis. The Adobe suite (Illustrator, Photoshop, Acrobat, etc.) and the increasing number of open-source (free or low-cost) image creation and manipulation programs open up more creative ways to create illustrations, maps, and other visual aids while still in the field, facilitating the "member checks" that ensure our findings reflect the local understanding.

- Mapping has always been central to anthropology, but Global Positioning Systems (GPS) and Geographic Information Systems (GIS) have opened levels of detail and sophistication that are not only conducive to ever more sophisticated maps but allow us to ask entirely new kinds of questions and display data in ways not previously possible. Apps for phones and tablets permit real-time mapmaking and make it possible to geolocate (geographically anchor) a place, event, or processes. The layout of interior spaces can be captured using cell phone or tablet computers with apps like Magic Plan (http://www.sensopia.com/), which can quickly create relatively accurate drawings of inside spaces.

- Little can be said in this short piece on the tremendous potential the digital world holds for collaboration. The rapid emergence and power of tools for sharing files and the capacity to work jointly and simultaneously on the same document (e.g., Google Drive, Dropbox, Mendeley, Zotero) and the ability to do data analysis "in the cloud" (e.g., Dedoose) makes real-time collaboration accessible to field workers and mentors/PIs/supervisors or other collaborators.

- Smart Pens (e.g., Notability, Livescribe) are digital pens that record handwriting strokes (using special paper) and sounds (via digital recorder) that automatically appear on one's tablet computer and can then be uploaded to Dropbox or Google Drive.

- The world of academic publishing is in a period of dramatic transition as digital media disrupt traditional approaches of print publication while also introducing new models of publishing. Blogs and other digital media allow us to quickly and much more widely share and disseminate our findings before, during, and after official publication. Some publishers and scholars are producing "digital abstracts" in which authors briefly discuss their work in a short (two- or three-minute) video clip posted on a journal's website and often the author's homepage.

John Brett is retired faculty in the Department of Anthropology, University of Colorado Denver. He received his PhD in 1994 from the Joint Program in Medical Anthropology at the University of California San Francisco and Berkeley. His primary research interests focus on food systems, food security, and food justice, as well as microfinance as a development enterprise.

References

Murthy, Dhiraj. 2008. Digital Ethnography: An Examination of the Use of New Technologies for Social Research. *Sociology* 42(5): 837–855.

Powis, Dick. 2013. Fieldwork in the Cloud: Training in Ethnographic Fieldwork with Global Technologies. http://anthropologyattacks.blogspot.com.br/2013/10/fieldwork-in-cloud-training-in.html?utm_content=bufferea85d&utm_medium=social&utm_source=facebook.com&utm_campaign=buffer. Accessed 8 November 2016.

Underberg, Natalie M., and Elayne Zorn. 2013. *Digital Ethnography: Anthropology, Narrative, and New Media.* Austin: University of Texas Press.

Wang, Tricia. 2012. Writing Live Fieldnotes: Towards a More Open Ethnography. *Ethnography Matters.* http://ethnographymatters.net/2012/08/02/writing-live-fieldnotes-towards-a-more-open-ethnography/. Accessed 8 November 2016.

Additional Resources

DiRT (Digital Research Tools) is a gold mine of different kinds of digital research tools of various kinds. http://dirtdirectory.org/. Accessed 8 November 2016.

Digital Media Commons at Rice University (http://dmc.rice.edu/), while reserved for staff and students of Rice University, nevertheless contains a wealth of publicly available information on a range of digital technologies. Accessed 8 November 2016.

Paulus, Trena, Jessica Nina Lester, and Paul Dempster. 2014. *Digital Tools for Qualitative Research.* Thousand Oaks, CA: Sage. Accessed 8 November 2016.

Lisa Spiro of Rice University produced a helpful Power Point on Digital Tools for Research and Teaching in Anthropology, available at: http://scholarship.rice.edu/bitstream/handle/1911/27211/DigitalAnthropology2009.pdf?sequence=1. Accessed 8 November 2016.

CHAPTER 9

Mapping Food and Nutrition Landscapes
GIS Methods for Nutritional Anthropology

Barrett P. Brenton

Maps are more than pieces of paper. They are stories, conversations, lives and songs lived out in a place and are inseparable from the political and cultural contexts in which they are used.

—Warren
Personal communication, 2004, cited in Rambaldi (2005: 5)

Spatial data and its visualization through maps has long been part of the research process in nutritional anthropology. One can hardly imagine a paper or presentation without a map to spatially anchor and contextualize the work. Consider the wide array of existing and potential applications for mapping food production, distribution, access, and consumption that are used to enhance our understanding of food systems from the micro-local to the macro-global level. Most sources of data on food systems, food environments, foodways, diet, and nutrition have a spatial component and thus can be mapped, qualitatively assigned themes and narratives, and/or quantified and statistically analyzed. Admittedly, maps are still produced primarily after the fact, as a product of data analysis and for the dissemination of results. Yet for non-geographers, their more recent methodological contribution as part of Geographic Information Systems (GIS), defined in more detail below, has made them an increasingly integral part of the process of data analysis in and of itself in a number of disciplines (Roberts 2011). This is especially true in the rapidly expanding work on mapping food systems in the context of emergency food crises, long-term sustainable development projects, and spatial memories of food and identity (e.g., Ahmed et al. 2014; Kremer and DeLiberty 2011; Morrison, Nelson, and Ostry 2011a, 2011b; Peters et al. 2009).

The proto-GIS work of physician John Snow's plot-mapping of cholera deaths and their relationship to contaminated water sources in mid–nineteenth-century London contributed early on to establishing modern principles of epidemiology, but Snow did not have the advantage of computer-generated algorithms to digitally produce, in real time, maps that can track Ebola outbreaks or drought crises requiring humanitarian food aid.

GIS can thus be incorporated into the fields of food studies and nutritional anthropology as an important research methodology for investigating and analyzing the spatial and temporal complexity of food systems, diet, and nutrition. Perhaps most popularized through the mapping of "food deserts" in both rural and urban contexts, highlighted in a case study below, GIS can be used as a powerful qualitative and quantitative research tool. This chapter will briefly review and introduce the practical use of GIS methodologies in food studies and nutritional anthropology. GIS holds great potential for integrating historical, ethnographic, and dietary spatial data on human foodways and nutrition. An additional emphasis of this chapter is to review commercial and open-source GIS programs, online mapping platforms, and low-threshold technologies and Participatory GIS used in the field for mapping landscapes of food and nutrition.

Given the possibility of mapping applications tailored to our needs, we must also remember that maps are not neutral constructs. Maps are clearly only as good as the information that is used to develop them. We can generally see how numerical statistical truths can be skewed toward a certain interpretation, and a similar fate can befall maps that "lie" (Monmonier 2005). The meaning they impart may or may not represent the communities we work with. In many regions the creation of maps may be seen as an extension of a centuries-old colonial enterprise and hegemonic control that seeks to document land use areas for tax revenue or resources to be exploited. Anthropologists, though generally aware of the ethical and logistical conundrums that come with knowledge production and its interpretation, must nonetheless be sensitive to the real concerns that can emerge during the research process. For these reasons and others a section of this chapter has been devoted to a discussion of Participatory GIS as an approach that seeks the full participation of the community in the research design, implementation, and interpretation of results stemming from being engaged with mapping methodologies (cf. Glantz and McMahan 2007; Herlinhy and Knapp 2003; Matthews, Detwiler, and Burton 2005; Nichter 2007; Warren 2004).

GIS Fundamentals

Geographic Information Systems (GIS) are just that: integrated systems based on spatially referenced geographic information. They are a method that allows for visualization, manipulation, analysis, and display of spatial data. This system is made possible through the use of computer software and hardware that stores and links the data needed to visualize any type of information that is coded with a geographic reference in the two dimensions of longitude and latitude (X and Y coordinates), with the possibility of adding a third dimension of altitude (Z coordinate), and even a fourth dimension of time (Chen and Clark 2013). It should be noted, though the details are beyond the scope of this chapter, that data may be drawn from several types of map projections. Most GIS software programs are equipped with the ability to adjust for any corrections that may be needed to align the data to conform to the same system.

These data are ultimately linked in a way that may utilize perhaps hundreds of files organized in dozens of folders to produce the map that appears on the screen. GIS analysis also provides the flexibility to query those tables of data to create different views as part of one's spatial analysis. The methodological key to a GIS analysis is the functionality of layers upon layers of visual information. A study on HIV/AIDS and food security might include developing a map depicting the following layers (and most likely many others): agro-ecological zones, soil nutrient levels, fertilizer use, rainfall, crop types and yields, livestock production, pest management, post-harvest loss, basic community demographics, HIV/AIDS morbidity and mortality rates, life expectancy, access to and use of anti-retroviral treatments, levels of community stigma, ethno-linguistic boundaries, dietary intake (calories, proteins, fats, carbohydrates, micronutrients), childhood growth indicators, parasitic load, water access, road access, emergency food distribution centers, income generating opportunities, market access, and so on. The advantages of GIS methodologies enable researchers to have a geo-referenced information system that can analyze and link all of these variables together for more evidenced-based meaningful results and targeted interventions.

Geo-referenced data for GIS are stored as Vector or Raster Data. Vector-based layers are comprised of feature or object classes based on their type of geometry (points, lines, or polygons). Each type of feature class is stored in an attribute table specific to its characteristics. For example, to understand the dynamics of a local food system, attribute tables may be used to generate layers based on the geometric concepts of points, lines, and polygons. Points indicate locations such as households, grocery stores, bodegas, and emergency food distribution centers; lines represent, for example, paths leading to healthy food locations, sidewalks, streets, roads, rivers, and bus and train routes. Polygons, in this case, are reference areas based on ecosystems, land usage, land ownership or tenure system, community garden plots, or political boundaries (zip code, census tracts, neighborhood, municipality, district, county, state, country, etc.).

Raster-based layers are comprised of a grid of cells consisting of pixels. Each cell has a specific value. The cells are used to create layers representing continuous data such as temperature, pollen count, soil pH, elevation, or satellite images and aerial photos.

We can visualize the relationships between these different types of spatial data and their corresponding attributes as a dynamic process, once they are brought together as layers of information. This is often achieved by switching layers on and off as part of the most basic form of qualitative visual analysis. One can monitor correlations between attributes or variables that occur as layers are made visible and then taken away across data fields. Regarding the local food system example above, one may want to view only households defined as food-insecure (point data) and the types of physical access (line data) and barriers (raster-data: aerial photos) those households have to community garden plots they can use (polygon data). Another example might look at the relationship between household food production in calories (point data); access to water sources for irrigation via wells (point data), rivers (line data), or lakes (polygon data); classification type and quality (i.e., pH levels) of soil (raster data) on arable land (polygon data); and crop yields (polygon data).

As part of an information system, GIS-generated maps are not static but dynamic. They are not simply a collection of pixels used to create a digital image, but rather layers of visual data producing an interactive map. Creating a GIS-based map thus requires the use of computer software that can store and retrieve these layers as tabular data. The main distinction that must be drawn at this time is between GIS utilizing stand-alone commercial or open-source software, and web-based GIS applications (a partial list of these can be found in the appendix to this chapter). The advantage of stand-alone desktop programs is that they make it possible to create a map encompassing endless amounts of data and layers with an infinite number of qualitative visual outputs based on your queries, and also possible to perform complex quantitative statistical analyses that correlate the relationship between fields (a full discussion of the many powerful geostatistical tools available is beyond the scope of this chapter). The industry leader of GIS software to date is the suite of ArcGIS programs developed by Environmental Systems Research Institute (ESRI) of Redlands, California (http://www.arcgis.com/).

The primary challenge of using these desktop applications is the very steep learning curve that faces users of most features of the programs, which were created by computer programmers and are generally neither user-friendly nor intuitive, as Microsoft Office products have become. Initially one cannot just click a map open and start adding data; rather, it has to be built literally from the ground up. For this reason it is often an interdisciplinary effort incorporating a geographer on the research team. Finding the exact type of data to fit research can also be difficult, and it may be available only for a fee. Commercial programs can also be cost-prohibitive for some organizations. However, many of the features of ArcGIS are mimicked by "open-source" programs like Quantum GIS that are downloadable at no cost (http://qgis.org/en/site/). Open-source software and data are created within a social justice framework that assumes information should be accessible and open to all, but they may not feature access to the same level of online support or program options offered by more expensive commercial products.

On the other hand, "free" web-based GIS has expanded dramatically over the past decade. It gives anyone with basic Internet access the opportunity to utilize interactive maps of locations around the world. Though commercial-based sites recoup their investment through advertising, users are generally limited to digital road maps and satellite and bird's-eye imagery, with limited options for incorporating their own data. Familiar sites are Google Maps (www.google.com/maps), and the downloadable Google Earth (www.google.com/earth/); Bingmaps (www.bing.com/maps); MapQuest (www.mapquest.com), and the open-source OpenStreetMap (www.openstreetmap.org).

Google Earth gives users the capacity to create basic food-system maps by adding placemark points, lines, polygons, and image overlays (with varying layers of transparency allowing sight of the underlying base map). Descriptors, images, and web links can be added to each of these. They can essentially function as a layer in a visual analysis of food landscapes, or be the basis of spatial food narratives. Screen-captured images of, for example, food insecurity maps from interactive GIS data portals like the ones discussed below and listed in the appendix, can be overlaid onto a food-system map. One can also combine satellite imagery with known street addresses using Google Earth to pinpoint geo-spatial coordinates (latitude, longitude, and elevation) of a specific location. A ruler allows measurement of distances but not area. These options have limitations when working in areas where low-resolution satellite imagery is projected, including a substantial part of the global South. For instance, in a community fishpond-mapping project I have been involved in with indigenous Shuar communities in the Ecuadorian Amazon, we needed greater spatial detail, a problem we solved by utilizing traditional contour-line maps as scanned images overlying the low-resolution satellite imagery. Finally, it is important to note that no tabular or integrated data is associated with these maps, so they provide nowhere near the same analytical power and flexibility of a desktop GIS program.

Google has also launched the site Google Maps Engine (http://mapsengine.google.com) (formerly Google My Maps). This platform provides additional options for creating and sharing custom maps and has good potential for developing a community-based food-mapping project. It differs from Google Earth mainly in that users can import basic spreadsheet table data files to create points or placemarks (e.g., CSV, TSV, KML, or XLSX file formats) enabling them to view a list of descriptors associated with each point (along with images and web links). Unfortunately image overlays are currently not an option. A group of users can log in to the website to edit and annotate the same map in a collaborative project to organize and meet changing community needs. Locations are mapped using place names or geo-referenced coordinates as one of the spreadsheet columns. The Lite version limits the map to 100 points per layer (15 columns maximum) and only three layers. Polygons can be drawn and area and distance can be measured, but they cannot be generated from the spreadsheet data. All of these options can be greatly expanded with the purchase of the Pro version. Hopefully Google will eventually launch a web-based mapping system that includes the combined benefits of both platforms. (NB: Unfortunately the site described above was discontinued by Google in 2016).

Besides the commercial and open-source programs and interactive mapping sites listed above, the other category of GIS data is the increasing number of web-based mapping platforms that are targeted to specific types of information. Many of these sites are of great use to nutritional anthropologists interested in sources of data, analytical inquiries, and qualitative visual analyses. They include, for example, a number of interactive sites sponsored by the United Nations Food and Agriculture Organization (FAO), World Food Programme (WFP), and World Health Organization (WHO); as well as interactive sites maintained by the U.S. Department of Agriculture (USDA), Centers for Disease Control (CDC), and U.S. Geological Survey (USGS). GIS capacity-building in countries throughout the world is also making governmental geo-referenced data increasingly available in relation to food system inquiries. Many NGOs are also creating web-based GIS platforms to increase awareness and advocacy surrounding their work. A list of such sites (by no means comprehensive) can be found in the appendix at the end of the chapter. Once again we must remind ourselves that maps are only as good as the data used to create them.

A caveat pertinent to all discussions of GIS-based methods and data collection is that rapid changes are taking place in the related supporting technologies. For that reason these discussions are often focused on the conceptual usage of methods that will remain somewhat consistent through time, regardless of dramatic technological shifts.

GIS Data Collection

A broad spectrum of methods exists for collecting spatially or geo-referenced data for GIS applications. As with all methods, some may be more appropriate than others given the spatial context and role of participants. Low to high thresholds of technology access must also be taken into account for any research design. Low-threshold technology data collection can be as fundamental as making pencil marks on a paper copy of a map or drawing a line in the sand. At the high end, access to the Global Positioning System (GPS) has revolutionized the ways in which spatial data can be accessed and recorded for specific locations. Also, a growing number of applications (apps) for smartphones and tablets can integrate GPS data with GIS functions. Accuracy and precision vary substantially (Rydlund and Densmore 2012). The use of basic mobile handheld GPS devices or smartphones and tablets (which are now both generally equipped with a GPS chip) can be used to identify a spot with accuracy within about 3 meters. This is most likely more than adequate for most food systems research. If more precision is needed, for example to track activity levels and distances traveled in real time, or to document the yield of a specific plant in a plot, differential-grade Global Navigation Satellite System (GNSS) equipment can be accurate within <1 meter by incorporating information from multiple satellites at once. Professional survey-grade GNSS equipment can provide an accuracy of within <1 centimeter, providing the greater spatial precision needed in, for example, the recovery of plant or animal food remains in an archaeological context. But as might be expected, the greater the accuracy sought, the higher the cost of the device.

Participatory GIS Mapping

GIS is an important tool for investigating and discussing social, cultural, political, economic, environmental, and public health concerns. To spatially represent and analyze indicators of human well-being, community stakeholders and decision makers are increasingly using GIS as a tool, generating maps that help identify community strengths and areas where development lags. This process provides an effective base for targeting investments in infrastructure to the places they can have the greatest impact. It involves assessments of both needs and assets (strength-based assessments). GIS mapping has great potential to fuel a participatory democratic process. When local communities are involved in collecting data and also have access to information about where they live, it becomes an instrument empowering a collective understanding of common spaces. Importantly, the process of community mapping of local food systems can help promote food justice.

Participatory mapping is one methodological approach that spans the continuum from low-threshold–appropriate technology to the building of capacity for integrating GIS software and online mapping applications. The process of map production revolves around the key element of community participation (IFAD 2009). It should represent the community's agendas with map content that reflects local knowledge, and should not be defined by compliance with traditional cartographic forms of conventional mapmaking. "Ground truthing" is an action-oriented term often used to bridge the gap between the abstract concept of a map and the reality or perceived truths on the ground (Vajjhala 2006; Walker et al. 2005). Many participatory mapping case studies have focused on access to and management of food and water resources (e.g., Herlinhy and Knapp 2003; Hesse 2013; Osha and Weiner 2006; Rambaldi 2005; Rambaldi et al. 2006; Rowley 2013). These strategies have great value for promoting more applied food studies and nutritional anthropology research.

The forum Integrated Approaches to Participatory Development (IAPAD) is devoted to promoting these methodologies (www.iapad.org). It holds that participatory avenues are a "… focal point for sharing lessons learned and innovation in practicing ethically-conscious community mapping and participatory GIS as means to add value and authority to people's spatial knowledge and improve bottom-up communication" (nl.linkedin.com/in/grambaldi). The IAPAD website contains numerous reports, case studies, and resource links concerning various locations around the world. IAPAD is also associated with other networks, such as the Open Forum on Participatory Geographic Information Systems (PGIS) and Technologies [www.ppgis.net), which includes sections in English, Spanish, Portuguese, and French. Particularly useful resources and a *Training Kit on Participatory Spatial Information and Management* (CTA 2010) for mapping food systems can be drawn from the following website (http://pgis-tk-en.cta.int/m01/u01.html). Some additional guiding principles and objectives in developing a research design that integrates participatory mapping within a community include helping communities become able to record and archive local knowledge for purposes of managing resources and addressing resource-related conflicts and challenges, communicating spatial knowledge to external agencies, and advocating for change through capacity building (IFAD 2009).

Participatory mapping tools can be as basic as hands-on mapping, where community members (or subsets of individuals based on levels of representation) literally draw or create spatial representations of how they see the world, say, by using sticks and pebbles on the ground or sketching it out on a blank roll of paper or whiteboard. Prompts for the group may be useful, for example, a series of questions related to land usage and food production or barriers to accessing food and water resources. Although this can be done individually, it is designed to be a process that involves multiple voices and opinions in dialogue as the map is created and edited. Conventional scale maps and images can be used as tools to start the conversation; then the participants can annotate them based on their own knowledge and perceptions of local food landscapes. Community members could also sketch pictures or take photos that add additional detail to articulation of the context and meaning of their food system map through "Geotagging." Another tool, the participatory 3-D model, can be produced using sculpting materials readily on hand (Rambaldi 2010; see also www.iapad.org). This method emphasizes the fact that people essentially do not view or perceive the world in two dimensions.

By definition, mapping tools utilizing participatory geographic information systems (PGIS) scale up the technology threshold by integrating the use of GPS and GIS software as part of the community discussions. Community members can use handheld GPS devices to mark specific locations and zones, and take part in managing and analyzing maps generated by the GIS program. Alternatively or in combination with desktop GIS software, a project might utilize web-based mapping platforms, which offer greater ease of access. Blended methods involving social media will also continue to transform how spatial data is collected. For example, some studies are using Twitter, where participants tweet about their local food environments (Chen and Yang 2011).

Regardless of how seemingly unconventional the mode of map production may be, the map can still be digitized and linked to a GIS database. Thus, different threshold levels may not be mutually exclusive and in fact may be integrated during fieldwork. The process of deciding what types of spatial data are collected and how is also central to understanding the potential role of participatory GIS methodologies in a project's research design.

Case Study: Mapping an Urban Food Desert

Defining Food Deserts

The mapping of "food deserts" has brought a great deal of attention to the use of GIS in understanding the spatial dynamics of food systems, particularly in urban areas. A food desert is generally defined as a geographic area with limited access to affordable healthy foods (e.g., fresh fruit and vegetables, whole grains, low-fat milk, etc.). The food desert is typically an area where local corner bodegas or convenience stores lack healthy foods and individuals face barriers that limit their ability to travel to the nearest large grocery store. Evidence of a spatial relationship between health disparities and obesity in low-income communities and their access to healthful food has spurred a number of public health intervention programs that seek to improve opportunities for healthy eating through changes in the food system that can happen by way of incentives for grocery stores to move into the desert areas, fresh fruit and vegetable "green cart" vendors, community gardens, farmer's markets, and nutrition education, to name but a few possibilities.

To standardize the concept of a food desert, the U.S Department of Agriculture (USDA) established that a community must be deemed low-income and have low access to a supermarket or large grocer. To be a low-income community, a census tract must have either a poverty rate of at least 20 percent, or a median family income at or below 80 percent of the area's median family income. To be considered a low-access community, at least 500 people and/or at least 33 percent of the census tract's population must reside more than one mile from a supermarket or large grocery store (for rural census tracts the distance is more than ten miles) (Dutko, Ver Ploeg, and Farrigan 2012; Ver Ploeg et al. 2012). In 2011 the USDA launched the Food Desert Locator, which by 2014 had been transformed into the *Food Access Research Atlas* (which now includes a more refined urban access distance of one half of a mile) (http://www.ers.usda.gov/data-products/food-access-research-atlas/go-to-the-atlas.aspx#.U-UgEPldWSo). An even wider set of statistics on food choices, health, and well-being, as well as community characteristics for all communities in the United States, can be found in the USDA *Food Environment Atlas* (http://www.ers.usda.gov/data-products/food-environment-atlas/go-to-the-atlas.aspx#.U-UgnvldWSo).

Redefining Food Deserts

While the USDA realizes that defining food deserts and food access is an evolving concept, numerous studies have either supported the concept, shown no relationship, or had mixed results (e.g., An and Sturm 2012; Coveney and O'Dwyer 2009; Donkin 1999; Feagan 2007; Gatrell, Reid, and Ross 2011; Lee 2012; Treuhaft and Karpyn 2010; Walker, Keane, and Burke 2010; Whalen and Seserman 2011). Studies by An and Sturm (2012) and Lee (2012) attracted a great deal of media attention by casting doubt on the food desert concept and what they claimed were misdirected policies that ensued based on unfounded correlations between obesity and access to healthy foods. Lee (2013) has even argued that food activism itself has led public health astray by putting more emphasis on transforming the food system than on individual behavior in the making of an obesity "epidemic." It is even possible that the ensuing backlash led to a rather sudden name change of the USDA's Food Desert Locator to *The Food Access Research Atlas*.

Given the polarized politics of this issue, it is unsurprising that the continued production of maps for action is an increasingly popular trend in the world of food justice and local food activism. Terms such as "citizen cartographers" and "citizen mapping" reflect a movement fueled by the ease of access to technologies reviewed above (GPS-enabled smartphones, mapping apps, web-based GIS through Google Maps and OpenStreetMap (an open-source online map with a history of involvement in social justice movements). This trend is also tied to the crowdsourcing of spatial data and the movement's expressed need for "ground-truthing" GIS metadata that can often mask local variation in food system dynamics.

Establishing an Urban Food Desert–Food Access Mapping Project

Within the context described above, several years ago I started formulating a set of methods for creating a food desert–food systems map as part of the Promoting Access to Healthy Eating and Nutritious Foods program in partnership with St. John's Bread and Life, an emergency food provider located in the Bedford-Stuyvesant section of Brooklyn. The primary goal of the project has been to support a sustainable and integral model of development that can best serve the health and nutritional needs of this community effectively and with dignity. A key focus of the collaboration is advocacy for a food-systems approach to community engagement that integrates food justice and food sovereignty as frameworks for responding to dietary health risks and access to nutritious foods in an urban food desert (Brenton 2012).

Nearly one in three of the over 300,000 inhabitants of this community live below the poverty line and rely heavily on community-based services. The food access reported by this same population provided only fair to poor diets, in terms of their healthfulness (NYC DOHMH 2012). St. John's Bread and Life serves a population of individuals and families living in poverty, people who have recently lost their jobs and are having difficulties providing food for their families, and people living with chronic physical or mental health problems who periodically need extra help. Approximately 30 percent of the residents are foreign-born, and the community struggles with a high degree of health disparities. Of the 42 neighborhoods in New York City, it has the 38th lowest life expectancy. Diet-related chronic diseases, including heart disease, hypertension, diabetes, and obesity, are a serious concern for this population. It has the highest mortality rate from heart disease in New York City, as well as high rates of adult obesity (>30 percent) and combined overweight and obesity (67 percent), and prevalence of Type II diabetes (>14 percent) (Matte et al. 2007; NYC DOHMH 2012; Zahilay 2010).

Against this background an initial survey was created for clients utilizing the food pantry at St. John's Bread and Life. In addition to basic demographic information, questions were asked about their general health status, food security, and dietary intake. A follow-up survey and interview was then designed with a focus on having the clients define healthy eating, access to healthy foods, and locations where they shopped. To enhance the degree of anonymity, they were not asked to provide a specific street address but only to give the closest street intersection to their residence. In theory this provided an accuracy of within half a city block and did not realistically compromise spatial accuracy.

Handheld GPS units and smartphones with GPS functions in combination with data from the Bed-Stuy Healthy Neighborhoods Map (City Harvest 2012) were used to geo-reference food retail locations within a one-mile radius of St. John's Bread and Life. Locations were tagged as bodegas, healthy bodegas, supermarkets, and healthy supermarkets using criteria developed by City Harvest and the NYC Department of Health and Mental Hygiene Healthy Bodegas Initiative (Graham et al. 2006; NYC CEO n.d.; NYC DOHMH and CEO 2010; Zahilay 2010).

This information was entered into an ArcGIS database to create a layer corresponding to these point locations. An additional layer was created for the cross-street location of each survey participant. The program was then able to map and determine the distance from each client's residence to each of the store locations. Alternatively, this process could have utilized an application such as Google Maps Engine or Google Earth to pin a place marker at the location of each tagged food retail location and survey participant. A measuring tool could then have been used to measure the distance to each location.

A Mixed-Mode Approach to Interpreting the Findings

The preliminary results, especially given the high density of retailers with and without healthy foods, unsurprisingly indicated that this neighborhood, like nearly all impoverished neighborhoods in NYC, did not fall into the USDA food desert urban classification of having to travel more than one mile (or even the revised half mile) for access to healthy food. Was there then no food desert? Was the desert only a mirage in what was actually a food swamp inundated with food access? From an anthropological perspective, the source of the answer was clear: go to the surveys, interviews, and local ethnographic context. Spatial constraints of food access cannot be defined by just a distance traveled. The clients perceived their food environment as a food desert because in many of the stores they shopped in healthy foods were not available, and if they were, they were not affordable.

Perhaps the most revealing narratives concerned the additional barriers they faced. These included public safety concerns about traveling the route needed to get to a store: many of the clients have physical and or mental disabilities that restrict the distances they can travel, and public transportation could require several transfers and backtracking to reach a store. For some it also involved a cost-prohibitive round trip. Then there were limitations on how much one could actually physically carry, especially on a crowded bus route, which made the decision to go to a specific store more arduous. Some culturally appropriate healthy ethnic food ingredients were only available in other neighborhoods that could take an hour or so to get to one way on public transportation. A NYC mobile Green Cart, part of an initiative to provide greater access to fresh fruits and vegetables in this neighborhood, is never seen near their residences but can only be found at the subway entrances, and though the rapid gentrification of the neighborhood has led niche organic health food stores to open nearby, they are far too cost-prohibitive. For these individuals the Bedford-Stuyvesant area is a "food desert" where they lack physical and economic access to fresh fruits and vegetables.

In summary, the brief lesson to be learned from this food desert–food systems mapping example is that GIS methods for nutritional anthropology are mixed-mode methods that must incorporate established spatial parameters that are informed by data as diverse as dietary intake, health status, and food access narratives of place.

Concluding Thoughts on the GIS Spectrum of Anthropological Inquiry for Food Studies and Nutritional Anthropology

GIS holds potential for anthropological and biocultural inquiry in a wide range of opportunities across the holistic traditional subfields of anthropology. Landscapes of food, diet, and nutrition can all be geo-referenced across time and space, from our evolutionary past to real-time monitoring of food security across the planet. We must, although it was beyond the scope of this chapter, imagine our ability to map the dietary isotopic signatures of our hominid ancestors as savannah replaced rainforest, or track the migration of early domesticated plants and animals through genomic expressions or linguistic variance. We should also envision the historical shift in landscapes of food that are still embedded in the ethnographic memories of kinship systems, life-cycle rituals of the secular and sacred, and political-economic obligations.

As research agendas are formulated to integrate GIS methods, some larger themes that emerge include the mapping of evolutionary nutrition decision-making maps, paleonutrition and the archaeology of foodways, centuries of the globalization of foodways, ethnic and regional foodways and cuisines, the language of food, and "traditional" foodways and cuisines giving new meaning to "local" and "locavorism."

We also have the potential to go beyond the fourth dimension of time to vertically integrate infinite layers of contextual data incorporating cognitive, conceptual, and network maps. While technology continues to transform our ability to map food landscapes with greater ease, we must remind ourselves that our species has had the same spatial cognitive wiring for nearly 200,000 years and thus must not lose sight of the biocultural context of geo-referenced knowledge embedded in traditions of space and place.

Barrett P. Brenton, PhD, is Professor of Anthropology and Director of the Center for Global Development at St. John's University in New York. As an applied nutritional anthropologist he has conducted fieldwork in communities across five continents on issues related to documenting, mapping, and promoting sustainable food systems. In addition to presenting numerous papers at national and international conferences he has published widely in the areas of dietary biodiversity, food insecurity, and diet-related health disparities. He is past president of the Society for the Anthropology of Food and Nutrition, and is a founding member of the AAA Presidential Task Force on World Food Problems.

Appendix

GIS Web Resources

The following is only a sample list of suggested GIS web resources useful for beginning a food systems mapping project. In these resources you will find geo-referenced information as diverse as soil growth potential, childhood malnutrition, food commodity imports, socioeconomic status, and ethnic identity. It is the ability to layer this data along with field-based evidence that makes GIS such a powerful methodological tool in nutritional anthropology. Also, a growing number of sites (not mentioned) provide access to spatial data for very specific research foci or locations. Depending on the level of GIS capacity building done to date, most countries now have their own GIS mapping centers or are at least working with partnering institutions that do.

The majority of the sites with web-based GIS data viewers listed below are either governmental or intergovernmental organizations (e.g., the United Nations) that provide access to primary data. Others are NGOs or research institutes that compile spatial data from multiple sources to create map infographics and interactive platforms for raising awareness through education and advocacy. Spatial data is increasingly becoming available in formats and files that can readily be downloaded as layers for GIS viewers (e.g., shapefiles, raster or vector files). In all cases users should be aware of the metadata tags for the spatial data found on the websites. This information will include the date of origin and source of the data used to generate the maps. In many situations there may be a time lag of several years between the most recent spatial data and the present date.

The following links provide access to data at no cost, but now there are also several commercial sites where information is consistently updated in a format that can easily be added as a layer to GIS platforms. This should be taken into consideration when putting together a research budget. Similarly, the list below holds examples of both commercial-grade and open-source GIS programs. An increasing number of research and educational institutions have GIS librarians and GIS labs that can be an important source of locating data, software, and support. However, many non-profit organizations or independent researchers may need to weigh the costs associated with utilizing GIS at different levels against the cost of accessing commercial rather than open-source programs and data. Open-source advocates feel that all data should be available in the public domain and are trying to meet that gap as an expression of social justice.

Web-Based Interactive GIS Data Viewers

- Center for Applied Research and Environmental Systems (CARES-University of Missouri)
  National Interactive Maps (U.S.): http://ims2.missouri.edu/tool/maps/default.aspx
- Consultative Group on International Agricultural Research (CGIAR)
  Consortium for Spatial Information (CSI): http://csi.cgiar.org/MapServices.asp
- Environmental Systems Research Institute (ESRI)
  Map Gallery: http://www.esri.com/esri-news/maps
- United Nations Food and Agriculture Organization (FAO)
  Agricultural Development Assistance Mapping (ADAM): http://www.fao.org/tc/adam/data/index.html

Agro-Maps: Global Spatial Database of Agricultural Land-Use Statistics: http://
    kids.fao.org/agromaps/
Country Profiles: http://www.fao.org/countryprofiles
FAOSTAT: http://faostat3.fao.org/faostat-gateway/go/to/browse/Q/*/E
Farming Systems and Poverty: http://www.fao.org/farmingsystems/regions_en
    .htm
GeoNetwork [Find and analyze geo-spatial data]: http://www.fao.org/geonet
    work/srv/en/main.home
Global Agro-Ecological Zones: http://gaez.fao.org/Main.html#
*Global Information and Early Warning System on Food and Agriculture
    (GIEWS):* http://www.fao.org/giews/english/index.htm
Hunger Portal: http://www.fao.org/hunger/en/
- United Nations Development Programme (UNDP)
    Human Development Indicators (HDI): http://hdr.undp.org/en/countries
- United NationsEnvironmental Programme (UNEP)
    Environmental Data Explorer (Geo Data Portal): http://geodata.grid.unep.ch/
- United Nations World Food Programme (WFP)
    Aid Professionals Map Centre: http://www.wfp.org/aid-professionals/map-
    centre
    Hunger Map: http://www.wfp.org/hunger/downloadmap
    WFP Food Procurement: http://one.wfp.org/country_brief/hunger_map/map/
    hungermap_popup/map_popup.html
- U.S. Agency for International Development (USAID)
    Foreign Assistance: http://www.foreignassistance.gov/web/OULanding.aspx.
    Famine Early Warning Systems Network (FEWSNET): http://earlywarning.usgs
    .gov/fews/mapviewer/?region=af
- U.S. Census Bureau/U.S. Department of Commerce
    American Fact Finder: http://factfinder2.census.gov/faces/nav/jsf/pages/index
    .xhtml
- U.S. Centers for Disease Control
    Diabetes Interactive Atlas: http://www.cdc.gov/diabetes/atlas/index.htm
- U.S. Central Intelligence Agency (CIA)
    The World Factbook: https://www.cia.gov/library/publications/the-world-
    factbook/
- U.S. Department of Agriculture (USDA)
    Economic Research Service (ERS) GIS Map Services and API User Guide: http://
    www.ers.usda.gov/developer/geospatial-apis.aspx#.U-dzL_ldWSp
    Farm Program Atlas: http://www.ers.usda.gov/data-products/farm-program-
    atlas.aspx#.U-dsdfldWSo
    Food Access Research Atlas (formerly the Food Desert Locator): http://www.ers
    .usda.gov/data-products/food-access-research-atlas.aspx

Food Environment Atlas: http://www.ers.usda.gov/data-products/food-environ
ment-atlas.aspx.

Geospatial Data Gateway: http://datagateway.nrcs.usda.gov/

Supplemental Nutrition Assistance Program (SNAP) Data System: http://www
.ers.usda.gov/data-products/supplemental-nutrition-assistance-program-
(snap)-data-system/go-to-the-map.aspx#.U-dxpfldWSo

- U.S. Geological Survey
  The National Map: http://nationalmap.gov/
  Global GIS: http://webgis.wr.usgs.gov/globalgis/index.html
- U.S. National Aeronautics and Space Administration (NASA)
  Earth Observing System Data and Information System (EOSDIS): https://earth
  data.nasa.gov/
  Socioeconomic Data and Applications Center (SEDAC): http://sedac.ciesin.org/
  maps/tools
- World Bank
  eAtlas of Millennium Development Goals: http://www.app.collinsindicate.com/
  mdg/en-us
  GINI Index: http://data.worldbank.org/indicator/SI.POV.GINI/countries?
  display=map
- World Health Organization (WHO)
  Global Health Atlas: http://www.who.int/globalatlas/default.asp
  Global Health Observatory (GHO)—Map Gallery: http://www.who.int/gho/
  map_gallery/en/
  Global Database on the Implementation of Nutrition Action (GINA): https://
  extranet.who.int/nutrition/gina/
  Nutrition Landscape Information System (NLIS): http://www.who.int/nutrition/
  nlis/en/
- Worldmapper Project
  Worldmapper: http://www.worldmapper.org/
  The World Population Atlas: http://www.worldpopulationatlas.org/index_map
  .htm

Food-Focused Interactive Web-Based GIS Data Viewers

- Center for Investigative Reporting
  Map: World Food Statistics: http://cironline.org/reports/map-world-food-
  statistics-2971
- Edible Geography
  United States of Food: http://www.ediblegeography.com/united-states-of-food/
- Feeding America
  Map the Meal Gap: http://feedingamerica.org/hunger-in-america/hunger-
  studies/map-the-meal-ap.aspx

- Foodmiles.com
  Food Miles Calculator: http://www.foodmiles.com/
- Guerilla Cartography
  Food: An Atlas: http://guerrillacartography.net/home.htm
- How Stuff Works
  World Food and Nutrition Map: http://maps.howstuffworks.com/world-food-nutrition-map.htm
- Integrated Approaches to Participatory Development (IAPAD) www.iapad.org
- Johns Hopkins Center for a Livable Future
  Maryland Food System Map: http://mdfoodsystemmap.org/
- Open Forum on Participatory Geographic Information Systems (PGIS) and Technologies www.ppgis.net
- Oxfam International
  Good Enough to Eat Map: http://www.oxfam.org/en/grow/good-enough-eat-map

Web-Based Interactive GIS Viewers with Limited Online Mapping Functions

- Bingmaps: www.bing.com/maps
- OpenStreetMap: http://www.openstreetmap.org/
- Google Earth: https://www.google.com/earth/
- Google Maps: www.google.com/maps
- Mapquest: www.mapquest.com

GIS Programs and Software

Open-source and "free" GIS programs and viewers
- ArcReader: http://www.esri.com/software/arcgis/arcreader
- ArcExplorer: http://www.esri.com/software/arcgis/explorer
- GRASS (Geographic Resources Analysis Support System): http://grass.itc.it/
- Geonetwork-Opensource: http://geonetwork-opensource.org/index.html
- GeoPackage-Open Geospatial Consortium (OGC): http://www.geopackage .org; http://www.opengeospatial.org/
- Open Source GIS: http://opensourcegis.org/
- Quantum GIS: http://qgis.org/
- uDIG (User-friendly Desktop Internet GIS): http://udig.refractions.net/

Commercial GIS program and viewer
- ArcGIS: http://www.esri.com/index.html; http://www.gis.com/.
- MapInfo: http://www.mapinfo.com/
- MyWorldGIS: http://www.myworldgis.org/
- Tatukgis: http://www.tatukgis.com/Home/home.aspx

References

Ahmed, Sohel, et al. 2014. Dining with Less Danger: Mapping Food and Environmental Hazards in Mathare, Nairobi. *IIED Briefing Papers*, March. London: International Institute for Environment and Development (IIED).

An, Ruopeng, and Roland Sturm. 2012. School and Residential Neighborhood Food Environment and Diet Among Californian Youth. *American Journal of Preventive Medicine* 42(2): 129–135.

Brenton, Barrett P. 2012. Promoting Food Security and Healthy Eating through Food Sovereignty: St. John's Bread and Life Digital Choice Food Pantry. Paper presented at Society for Applied Anthropology 72nd Annual Meeting, Baltimore, MD.

Chen, Xiang, and Xining Yang. 2011. Does Food Environment Influence Food Choices? A Geographical Analysis through "Tweets." *Applied Geography* 51: 82–89.

Chen, Xiang, and Jill Clark. 2013. Interactive Three-Dimensional Geovisualization of Space-Time Access to Food. *Applied Geography* 43: 81–86.

City Harvest. 2012. Bed-Stuy Healthy Neighborhoods Map. In *Healthy Neighborhoods Resource Guide: Bed Stuy*. New York: City Harvest.

Coveney, John, and Lisel A. O'Dwyer. 2009. Effects of Mobility and Location on Food Access. *Health & Place* 15: 45–55.

CTA (Technical Centre for Agricultural and Rural Cooperation). 2010. *Training Kit on Participatory Spatial Information Management and Communication*. Wageningen, Netherlands: Technical Centre for Agricultural and Rural Cooperation (CTA) and Rome: International Fund for Agricultural Development (IFAD).

Donkin, Angela J. M., et al. 1999. Mapping Access to Food at a Local Level. *British Food Journal* 101 (7): 554–564.

Dutko, Paula, Michele Ver Ploeg, and Tracey Farrigan. 2012. *Characteristics and Influential Factors of Food Deserts*. Economic Research Report (ERR-140). U.S. Department of Agriculture, Economic Research Service.

Feagan, Robert. 2007. The Place of Food: Mapping out the 'Local' in Local Food Systems. *Progress in Human Geography* 31(1): 23–42.

Gatrell, Jay D., Neil Reid, and Paula Ross. 2011. Local Food Systems, Deserts, and Maps: The Spatial Dynamics and Policy Implications of Food Geography. *Applied Geography* 31 (4): 1195–1196.

Glantz, Namino, and Ben McMahan. 2007. The Anthropology-Map Merger. *Practicing Anthropology* 29(4): 4–5.

Graham, R., et al. 2006. *Eating In, Eating Out, Eating Well: Access to Healthy Food in North and Central Brooklyn*. New York: New York City Department of Health and Mental Hygiene.

Herlinhy, Peter H., and Gregory Knapp, eds. 2003. Participatory Mapping of Indigenous Lands in Latin America. Special issue, *Human Organization* 62(4).

Hesse, Ced. 2013. Maps that Build Bridges. *Reflect and Act* (December). London: International Institute for Environment and Development (IIED).

IFAD (International Fund for Agricultural Development). 2009. *Good Practices in Participatory Mapping*. Rome: International Fund for Agricultural Development.

Kremer, Peleg, and Tracy L. DeLiberty. 2011. Local Food Practices and Growing Potential: Mapping the Case of Philadelphia. *Applied Geography* 31(4): 1252–1261.

Lee, Helen. 2012. The Role of Local Food Availability in Explaining Obesity Risk Among Young School-Aged Children. *Social Science and Medicine* 74(8): 1–12.

———. 2013. The Making of the Obesity Epidemic. *Breakthrough Journal* 3). Published online at: http://thebreakthrough.org/index.php/journal/past-issues/issue-3/the-making-of-the-obesity-epidemic.

Matte, Thomas, et al. 2007. *Obesity in Bedford-Stuyvesant and Bushwick: A Look Across Generations.* New York: New York City Department of Health and Mental Hygiene.

Matthews, Stephen A., James E. Detwiler, and Linda M. Burton. 2005. Geo-Ethnography: Coupling Geographic Information Analysis Techniques with Ethnographic Methods in Urban Research. *Cartographica* 40(4): 75–90.

Monmonier, Mark. 2005. Lying with Maps. *Statistical Science* 20(3): 215–222.

Morrison, Kathryn T., Trisalyn A. Nelson, and Aleck S. Ostry. 2011a. Mapping Spatial Variation in Food Consumption. *Applied Geography* 31(4): 1262–1267.

———. 2011b. Methods for Mapping Local Food Production Capacity from Agricultural Statistics. *Agricultural Systems* 104(6): 491–499.

Nichter, Mark. 2007. Forward: Mapping Communities; Strengthening Research through Participatory GIS. *Practicing Anthropology* 29(4): 2–3.

NYC CEO (New York City Center for Economic Opportunity). n.d. *Healthy Bodegas Initiative: Adopt-a-Bodega Toolkit.* New York: NYC CEO.

NYC DOHMH (New York City Department of Health and Mental Hygiene). 2012. *NYC Community Health Survey 2012.* New York: NYC DOHMH.

NYC DOHMH and NYC CEO. 2010. *New York City Healthy Bodegas Initiative 2010.* New York: NYC DOHMH/CEO.

Osha, Jen, and Daniel Weiner. 2006. Participatory GIS—A Paradigm Shift in Development? *Directions Magazine,* 14 December 2006. Published online at: www.directionsmag.com/entry/participatory-gis-a-paradigm-shift-in-development/122968.

Peters, Christian J., et al. 2009. Mapping Potential Foodsheds in New York State: A Spatial Model for Evaluating the Capacity to Localize Food Production Renewable Agriculture and Food Systems. *Renewable Agriculture and Food Systems* 24(1): 72–84.

Rambaldi, Giacomo. 2005. Who Owns the Map Legend? *URISA Journal* 17(1): 5–13.

———. 2010. *Participatory 3-Dimensional Modeling: Guiding Principles and Applications.* Wageningen, Netherlands: Technical Centre for Agricultural and Rural Cooperation (CTA).

Rambaldi, Giacomo, et al. 2006. *Mapping for Change: Practice, Technologies and Communication.* London: International Institute for Environment and Development (IIED) and Wageningen, Netherlands: The Technical Centre for Agricultural and Rural Cooperation (CTA).

Roberts, Shadrock. 2011. What it Means to Think Spatially. *Frontlines: Climate Change/Science & Technology* (June/July). U.S. Agency for International Development (USAID).

Rowley, Tom. 2013. Participatory Digital Map-Making in Arid Areas of Kenya and Tanzania. *Participatory Learning and Action* 66: 51–56. http://pubs.iied.org/cover_l/G03659.jpg

Rydlund, Paul H. Jr., and Brenda K. Densmore. 2012. *Methods of Practice and Guidelines for Using Survey-Grade Global Navigation Satellite Systems (GNSS) to Establish Vertical Datum in the United States Geological Survey.* U.S. Geological Survey Techniques and Methods, Book 11- D1. Reston, VA: United States Geological Survey.

Treuhaft, Sarah, and Allison Karpyn. 2010. *The Grocery Gap: Who has Access to Healthy Food and Why it Matters.* Oakland, CA: Policy Link and Philadelphia, PA: The Land Trust.

Vajjhala, Shalini P. 2006. "Ground Truthing" Policy: Using Participatory Map-Making to Connect Citizens and Decision Makers. *Resources* 162: 14–18. Washington, D.C.: Resources for the Future.

Ver Ploeg, Michele, et al. 2012. *Access to Affordable and Nutritious Food: Updated Estimates of Distance to Supermarkets using 2010 Data.* Economic Research Report (ERR-143). U.S. Department of Agriculture, Economic Research Service.

Walker, Renee E., Christopher R. Keane, and Jessica G. Burke. 2010. Disparities and Access to Healthy Food in the United States: A Review of Food Deserts Literature. *Health & Place* 16: 876–884.

Walker, Wendy M., et al. 2005. *Ground-Truthing: Mapping Mobility and Access in Rural Lesotho.* Washington, DC: World Bank.

Warren, Stacey. 2004. The Utopian Potential of GIS. *Cartographica* 39(1): 5–16.

Whalen, Elizabeth, and Michael Seserman. 2011. *Looking for an Oasis in a Food Desert: Low Income New Yorkers Lack Access to Healthy Food.* New York: New York Action Center, American Cancer Society.

Zahilay, Grimay. 2010. Community Food Assessment: Bedford Stuyvesant. New York: City Harvest.

CHAPTER 10

Photo-Video Voice

Helen Vallianatos

Introduction

Participatory visual methods share a commitment to engaged, collaborative research paradigms that honor participants' opinions and experiences while striv-
ing towards social change. Photovoice as a distinct method is credited to Caroline
Wang and Mary Ann Burris's (1994, 1997) work on reproductive health issues
with women in China. They defined photovoice as "the process by which people
identify, represent, and enhance their community through specific photographic
technique" (Wang and Burris 1997: 369). The purpose of photovoice is to have
participants reflect upon and record various aspects of an issue or problem, and
to recognize locally available opportunities and challenges alike that can provide building blocks for solutions to the issue or problem under investigation.
Through discussion of the photographs and associated narratives, dialogue is promoted. The evocative power of images also makes this a tool that effectively en-
gages a variety of stakeholders, including policy makers.

More recently, researchers working predominantly on health and development issues developed videovoice, building upon photovoice as well as participatory media/video methodologies (e.g., Catalani et al. 2012; Chávez et al. 2004).
This method resembles photovoice in that it intertwines research and advocacy
while relying on participants' expertise and knowledge, which participants themselves document using video cameras. It differs in that it can capture movement,
sound, and interactions and relationships between subjects, including people,
animals, objects, or the environment. Like photovoice, videovoice—also called
participatory video—has been found to facilitate empowerment and community
collaborations (White 2003). As evocative as photographs are, video may be an
even more powerful mode for dissemination, especially considering the range of
means for broadcasting findings (e.g., via YouTube and other Internet platforms,
as well as more traditional means like television and theatres).

Theoretical Origins

Photovoice was developed by Caroline C. Wang and Mary Ann Burris (1994, 1997), who incorporated three main sources: (1) theoretical literature on education for critical consciousness (Freire 1970), feminist theory (Wang and Burris particularly drew on Weiler 1988 and Kramarae and Spender 1992), and documentary community photography (e.g. Hubbard 1991; Spence 1995); (2) efforts of feminist scholars, community photographers and participatory educators to challenge assumptions about representation and authorship; and (3) their experience conducting research on the Ford Foundation-supported Yunnan Women's Reproductive Health and Development Program. In bringing together these sources and experiences, Wang and Burris developed a method that explicitly aims to challenge traditional authoritative knowledge by privileging the embodied, experiential knowledge of participants. In other words, power dynamics of knowledge creation are reversed, or at least challenged, when the expert is the participant, not the researcher. Acknowledging the value and importance of *all* participants' voices, and creating a space to share these opinions and experiences, is a critical aspect of this method. Oftentimes, participants who are empowered to be heard may otherwise have had little opportunity or means to voice their opinions (Molloy 2007; Wang, Burris and Xiang 1996). Wang and Burris promoted dialogue through group discussions in which participants shared their photos and stories. Participants reflect upon the social, political, economic, and cultural realities influencing their lives, raising consciousness around the problem or issue at hand (Carlson, Engebretson, and Chamberlain 2006; Molloy 2007). While listening to one another, people may recognize shared experiences or similar problems and, most importantly, share information on coping strategies or ideas for solutions. From these discussions, then, grassroots inspirations for dealing with an issue or problem may emerge (Carlson et al. 2006). Consequently, photovoice has been widely applied in participatory research and in both scholarly and applied social justice work.

The goals of photovoice, (and videovoice by extension), as summarized by Wang and Redwood-Jones (2001), are

1. To enable people to identify and reflect upon their community's strengths and concerns,
2. To promote critical dialogue on issues or problems through discussions of photographs,
3. To reach policy makers.

Social action and change inform this method, from its development through to its application. Social change can begin with personal, individual reflections and raised consciousness that may lead to behavioral changes or altered ideas, and continue in the form of community mobilization based on critical discussions and engagement amongst participants and with other community members and policy makers.

Steps and Variations

The very nature of this method makes it most useful for participatory research. Therefore the research question/issue ought to evolve from discussions with various stakeholders in the community. Some researchers develop a guiding or advisory committee consisting of various community leaders and stakeholders to participate in the research process, from design through analysis and dissemination (e.g., Nykiforuk et al. 2012; Wang and Redwood-Jones 2001). As in any group interview, a group must be constructed with care to ensure no one is silenced or marginalized in the discussions. For further information on conducting group interviews the reader is referred to texts on focus group methodologies, such as Morgan (1997) and Barbour and Kitzinger (1999).

The first group discussion with participants can be an opportunity to begin conversations on the question or issue of interest, as well as introduce ways of using visual techniques to share ideas. The length and content of this meeting will depend on the needs of the project and participants. For instance, some participants may need training in the use of cameras or video. A discussion on the "frame" of the photo or video—that is, on the importance of considering what the photograph or video captures or excludes—may be necessary. This may be particularly important for projects investigating more abstract concepts, where participants may need to be encouraged to think about how to visually represent intangible concepts (see, e.g., Yohani 2008). A discussion about framing visual images and creative, symbolic representations may also be necessary depending on the ethical requirements of the project, such as avoiding identifiable images of children. The ethics of taking photographs and of the research process needs to also be discussed, of course when informed consent is obtained prior to participation, but again at this stage, when questions may emerge as participants consider how to visually represent their opinions, ideas, and experiences. At the end of this discussion, participants may be given a guideline of the kinds of photographs to be taken. For example, in a research project investigating pregnant women's food practices, women were instructed to photograph "all meals and snacks (including drinks) during a three-day period (including one weekend day) and other foods they perceive to be healthy/unhealthy for consumption during and after pregnancy," and were given guidelines to include foods that should be eaten and avoided while pregnant, after birth, and so forth (Higginbottom et al. 2011: 106–107). For other projects, though, it may be preferable to avoid influencing what kinds of photographs or videos are taken and thus not to provide specific guidelines, so that participants can have free rein to capture visual images that speak to their stories, experiences, or opinions of a particular issue or problem. Researchers may also choose to avoid defining key terms, in order to learn how participants think about and experience such concepts. For example, Gosselink and Myllykangas (2007) purposefully refrained from defining the concept of "leisure" in order to capture participants' perceptions of what leisure entails.

Participants need time to capture images, but a time limit is advisable, as are check-ins or reminders for participants during this phase. The length of the photo-taking period will depend on the project goals and design. Many projects give participants a couple of weeks or so to take photos (e.g., Nykiforuk, Vallianatos, and Nieuwendyk 2011), but others may take longer, meeting repeatedly during this phase to discuss photos taken and then taking time to shoot further photos (e.g. Mamary, Mccright, and Roe 2007; Wang and Redwood-Jones 2001). More time and repeated efforts may provide opportunities for participants to improve their skills at photography/videography, and in turn affect the evocative and/or creative nature of the images.

The next phase is the discussion(s), when images are shared. Whether participants are able to share all their photographs depends on the number of photographs taken and the time available for discussion. Film footage obtained through videovoice can be quite lengthy, so in many studies participants are asked to select key images to share—for example, a few photographs (e.g., Nykiforuk et al. 2011) or a short clip, no longer than five minutes (e.g., Catalani et al. 2012). These may be chosen because they best represent a participant's experiences or ideas, or because the participant likes the aesthetics of the image—what is fundamental here is that it is the participant's choice. Participants then share stories explaining the image. Wang (2006: 151) provided the mnemonic SHOWeD to assist with framing stories:

- What do you *S*ee here?
- What's really *H*appening here?
- How does this relate to *O*ur lives?
- *W*hy does this situation, concern, or strength exist?
- What can we *D*o about it?

When images are shared in a group context, facilitators need to watch the time to ensure that all have the opportunity to convey their images and stories, and to allow other participants to ask questions and discuss the images. Many studies have rounds: participants take turns sharing one image with the group; after all have had a chance to share one image, the round starts again with the second group (e.g., Wang 2006). Other studies involve one-on-one discussions between the participant and the researcher, which allow participants to share in-depth stories using most, if not all of their images, and make connections between images.

The group discussion happens later at a public sharing of the images, for example a presentation at a public library. This allows not just participants but other community members too to engage with the images and stories, thereby broadening the group of people with experience of the issue and opinions on solutions (e.g., Nykiforuk et al. 2011).

Data analysis, like other qualitative methods, is an iterative process that takes place during data collection. The participatory approach means that analysis is done in collaboration with participants. It begins with participants selecting images and then contextualizing them through stories and discussions (Wang and Burris 1997). This connection between images and narratives is critical to understanding the issues under investigation. In other words, the images are not analyzed separately, and their quality or aesthetic value is a trivial factor in the analysis. What is essential in this method is the participants' meanings and knowledge, which emerge as the stories, explanations, and discussions of their images make issues and themes apparent (Wang and Burris 1997). Qualitative data analysis software, such as Atlas-Ti, is helpful for data management, especially when working in a collaborative team context. For example, this software allows interviews and photographs to be linked and both text and image content to be coded.

Thus, photo/videovoice promotes dialogue through discussion of images and can be part of a process (e.g., during individual or focus group interviews) or of the larger community discussions (i.e., when images are displayed, distributed, or screened in public spaces) that are critical for social action. Efforts to include all stakeholders, including policy makers, in these discussions are imperative for change to occur. Appendix 1 summarizes the key steps in designing a photo-video voice project.

Ethical Considerations

A number of ethical issues are inherent in this method. Images, whether in photographs or videos, are not just snapshots of an objective truth, but rather are composed by the photographer/videographer. What is captured in the frame, what is left out, and the contexts of the images reflect the photographer's or videographer's values. Furthermore, viewers emplace their own values onto the images in the process of interpretation. Careful consideration of ethical dilemmas is therefore essential, especially when working with marginalized communities and people.

As in any research, informed consent is required before participation (see Whiteford and Trotter 2008). However, further consents are necessary in photovideo voice. In the project description, along with the regular information required by institutional ethics boards, the process of photo-video voice and the participant's role therein need to be elaborated, and the potential uses of the images need to be demarcated (e.g., for research or educational purposes, etc.). Participants typically are offered copies of the images (either hard copies, digital copies, or negatives). The participants are the authors of the images, so not only is their permission needed to use the images, but they also have to be given the opportunity to say which images may be disseminated and which, if any, they wish to keep private. For example, Catalani and colleagues (2012) practiced inclusive editing in developing the final film footage to ensure that privacy, representation, and authorship issues were addressed. Furthermore, participants may wish to be credited as authors of the images. Issues of anonymity arise, for confidentiality and anonymity are potentially breached when pseudonyms are used in the text but not for the images. Some wish to have their images and words credited; others prefer to use pseudonyms. One solution is to maintain anonymity in the text and images but recognize image authors in the acknowledgements section, without specifying which images are whose. Participants need to make informed choices, so time must be taken to discuss the options and ramifications of various choices. Of course, when working with youth, parental consent and participant assent are required as well.

Further consents may be required if participants take photographs of other people. In this form of consent an individual participant's permission is obtained prior to her or his inclusion in photographs or video. Although institutional ethics boards may not require this in public spaces, Wang and Redwood-Jones (2001: 565) emphasize that it is important to go beyond ethics requirements and emphasize respect for privacy. They provide an example: an individual may be in a public place, yet not wish another to know that she or he was in a particular location at a particular time. Consequently, as a rule of thumb, Wang and Redwood-Jones recommend that all participants obtain permission prior to recording any images. The only exceptions would concern individual faces that are unrecognizable or a person who entered the frame inadvertently. In some projects, during the informed consent discussion participants are told not to take identifiable images of people, as in the study of Higginbottom and colleagues (2011). Wang and Redwood-Jones (2001) recommend that photovoice training begin with discussion of images, the power of representation/images, and ethics. Readers are referred to guidelines developed by Wang and Redwood-Jones (2001: 570) for best practices in photovoice ethics.

A final note on ethical practice in work with marginalized peoples relates to managing expectations for social change. The onus for coming up with and implementing potential solutions ought not to be a burden shared only by participants, who might be blamed if the change does not meet expectations. This method was developed to explicitly include an array of voices and opinions not typically heard, but other stakeholders—policy makers, media, and others—need to be part of the process of change. Prins (2010) warns researchers about the potential for unexpected consequences when this method fails to erase power differentials, and shares a case study of how images were viewed as surveillance, not empowerment. Carlson and colleagues (2006) emphasize that when working with historically oppressed populations, active facilitation on the researchers' part is crucial to support ongoing learning, reflection, participation, and action.

Applications

The participatory nature and evocative findings of photo-video voice have led to high uptake of the method among organizations working to support community development and social change. One such organization is *PhotoVoice: Participatory Photography for Social Change* (www.photovoice.org), based in the United Kingdom. At its website, readers will find a wide variety of examples as well as resources and training opportunities. Other organizations that have provided guidebooks and training for community members and organizations include IDEO (www.ideo.org/stories/introducing-photovoice), Heal-Chi Photovoice Project: Train the Trainer (norcalheal.cnr.berkeley.edu/docs/Photovoice_Training .pdf), Community Tool Box (ctb.ku.edu/en/table-of-contents/assessment/assess ing-community-needs-and-resources/photovoice/main; note that there are many other resources on community building and activism at this site), Kids With Cameras (kids-with-cameras.org/home/), and the Prairie Women's Health Centre (Palibroda 2009). Many organizations have used social media and YouTube to disseminate their findings; readers will find a rich variety of topics at this site.

Conclusion

Photo-video voice is a participatory research method used to elicit experiences, perspectives, and ideas from people who may previously have had limited opportunities to share their knowledge. Because this method does not require literacy, it can be used with those with limited literacy skills and diverse age groups (e.g., Gosselink and Myllykangas 2007; Wang 2006; Yohani 2008). The method can be altered to meet specific community needs and contexts, from providing snapshots of a particular moment in time and space to conducting a longer-term examination of a particular issue. Examples of the range of work undertaken using this method include not only public health research (beginning with Wang and Burris 1994, and now covering a range of issues exemplified by Gosselink and Myllykangas 2007; Higginbottom et al. 2011; Mamary et al. 2007), but also experiences of violence (e.g., Lykes, Blanche, and Hamber 2003), discrimination (e.g., Graziano 2004), identity and community (e.g., McIntyre 2003; Side 2005), and other topics related to social justice. Anthropological perspectives on meanings of images, image technologies, and the sociocultural contexts of taking and interpreting photos/images will add to the literature on this rapidly growing methodology.

Helen Vallianatos is Associate Professor of Anthropology at the University of Alberta, Canada. Her research and teaching focus on the topics of food, gender, body, and health. Examples of her research range from her early work on food consumption during pregnancy in New Delhi, India, examining how a confluence of individual, community, and political-economic factors shaped women's food practices and nutritional health status (*Poor and Pregnant in New Delhi, India,* available through Left Coast Press), to recent and ongoing collaborative interdisciplinary research on family food practices (*Acquired Tastes: Why Families Eat the Way They Do,* available through University of British Columbia Press*)*, to ways place shapes health practices and behaviors, and the food and health experiences and needs of various immigrant communities. Much of this collaborative work involves use of photo elicitation and photovoice methods.

Appendix. Key Steps in Designing a Photo-Video Voice Study

1. Community consultation and research question development
2. Plan photo-video voice project and obtain research ethics
   i. Other applicable institutional ethics permissions must be also sought and cleared (e.g., from a school board, if working in a school).
3. Recruitment and obtaining informed consent
4. First interview and discussion on photography/videography (e.g., how to take photos/videos)
   i. Discussion on how/what images to capture depends on the nature of the project. Limited instructions may be desirable.
5. Image-taking
   i. Remember check-ins and have a set timeline for this task.
6. Discussion/selection of images
   i. In some studies, steps 5 and 6 are repeated over a period of time.
7. Larger community discussions
8. Data analysis
   i. Analysis is an ongoing process in conjunction with data collection.
9. Dissemination of findings within the community
10. Policy change and social action

References

Barbour, Rosaline S., and Jenny Kitzinger. 1999. *Developing Focus Group Research.* Thousand Oaks, CA: Sage.

Carlson, Elizabeth D., Joan Engebretson, and Robert M. Chamberlain. 2006. Photovoice as a Social Process of Critical Consciousness. *Qualitative Health Research* 16: 836–852.

Catalani, Caricia E. C. V., Anthony Veneziale, Larry Campbell, Shawna Herbst, Brittany Butler, Benjamin Springgate, and Meredith Minkler. 2012. Videovoice: Community Assessment in Post-Katrina New Orleans. *Health Promotion Practice* 13: 18–28.

Chávez, Vivian, Barbara Israel, Alex J. Allen, Maggie F. DeCarlo, Richard Lichtenstein, Amy Schulz, Irene S. Bayer, and Robert McGranaghan. 2004. A Bridge Between Communities: Video-Making Using Principles of Community-Based Participatory Research. *Health Promotion Practice* 5: 395–403.

Freire, Paulo. 1970. *Pedagogy of the Oppressed.* New York: Seabury.

Graziano, Kevin J. 2004. Oppression and Resiliency in a Post-Apartheid South Africa: Unheard Voices of Black Gay Men and Lesbians. *Cultural Diversity and Ethnic Minority Psychology* 10(3): 302–316.

Higginbottom, Gina M. A., Helen Vallianatos, Joan Forgeron, Donna Gibbons, Rebecca Mahli, and Fabiana Mamede. 2011. Food Choices and Practices During Pregnancy of Immigrant and Aboriginal Women in Canada: A Study Protocol. *BMC Pregnancy and Childbirth* 11: 100–110.

Hubbard, Jim. 1991. *Shooting Back: A Photographic View of Life by Homeless Children.* San Francisco: Chronicle.

Gosselink Carol A., and Sue A. Myllykangas. 2007. The Leisure Experiences of Older U.S. Women Living with HIV/AIDS. *Health Care for Women International* 28: 3–20.

Kramarae, Cheris, and Dale Spender, eds. 1992. *The Knowledge Explosion: Generations of Feminist Scholarship.* New York: Teacher's College Press.

Lykes, M. Brinton, Martin T. Blanche, and Brandon Hamber. 2003. Narrating Survival and Change in Guatemala and South Africa: The Politics of Representation and a Liberatory Community Psychology. *American Journal of Community Psychology* 31(1/2): 79–90.

Mamary, Edward, Jacqueline Mccright, and Kevin Roe. 2007. Our Lives: An Examination of Sexual Health Issues Using Photovoice by Non-Gay Identified African American Men Who Have Sex with Men. *Culture, Health & Sexuality* 9: 359–370.

McIntyre, Alice. 2003. Through the Eyes of Women: Photovoice and Participatory Research as Tools for Reimagining Place. *Gender, Place and Culture* 10(1): 47–66.

Molloy, Jennifer K. 2007. Photovoice as a Tool for Social Justice Workers. *Journal of Progressive Human Services* 18(2): 39–55.

Morgan, David L. 1997. *Focus Groups as Qualitative Research.* 2nd ed. Thousand Oaks, CA: Sage.

Nykiforuk, Candace I. J., Donald Schopflocher, Helen Vallianatos, John C. Spence, Kim D. Raine, Ronald C. Plotnikoff, Eric VanSpronsen, and Laura M. Nieuwendyk. 2012. Community Health and Built Environment: Examining "Place" in a Canadian Chronic Disease Prevention Project. *Health Promotion International* 28(2): 257–268.

Nykiforuk, Candace I. J., Helen Vallianatos, and Laura M. Nieuwendyk. 2011. Photovoice as a Method for Revealing Community Perceptions of the Built and Social Environment. *International Journal of Qualitative Methodology* 10(2): 103–124.

Palibroda, Beverly, with Brigette Krieg, Lisa Murdock, and Joanne Havelock. 2009. *A Practical Guide to Photovoice: Sharing Pictures, Telling Stories and Changing Communities.* Winnipeg, Manitoba: Prairie Women's Health Centre.

Prins, Esther. 2010. Participatory Photography: A Tool for Empowerment or Surveillance? *Action Research* 8: 426–443.

Side, Katherine. 2005. Snapshots on Identity: Women's Contributions Addressing Community Relations in a Rural Northern Irish District. *Women's Studies International Forum* 28(4): 315–327.

Spence, Jo. 1995. *Cultural Sniping: The Art of Transgression.* New York: Routledge.

Wang, Caroline. 2006. Youth Participation in Photovoice as a Strategy for Community Change. *Journal of Community Practice* 14: 147–161.

Wang, Caroline, and Burris, Mary Ann. 1994. Empowerment through Photo Novella: Portraits of Participation. *Health Education Quarterly* 21: 171–186.

Wang, Caroline, Mary Ann Burris, and Xiang Yue Ping. 1996. Chinese Village Women as Visual Anthropologists: A Participatory Approach to Reaching Policy Makers. *Social Science and Medicine* 42: 1391–1400.

Wang, Caroline, and Burris, Mary Ann. 1997. Photovoice: Concept, Methodology, and Use for Participatory Needs Assessment. *Health Education & Behavior* 24: 369–387.

Wang, Caroline, and Yanique A. Redwood-Jones. 2001. Photovoice Ethics: Perspectives from Flint Photovoice. *Health Education and Behavior* 28: 560–572.

Weiler, Kathleen. 1988. *Women Teaching for Change: Gender, Class, and Power.* South Hadley, MA: Bergin and Garvey.

White, Shirley A. 2003. *Participatory Video: Images that Transform and Empower.* Thousand Oaks, CA: Sage.

Whiteford, Linda M., and Robert T. Trotter II. 2008. *Ethics for Anthropological Research and Practice.* Long Grove, IL: Waveland Press.

Yohani, Sophie C. 2008. Creating an Ecology of Hope: Arts-Based Interventions with Refugee Children. *Child & Adolescent Social Work Journal* 25(4): 309–323.

CHAPTER **11**

Digital Storytelling
Using First-Person Videos about Food in Research and Advocacy

Marty Otañez

Introduction

Stories about food, especially those with moving images, are among the most popular in cultures around the world. This chapter presents an introduction to digital
food stories in anthropology research projects. A digital story is a first-person video
about three minutes long with voice narration, personal photographs, video footage, and background music. Digital storytelling is a process in which individuals
create and narrate their own stories instead of researchers telling stories about
or for them. A challenge for anthropologists and social scientists is recognizing
that digital storytelling is not about making videos about other people. It is a
method and process for sharing our own stories and using our skills to create a
platform for community collaborators to make their own visual narratives. Anthropologists and community members express a growing interest in digital storytelling, recognizing that media-making skills and short videos augment the
peer-reviewed papers that traditionally emerge from academic-community projects. Videos and basic proficiency in image-making that emerge through these
projects offer individuals tangible products that tend to be more practical for research participants than written text publications. Also, students of culture often
desire training in visually based research strategies to critically understand their
personal research experiences and to effectively circulate anthropological findings
to broader audiences. This chapter is designed to help students and researchers
engage in digital storytelling through story development, image selection, video
editing, and screening of digital stories in diverse settings. My hope is that a
hands-on introduction to first-person video creation will equip individuals with
an understanding of digital storytelling as a method for research.

Digital storytelling is a blossoming field of inquiry and practice among anthropologists and other social scientists who desire to conduct image-driven, ethnographic, activist, and public projects. Individuals apply digital storytelling to gender justice (Hill 2010), pedagogy (Fletcher and Cambre 2009), visual-based theory (Benmayor 2009), and new media technology (Biella 2008). Digital storytelling overlaps with and is historically linked to photovoice approaches (Castleden 2008), telenovelas (Tufte 2000), video diaries (Roberts 2011), "tabletop videos" (Maier and Fisher 2006) and therapeutic films (Johnson 2008). In the area of health, digital storytelling is presented as a compelling method and intervention in community-based participatory research (Gubrium and Turner 2011) with implications for the decolonization of research (Salazar 2005; Willox 2012). Individuals with expertise in ethnographic film and documentary video address contexts in which digital storytelling is performed, covering the politics of representation (Rony 1996), videography in fieldwork (Barbash and Taylor 1997), ethics in visual research (Wiles 2011), auto-ethnography (Russell 1999), visual illness narratives (Chalfen 2010), digital visual ethnography (Pink 2011), visual sovereignty (Raheja 2011), and future visions of visual anthropology (Coover 2009). This chapter expands the literature on visual-based research methods by focusing on digital food stories and key activities to conduct digital storytelling research.

Origins: The Story Center

Story Center (storycenter.org), formerly called the Center for Digital Storytelling, a Berkeley-based nonprofit organization that administers fee-based workshops, pioneered digital storytelling in the 1980s. In 2013 Story Center started a series of food-themed digital storytelling workshops that evolved into a food story YouTube playlist (http://tinyurl.com/CDSFood). My approach to digital storytelling in teaching and research projects is influenced by the Story Center. Each Story Center digital storytelling workshop typically includes ten individuals in three successive days (24 hours) of instruction. Story Center co-facilitators elicit digital stories from participants who produce videos in a professional, broadcast-quality format. Unlike traditional documentary and ethnographic video making, which reports on different cultures and leaves control of the creative process in producers' hands, the digital storytelling model prioritizes personal narrative and the experience of visual storytelling in a group setting. The approach has its faults— specifically, individuals who participate in the digital storytelling process may experience discomfort sharing a private moment among strangers and writing a script using the first-person format (Smilack 2013).

The Story Center's approach to digital storytelling comprises seven steps: owning your own insights, owning your emotions, finding the moment, seeing your story, hearing your story, assembling your story, and sharing your story (Lambert 2010). Technology is secondary; the main goal is for individuals to make their voices heard, seen and influential through the digital storytelling process. From 1994 to 2014, Story Center staff and affiliates helped individuals create and produce more than twenty thousand digital stories in community-based workshops in 45 US states and more than 20 countries as diverse as Brazil, Korea, and Uganda.

In 2008, I was introduced to the Story Center model by a professional videographer who worked on occasion with the organization. The model offered an alternative to the traditional documentary video approach that I had used since 2000, when I turned my dissertation research in cultural anthropology at the University of California, Irvine, into a video called *Thangata: Social Bondage and Big Tobacco in Malawi* (http://bit.ly/12j1TGu). With virtually no formal training as a documentary or ethnographic filmmaker, I embraced digital media strategies to reach non-academic audiences and explore digital storytelling as a medium for policy change. Digital storytelling then represented, and continues to develop as, a method for qualitative research that is sensitive to community members' interests, adding transparency to ethnographic practice (Otañez and Guerrero 2015; Otañez and Lakota 2015).

Seven Key Activities in Digital Storytelling

Individuals involved in digital storytelling workshops in research projects perform seven key activities in the creation of their videos. The activities overlap with, but are qualitatively different from, the Story Center's seven digital storytelling steps. The key activities are fluid and adjusted as needed to accommodate participants' interests and skills. The activities are designed for the workshop model but may easily be applied to the one-on-one approach to digital storytelling. Based on my experience, nearly everyone who creates digital stories has little or no experience in the first-person approach to digital storytelling. The activities provide guidance on addressing anxieties associated with sharing personal narratives in a public setting and challenges encountered in learning software applications for video editing. At the start of a workshop, individuals are reminded that instruction in digital storytelling prioritizes story identification and script-writing skills, placing relatively low value on video editing skills. Researchers and co-facilitators inform individuals who are preparing to make videos that the most compelling stories are the ones that have never been told before.

In activity one, each participant identifies an idea for a digital story and produces an initial script of at least 250 words. About one week before the start of the workshop, individuals receive a story prompt to facilitate story ideas. Story prompts typically express a project theme such as 'Share a story about a recent health problem you experienced.' In practice many individuals arrive at a workshop with little or no idea about a story to share. Actual story scripts are written in English. Participants who speak a language other than English as their first language may record audio narration in their primary language, adding subtitles for English speakers. Researchers need to be clear about who likely participants may be and plan to include a co-facilitator with the appropriate language skills to assist non-English speaking individuals.

In activity two, individuals participate in a story circle, where storytellers share scripts in a group setting and provide oral feedback to peers. Approximately fifteen minutes are allotted for the sharing of each individual's story and subsequent constructive input from participants and co-facilitators. The story circle is the activity that builds collective consciousness among participants, which storytellers draw upon in the digital storytelling process (Gubrium 2009). An outsider who fails to see the circle as a space where participants take ownership of their narratives and build group solidarity might view a story circle as a group therapy session. In a limited sense, a story circle is indeed imbued with therapeutic possibilities, as individuals share stories that have remained private up to that point and receive positive reinforcement from others in story sharing. Digital storytelling's potential to contribute to therapy and personal wellness is an area that requires more attention from anthropologists.

Opening remarks by co-facilitators emphasize that individuals in the circle are expected to be listeners and reviewers whose comments allow storytellers to develop the best story script they wish to make. To encourage peer-to-peer teaching, people in story circles are asked, with regard to their comments about draft scripts of others in the group, to see themselves as on equal footing with the co-facilitators. Acknowledging power relations between participants and co-facilitators helps participants refrain from acting in deference to co-facilitators and recognize that participants' comments are as valuable as co-facilitators'. Sample questions for an individual in a story circle might include: Are there specific sections in your story that you wish to receive feedback on? What do you see as the main message of your story? What images do you want to use to tell your story? What is the title of your digital story?

Next (activity three), each storyteller polishes her or his script and begins to think about imagery. Co-facilitators inform storytellers that the script writing process may take up four hours after the end of the circle, with multiple versions being drafted before recording audio. The process may start with a script reaching 1,000 words in order to find the story, which is then synthesized to 250 words in preparation for recording the voiceover. In activity four the co-facilitator, using a professional microphone and digital audio device or a laptop computer, records the participant reading the script. Prior to recording, the co-facilitator and the participant review the script, making last-minute adjustments to ensure the storyteller's voice is prominent in the narrative. In preparation for the recording, individuals are encouraged to speak in their conversational voice, demonstrate emotion, and speak slowly. It is not unusual for storytellers to record a reading of the script two or more times before capturing a quality audio narration. Storytellers leave the session with a copy of their audio file on a flash drive that they transfer to a laptop to begin video editing.

Activity five covers video editing with media resources such as photographs, video excerpts, instrumental music, and sound effects. Prior to the workshop, participants are encouraged to bring ten or more personal photographs or video excerpts, label media with one or two key words, and organize media in a master project folder stored on a flash drive or in an online cloud storage platform. Each project folder includes subfolders labeled "Imagery," "Audio," and "Miscellaneous" to organize media. Storytellers are allowed to use media from their own personal collections and learn basic skills to obtain photos and video excerpts created specifically for their projects. With brief instructions and discussion about using individuals' own cameras and mobile devices, digital storytellers learn to take their own photographs and video excerpts and gather imagery from personal media collections. A scanner is available to digitize photographs and other print media such as news clippings, food recipes, and diary entries. Basic proficiency in Adobe Photoshop or other image editing programs may help digital storytellers enhance the aesthetic look of the most generic photographs. Personal video in the form of videocassettes and other media formats will likely require professional digitization fee-based services and need to be completed prior to the workshop. Individuals in need of media for their projects have options to use their own mobile devices or borrow digital still and video cameras.

I prohibit individuals from using media that they did not create or own, such as copyrighted and copyright-free media found on the Internet. This approach reinforces the originality in digital stories and encourages the maker to see the piece as art rather than a video stitched together using images and music the maker does not own. The media policy is a vehicle to discuss with individuals options available to them for producing drawings and gathering photos and video shots that are metaphorical and symbolic and less literal and explicit. The restriction on Internet-based media is a challenge for most community members, who are increasingly adept at finding and capturing media online. I also prohibit storytellers from using images from Facebook and other social media sites because the sites recompress media, downgrading image quality and adding to pixilation of photographs. Numerous sites on the Internet provide copyright-free photographs (e.g., flickr.com, istockphoto.com, archive.org). In the past I allowed individuals to obtain images for their videos from these sites with appropriate accreditation. In 2012, though, wanting to see more original and less corporate-looking media-driven work, I required participants to obtain photographs and video excerpts from their own collections or create them as needed for their projects. However, I make exceptions when the design of a video such as a mash-up or parody is compelling justification for the use of media not owned by a storyteller. In terms of the possibility of publication of digital stories in scholarly outlets, original work is easier to publish than copyrighted materials because publishers generally request permission from the individuals who originally created the media used in a digital story.

In discussions about audio, community members learn that audio tracks in the form of instrumental songs and sound effects are characters in digital stories. In videos, instrumental tracks are preferred to songs with lyrics because the latter can sometimes compete with the audio narration. Storytellers learn at the beginning of the creative process to identify the audio feel of their stories and obtain the appropriate audio tracks before assembling their videos. Also, they learn that oftentimes silence (e.g., no background music or sound effects) is a powerful character in a digital story. Another lesson is that individuals should not feel compelled to integrate songs and effects without considering these media's relationship to the narrative and emotional essence of the video. Digital stories without songs and sound effects are appropriate. An effective digital storyteller imports the background music and/or sound effect into the video editing program and begins to build a project with audio narration and imagery, using the audio as the basis for editing decisions. These activities are consistent with the notion that viewers will put up with mediocre visual imagery but do not tolerate inferior audio tracks. Many participants are familiar with web resources that provide copyright-free music and sound effects (jamendo.com, soundcloud.com, archive.org). My policy on background music and sound effects is the same as the policy for photographs and video excerpts: digital storytellers are encouraged to use copyright-free audio as background music and sound effects. Apple Garage Band and an increasing number of other fee-based and free music software programs allow individuals to make their own instrumental audio tracks and sound effects. Storytellers are encouraged to explore their social networks for musicians and singers, collaborating with them to create original soundtracks.

Activity six includes video editing. Media resources are imported into the video-editing program, and participants assemble their digital stories. Participants learn to edit around their audio narration and any instrumental music and sound effects in their projects. The editing process includes arranging imagery in a timeline, applying transitions, adding credits, and adjusting audio to ensure levels are smooth and consistent. Participants export their video projects from the editing program into a QuickTime movie file and back up their project folders with media on a flash drive or upload them to an Internet storage service such as Dropbox. At this phase of the digital storytelling process, participants learn about the importance of backing up media files, both for archival purposes and in anticipation of the inevitable technological problems that accompany any media making.

From 2000 to 2013, I used Apple's proprietary Final Cut video editing program. It meets movie industry standards for broadcast-quality videos and is a more robust program than Apple's consumer-friendly iMovie. Moreover, Final Cut can be learned by individuals with no knowledge of video editing. However, I have migrated from Final Cut to Adobe Premiere, not only to take advantage of emerging opportunities for video editing through the cloud, but also in response to community members who stated that Final Cut only works on the Apple platform, but they primarily use PC operating systems. A wide range of free and fee-based video editing software programs are available for Mac and PC users. Mac users may want to try iMovie and Premiere. PC users may want to try Premiere, Las Vegas, Avid, Movie Maker, Photo Story, and LoiLoScope. WeVideo and Splice are representative applications for mobile devices that emerging digital storytellers may want to explore. Hubert Knoblauch (2014) and Britta Meixner (2014) provide a useful overview of video tools and qualitative software associated with digital media. Video programs are changing rapidly as new developments in online platforms for participatory video production integrate web editing and mobile devices.

In activity seven, individuals screen their digital stories in a group setting. Screenings are celebratory, and workshop organizers provide snacks and beverages. Prior to the screening, co-facilitators inform project participants that they may make a few remarks about their story and their experience of the digital storytelling process, and that it is not necessary to apologize or make excuses for the quality of their videos. This partly addresses both the compressed time frame of the workshops where digital stories are produced and some individuals' lack of confidence in their video-making skills or anxiety about sharing their story publicly. Overall, a general feeling of excitement fills the room as the first-time video makers watch their videos on a big screen. Brief discussions follow each digital story, with individuals providing feedback on the overall quality of the imagery, audio, and messaging. It would not be an overstatement to say that by the end of the screening, a heightened sense of accomplishment runs through storytellers and co-facilitators. Participants complete a short evaluation to give feedback on the workshop and their individual experiences. Before departing, they receive a copy of their story on a DVD or flash drive, and a gift card.

Digital Storytelling as a Research Process

Anthropologists with an interest in food and other cultural issues use digital storytelling in systematic investigations to create generalizable knowledge. In anthropology at the University of Colorado, Denver (UCD) I have integrated the Story Center's model into ethnographic research projects focused on health equities among Latinos and other marginalized groups. Through different research projects, and in collaboration with study participants and Story Center co-facilitators retained for some of the projects, I administered eight digital storytelling workshops and oversaw the production of more than seventy digital stories between 2008 and 2014. The Colorado Multiple Institutional Review Board approved my use of human subjects for digital storytelling as a research method. Funding for projects has come from the Ford Foundation, the Colorado Clinical and Translational Sciences Institute, the Colorado Department of Public Health and Environment, the UCD Latino Research and Policy Center, and the UCD Undergraduate Research Opportunity Program. At the same time, in projects assigned for my university courses I provide students with options for creating scholarly digital stories. Some examples of the student videos are uploaded on my blog, sidewalkradio.net. Applying the method in both the classroom and research settings allowed me to develop my own style of co-facilitation with storytellers and expand my technological skill set enough to enable me to administer digital storytelling workshops without assistance from professional co-facilitators. Researchers and students who are highly proficient in video editing may find it easier to multitask in digital story production and ethnographic research activities.

In my digital storytelling research projects, individuals integrated a range of food topics in their digital stories. Digital storytelling is, after all, a research tool for collecting information such as participants' narratives, the images they select to visually tell their stories, and their perceptions of health and wellness prior to and after completing their digital stories. The qualitative tool is designed for sampling a small population through participatory and visual methods, producing short personal stories in participants' own words in a group setting. The repository of stories and the participants' lived experiences in video-making become cultural information that can be further examined in interpretive, narrative, and visual ethnographic content analyses. Digital storytelling is reconfiguring the rules and protocols of human subjects committees that recognize the intersection of visual strategies and evidence-based research, including the ethical implications for research participants who wish to reveal personal identifiers in videos that will be screened in diverse settings and social media platforms.

In *The American Dream* (vimeo.com/9354534), Philip talks about the lack of human rights among immigrant sheepherders in Colorado, showing the links between individuals involved in animal husbandry and social justice advocacy. Jeff, a hepatitis C patient in urgent need of a soda pop, receives a second chance at life with a liver transplant in a digital story called *Donation* (vimeo .com/25169192). Another community member produced *Las Abuelas*, about tortillas and family memory (vimeo.com/26812318). In *There Is No Tri, Just Do!* (vimeo.com/9354148), Leslie narrates a story about herself and other Latinas who created the Hermanas triathlon team to combat overeating, integrating the message "*Hermanas* want to be healthier." Harsh working conditions and poor health care of farm workers in tobacco and other field crops in the United States form the backdrop of Anne's story of Latino immigrants in *What Price Freedom* (vimeo.com/9353463).

Additional activities besides those discussed earlier are needed to apply the digital storytelling method in research projects. These activities mainly involve recruiting participants, administering workshops, and disseminating digital stories. Recruitment is done through traditional channels, such as email listservs within the university and in networks of community leaders, using new and existing contacts. Recruitment starts no more than a month before a workshop is scheduled. Each participant is required to commit to the entire training, held on three consecutive days (e.g., 9 a.m. to 5 p.m., Thursday through Saturday). Recruitment is difficult, primarily because of the demanding schedules of most community members, who are already experiencing time limitations due to professional and personal demands. To accommodate the shortage of time among potential participants, it may be necessary to adjust the workshop schedule, for example, by conducting the instruction over eight days or limiting the entire workshop to two days and adjusting the number of hours of instruction accordingly. I am convinced that the three-day workshop (twenty-four hours of instruction), though time-consuming, is the model likeliest to produce the most compelling digital stories and build group solidarity through shared experiences with digital media and personal narrative. If appropriate funding is available, individuals receive a $250 gift card (approximately $10 per hour of attendance) for a participating in a digital storytelling workshop.

In the first hour of a digital storytelling workshop, participants receive information about consent and media release forms. The basic principle, which is explicit in the forms, is that each participant will have at least four opportunities to end participation in the study: during the initial consent process in the first hour of the workshop, at any time during the workshop, in the last hour of the workshop after the digital stories have been screened by the group, and at any time in the future. Participants may revoke participation by informing the researchers or their assistants. Participants are also informed that the digital stories produced in the workshop will be uploaded to the Internet only with their consent. Additionally, the researcher explains that whereas digital stories can be taken down after they are uploaded, there can be no guarantee that someone else has not downloaded the video files. In my digital storytelling research projects with seventy community members from the fall of 2008 through the spring of 2014, four participants who created digital stories did not consent to upload their videos to the Internet, although within twelve months of the end of the workshop, two of those four requested that I upload their digital stories after all. It is possible that all individuals, after completing their digital stories, may revoke their participation in a research project, whereupon scholars are obliged to follow their wishes. My experience with project participants demonstrates that given the chance, people want their digital stories shared and shared widely via the Internet and other channels.

It is self-evident among media makers that the videos created by storytellers may wind up with limited visibility unless there has been a strong dissemination plan from the outset of the project. My dissemination plan is multipronged and continuously evolving based on new dissemination opportunities. After a workshop, digital stories are uploaded to a website where they are available free of charge for viewing and downloading. In cases where individuals revoke their participation in a digital storytelling research project or do not wish videos screened widely, the web link can be password-protected (Vimeo.com) or limited to individuals who receive the link from the storyteller (Youtube.com). Other venues for dissemination include screenings of digital stories in university and professional conference presentations, and community events such as church meetings where individuals receive a compilation DVD. On several occasions I invited digital storytellers who participated in my research projects to accompany me to invited presentations. At events where videos were screened, storytellers discussed their digital storytelling projects and experiences with audience members. The process was invaluable to me because audience members' conversations with actual digital storytellers drew out additional details of the stories. I believe that the interface between audience members and storytellers reveals the power personal narratives have to connect us on a human level beyond what is possible during the standard PowerPoint presentation performed by a lone anthropologist. In my current digital storytelling research projects, I arrange to share creative work in public screenings of videos with free food at a local theater. The screenings are integrated into the research design as opportunities to collect data on audience perceptions of first-person videos via surveys of audience members conducted before and after the screenings, and videotaped post-screening discussions with audience members and digital storytellers.

The intent of my digital storytelling research projects has been to influence the landscape in which decisions that influence the lives of individuals in marginalized communities are made. Virtually all my work has been designed to increase public awareness about health issues such as tobacco use, breast cancer, viral hepatitis, and sexual and reproductive health-care access and justice. One possibility for extending the policy implications of digital storytelling as a research method is to screen digital stories for audiences of decision makers and legislators. In collaboration with storytellers, community leaders, and scholars, two or more first-person videos about urban gardening and food deserts, for example, can be integrated into a one-hour lunch and learn session with invited city councilors, staff members, and other decision makers. Handouts in the presentation may include a one-page, two-sided video viewing guide (i.e., a policy brief) with a description of the digital story, background on issues raised in the video, discussion questions, and contact information for the sponsoring group. To obtain ethnographic data and measure the efficacy of such encounters, brief surveys may be administered before and after they take place, and conversations among storytellers and decision makers may be video recorded. In addition to receiving a compilation DVD with digital stories, decision makers and their staff members can sign a form letter to demonstrate their support for the issues raised by storytellers and commit to participating in a follow-up interview about their perceptions of the impact of the session and digital stories they watched (e.g., three months after the screening). Data, including signed letters, provide metrics on project effectiveness. Activities involving interaction with decision makers build leadership among storytellers and researchers, and increase the strength of policy-influencing digital storytelling in anthropology.

Digital Food Stories: A Brief Overview of Interventions Using the First-Person Video Approach

In 2013 and 2014, the Story Center administered a series of food-themed workshops in New Orleans, Louisiana, and Lyons, Colorado. In September 2014, the Story Center ran the Food Preservation Snapshot Story Retreat, which included a module on tomato canning with community members. The event description addresses themes of the retreat: "Childhood memories of canning garden vegetables? Jam from pick-your-own berry patches? Foraging for elusive mushrooms? Rogue pressure-cookers gone wild? Learn how to shape your food preservation experiences into stories that nourish, instruct, and delight" (Story Center 2014). The retreat offers an innovative way to apply the method with diverse community members and learn how personal videos influence food cultures.

One of the initial Story Center food workshops in New Orleans in March 2013 was framed in terms of food exploration and identity formation: "All of us live in a food story of some kind: our comfort food, the food(s) that define us, our favorite meal and how it changed us, things that happened to us while eating. All of these stories inform our largest story" (Story Center 2014). Individuals with expertise in digital storytelling, media art and performance, and cultural activism co-facilitated the workshop, providing inspiration to participants through visits to key culinary sites in the Marigny, Bywater, and French Quarter neighborhoods. Eleven participants used iPhones to obtain images and edit their digital stories. Claire, one of the workshop participants, created *We Come From the Water* (https://vimeo .com/61549984). She narrates her dislike for seafood and her efforts to find acceptance in her new home in New Orleans. In her digital story Claire says,

> I've used food as a way to immerse myself in new communities of people and I've chased the elusive idea of culture like something I can trap and boil myself into, hungry for a place and a people to call home. But my relationship with New Orleans' food has been more defined by what I don't eat than what I do. (Bangser 2013)

The storyteller discusses her distaste for seafood, relating it with levity to her urinating in the ocean as a child. The real story is about Claire's admiration of a range of diverse food and her determination to find her place in the local community. Claire has already traveled to several different places in the relatively short span of her life so far. She says, "New Orleans is the first place in years where I feel I really might stay if it will let me stew in my own way." The narrative occurs over a series of three photographs and one video clip showing a close-up shot from above of the storyteller in sandals pedaling a red bicycle. The bicycle excerpt is juxtaposed with images: a mound of cooked crawfish spread over newspaper, the storyteller and her friend wearing homemade crawfish hats, a small wooden deck on the bayou with a sunset in the background. The moving bicycle is a metaphor of the storyteller's ongoing journey to find her own community, one that will work with her as she tries to develop an appreciation for food that she describes as "gross."

Emerging digital storytellers and researchers may want to explore additional projects focused on culture and food-themed digital storytelling on their own. Nina Shapiro-Perl, a professor and professional filmmaker at American University, integrates digital storytelling in her teaching and research. In the course "Unseen and Unheard: Documentary Storytelling in the *Other* Washington," Professor Shapiro-Perl oversees collaborative projects with students and African-American community members to document "the lives of people of Washington—all too often unseen and unheard." Performing creative tasks with the Smithsonian Anacostia Community Museum, storytellers and their videos address the intersection of food justice, poverty, and homelessness in *Brainfood. Eat. Learn. Cook* (http://tinyurl.com/mxwwmme), *Giving Them Strength* (http://tinyurl.com/mwtk9wx), and *A Wider Circle* (http://tinyurl.com/k59e7qv). The strength of Shapiro-Perl's approach is the use of collaborative storytelling and digital storytelling as community-driven documentaries.

In 2011, community leaders and researchers with the Native American/Alaska Native STEM (Science, Technology, Engineering, and Mathematics) Pipeline Program and the University of Washington School of Public Health with a grant from the National Institutes for Health produced digital stories about traditional Native diet and nutrition (http://tinyurl.com/mjog6g9). Storytellers used personal narratives and family photographs of "learning how to make fry bread from a parent or grandparent, cooking salmon, picking berries for a pudding and learning Lakota language for food, or brewing a plant based tea for an uncle with cancer" (Native Youth Enrichment Program 2012). The digital storytelling research project contributed to participants' awareness of dietary choices and increased storytellers' and families' knowledge about food and the environment (Carlson and Olsen 2011). Drawing attention to urban food initiatives, the city of Toronto, Canada, in partnership with the Story Center and United Way Toronto, created eleven videos (http://tinyurl.com/my4otkc). In *The Big G: Our*

Soil Creation Legacy, produced by four individuals at the George Harvey Collegiate Institute, the storytellers discuss the beautification of a secondary school through a garden. The garden was integrated into the curriculum, with students obtaining measurements for wood boxes and learning about the nutrition content of vegetables produced in the garden. *The Big G* is an example of an emerging form of collaborative digital storytelling where multiple individuals and their voices are stitched together into a compelling narrative.

Creative Narrations (creativenarrations.net), a social change consulting firm specializing in multimedia support and training for nonprofit and educational institutions based in Seattle, Washington, is at the forefront of digital food stories and policy change. The group's strategy is to educate and engage community members to create sustainable changes in policy, the food system, and the environment to reduce health inequities (Freidus 2013). Through the firm's Mapping Our Voices for Equality project, Creative Narrations worked with individuals to create digital stories about healthy food choices and options. Digital storytellers and their videos were screened at a community forum organized by Creative Narrations, where community members, parents, and decision makers discussed ways to address food inequities in the neighborhood called South Park. In *We Are What We Eat* (Box 1), one of the digital stories screened at the forum, Paulina discusses access issues associated with healthy food choices at corner stores in her community. As a result of viewing the video and participating in the forum, Stockbox, a small mobile produce business, decided to launch a mobile produce stand in South Park. Carrie Ferrence, the owner of Stockbox, said, "Attending the MOVE forum in South Park was the tipping point for us in deciding to open up our first store in this neighborhood" (Freidus 2013). Creative Narrations' policy interventions extend to nutrition and physical activity in local schools. At the same community forum discussed above, Concord International Elementary School in 2012 was inspired to create policies called "Healthy Celebrations" and "Recess Before Lunch" to reduce food waste and improve classroom performance. The policy successes of Creative Narrations and its community collaborators are examples anthropologists can learn from to scale up digital food storytelling as a policy intervention.

Anthropologists and food researchers with an interest in innovative uses of social media may want to explore PoliCultura (policulturaportal.it/eng), a large-scale digital storytelling initiative based in Milan, Italy. From 2007 to 2012, the initiative helped digital storytellers 5–18 years old produce 844 videos using an approach in which individuals are encouraged to interact with local institutions, authorities, and experts; involve parents and grandparents; and share digital stories through an international portal with their peers during and after school hours (Di Blas and Paolini 2013). With funding from the Italian National Association of Organic Agriculture, the project generated digital stories through food-related question prompts: "What is your relationship with food? What do you eat (at

---

Figure 11.1.   *We Are What We Eat: One Family's Quest for a Healthy Home,*
Transcript by Paulina Lopez, May 2010 (http://tinyurl.com/7zaoxwy)

You are what you eat and you will be what you ate. This is the phrase my mother always told me when growing up. I never really understood and I even thought it was one more of her exaggerations. I currently live in a prominent Latino neighborhood called South Park. I think it took us like two months since we lived here to realize that we had to always use a car in order for us to get milk, bread, eggs—all of the basics. When I had my first child, it was what struck me the most— "There is no market?" I thought. I just want to buy a tomato for my stew and I have to dress the baby, put him in the car seat, ride in the car, and bear with his crying to go somewhere for at least four miles. Hmm. What a headache.

I remember growing up back home in Quito, Ecuador. Our family always went walking to the markets or grocery stores. It was not as scary and we knew we would certainly find everything we were looking for. But the first time I went to the store here I was scared. The store was very dark and maybe about five people in line buying just beer. They smelled like cigarettes and everyone looked and smelled like if they had slept in a bar. I did not want to go back there and let alone to take my babies to witness that.

I have to say I have seen changes lately. The last time I visited the same store instead of candy to our eyes the first things we could see were vegetables and fruits. Wow. A little change can truly make an impact. This time, even my son Gabriel, the first thing he said as we walked in was, "I want a banana, mommy." Ahh. I was so happy. We are a small community but it will be much different if we will have healthier choices for our family. We would like to live longer as well. And we want our children to always have a choice to live and eat healthy. Now, I really understand what my mother was referring to: I think we should all have the same right to be what we eat, if we can eat healthy and if we have the opportunity.

---

home, at school)? How do you choose your food? What do you know about the way vegetables are grown or animals are bred?" (Di Blas and Paolini 2013, 18).

PoliCultura is carving out new areas in digital food storytelling by working with individuals as young as five years old and maintaining a repository of videos on a website where visitors may search by keywords (e.g., nutrition, recipe), place (e.g., city, country) and grade level (e.g., secondary school student, senior student). The website is an interactive search engine that allows visitors to access and view hundreds of digital stories and video descriptions that will whet users' appetites interest in food and other cultural issues.

Marty Otañez is Associate Professor in the Anthropology Department, University of Colorado, Denver. He examines digital storytelling as a research method and solidarity-building process to promote health equities among communities of color. Also, he studies diverse ways to bring digital media, visual sovereignty, and a community-wellness perspective to the social sciences and public health applications. Marty co-edited *Participatory Visual and Digital Research in Action*

(Walnut Creek, California: Left Coast Press, 2015) and operates the Coalition for Excellence in Digital Storytelling blog, www.dscoalition.org.

References

Bangser, Claire. 2013. We Come from the Water. 2:15 min. Story Center. Berkeley. https://vimeo.com/61549984. Accessed 15 January 2014.

Barbash, Ilisa, and Lucien Taylor. 1997. *Cross-Cultural Filmmaking: A Handbook for Making Documentary and Ethnographic Films and Videos*. Berkeley: University of California Press.

Benmayor, Rina. 2009. Theorizing through Digital Stories: The Art of "Writing Back" and "Writing for." In *From the Difference that Inquiry Makes: A Collaborative Case Study on Technology and Learning, from the Visible Knowledge Project*, ed. Randy Bass and Bret Eynon, 4–20. Washington, DC: Center for New Designs in Learning and Scholarship.

Biella, Peter. 2008. Elementary Forms of the Digital Media: Tools for Applied Action Research in Visual Anthropology. In *Viewpoints: Visual Anthropologists at Work*, ed. Mary Strong and Laena Wilder, 363–389. Austin: University of Texas Press.

Carlson, Dara, and Polly Olsen. 2011. Teaching Traditional Diet and Environmental Justice to Urban Youth Participating in the Native Youth Enrichment Program's Digital Storytelling Workshop. Practicum Poster presented at the School of Public Health, University of Washington. http://tinyurl.com/kxv2rqx Accessed 11 April 2014.

Castleden, Heather, Theresa Garvin, and Huu-ay-aht First Nation. 2008. Modifying Photovoice for Community-Based Participatory Indigenous Research. *Social Science and Medicine* 66: 1393–1405.

Chalfen, Richard, with Laura Sherman and Michael Rich. 2010. "VIA's Visual Voices: The Awareness of a Dedicated Audience for Voices in Patient Video Narratives." *Visual Studies* 25(3): 201–209.

Coover, Roderick. 2009. On *Verite* to Virtual: Conversations on the Frontier of Film and Anthropology. *Visual Studies* 24(3): 235–249.

Di Blas, Nicoletta, and Paola Paolini. 2013. Beyond the School's Boundaries: PoliCultura, a Large-Scale Digital Storytelling Initiative. *Educational Technology & Society* 16(1): 15–27.

Fletcher, Christopher, and Carolina Cambre. 2009. Digital Storytelling and Implicated Scholarship in the Classroom. *Journal of Canadian Studies* 43(1): 109–130.

Freidus, Natasha, with Seth Schromen-Wawrin, Samantha Benson, Nicole Sadow-Hasenberg, and Afsaneh Rahimian. 2013. Mapping Our Voices for Equality: Stories for Healthier Policies, Systems and Environments in King County, Washington. In *Experiencing Digital Storytelling*, ed. Maria Alcantud-Diaz and Carmen Gregori-Signes. 98–115. Valencia, Spain: JPM Ediciones.

Gubrium, Aline. 2009. Digital Storytelling as a Method for Engaged Scholarship in Anthropology. *Practicing Anthropology* 31(4): 5–9.

Gubrium, Aline, and K. C. Nat Turner. 2011. Digital Storytelling as an Emergent Method for Social Research and Practice. In *The Handbook of Emergent Technologies in Social Research*, ed. Sharlene Nagy Hesse-Biber. 469–491. New York: Oxford University Press.

Hill, Amy. 2010. Digital Storytelling for Gender Justice: Exploring the Challenges of Participation and the Limits of Polyvocality. In *Confronting Global Gender Justice: Women's Lives, Human Rights*, ed Debra Bergoffen, Paula Ruth Gilbert, Tamara Harvey, and Connie McNeely, 126–140. London: Routledge.

Johnson, J. Lauren. 2008. Therapeutic Filmmaking: An Exploratory Pilot Study. *The Arts in Psychotherapy* 35: 11–19.

Knoblauch, Hubert, with Rene Tuma and Bernt Schnettler. 2014. Video Analysis and Videography. In *The SAGE Handbooks of Qualitative Data Analysis*, ed Katie Metzler, 435–449, London: Sage.

Lambert, Joe. 2010. *Digital Storytelling Cookbook*. Berkeley, CA: Digital Diner Press. http://tinyurl.com/lvy8r3d. Accessed 23 November 2013.

Maier, Robert, and Mercedes Fisher. 2006. Strategies for Digital Storytelling Via Tabletop Video: Building Decision Making Skills in Middle School Students in Marginalized Communities. *Journal of Educational Technology Systems* 35(2): 175–192.

Meixner, Britta, with Katarzyna Matusik, Christoph Grill, and Harald Kosch. 2012. Towards an Easy to Use Authoring Tool for Interactive Non-Linear Video. *Multimedia Tools and Applications* 70(2): 1251–1276.

Native Youth Enrichment Program. 2012. Digital Story Telling. http://youth.iwri.org/digital-story-telling. Accessed 19 February 2014.

Otañez, Marty, and Andrés Guerrero. 2015. Digital Storytelling and the Viral Hepatitis Project. In *Participatory Visual and Digital Research in Action,* ed. Aline Gubrium, Krista Harper, and Marty Otañez, 57–70. Walnut Creek, CA: Left Coast Press.

Otañez, Marty, and Wanda Lakota. 2015. Digital Storytelling: Using Videos to Increase Social Wellness. In *Video Filmmaking as Psychotherapy: Research and Practice,* ed. Josh Cohen and J. Lauren Johnson, 119–130. New York: Routledge.

Pink, Sarah. 2011. Digital Visual Anthropology: Potentials and Challenges. In *Made to be Seen: Perspectives on the History of Visual Anthropology,* ed. Marcus Banks and Jay Ruby, 209–233. Chicago: University of Chicago Press.

Raheja, Michelle. 2011. *Reservation Reelism: Redfacing, Visual Sovereignty and Representations of Native Americans in Film*. Lincoln and London: University of Nebraska Press.

Roberts, Jane. 2011. Video Diaries: A Tool to Investigate Sustainability-Related Learning in Threshold Spaces. *Environmental Education Research* 17(5): 675–688.

Rony, Fatimah. 1996. *The Third Eye: Race, Cinema and Ethnographic Spectacle*. Durham, NC: Duke University Press.

Russell, Catherine. 1999. Autoethnography: Journeys of the Self. In *Experimental Ethnography*, ed. Catherine Russell, 275–314. Durham, NC: Duke University Press.

Salazar, Juan. 2005. Digitising Knowledge: Anthropology and New Practices of Digitextuality. *Media Information Australia* 116: 64–74.

Smilack, Jacqueline. 2013. "Steeped in History, Light on Technology: A Genre Analysis of Digital Storytelling Guidebooks." Master's thesis, University of Colorado, Denver.

Story Center. 2014. *Savory Story Series*. Berkeley, CA: Story Center. http://storycenter.org/savory-story-series. Accessed 19 May 2014.

Tufte, Thomas. 2000. *Living with the Rubbish Queen: Telenovelas, Culture and Modernity in Brazil*. London: John Libbey.

Wiles, Rose, with Andrew Clark and Jon Prosser. 2011. Visual Research Ethics at the Crossroads. In *The SAGE Handbook of Visual Research Methods,* ed. Eric Margolis and Luc Pauwels, 685–706. Los Angeles, CA: Sage.

Willox, Ashlee, with Sherilee Harper and Victoria Edge. 2012. Storytelling in a Digital Age: Digital Storytelling as an Emerging Narrative Method for Preserving and Promoting Indigenous Oral Wisdom. *Qualitative Research* 13(2): 127–147.

CHAPTER 12

Accessing and Using Secondary Quantitative Data from the Internet

James Wilson and Kristen Borre

Introduction

The nutritional anthropologist develops research problems within the context of existing food, nutrition, agricultural, ecological, socioeconomic, and health data. Whether planning a rapid assessment of nutritional deficiencies in a village, a study of urban food deserts in ethnic neighborhoods, or an exploration of immigrant children's dietary patterns and food preferences, a researcher will need to inform, place, and interpret the research in the context of the social, demographic, and economic structures and patterns of the community, region, political entity, state, or globalized market. By doing so the nutritional anthropologist helps meet the needs of globalized communities, allowing others to ascertain the appropriate application of his or her findings to their research, policy development, and/or interventions and programs. This chapter will guide the researcher in accessing and transforming publicly available online data to develop research ideas, support theses, and assess the significance of food and nutrition problems. These data are especially important to establish policies to improve the diet and health of populations and to serve as baselines for program planning, development, and evaluation. The applied nutritional anthropologist working for nonprofit agencies, NGOs, and government organizations is often required to be able to access and manipulate these online databases. The guidance offered here will encourage and steer the secondary database novice to discover existing, verified facts related to a population's or community's food and nutritional status.

The data described in this chapter have been vetted by means of peer review or evaluated by research institutes, universities, and consulting partners. Data collected and managed by institutions and research programs and made available to others are known as secondary data. These data are usually accompanied by supporting information detailing their provenance and caveats about their use. This information is often referred to as metadata. Generally, data are aggregated at scales larger than communities and villages, but they do have value for the anthropological researcher working at a local scale. Data collected at the county, district, state, provincial, or even national scale can provide context and reference by which to establish benchmarks and can also be used to make comparisons among more localized study scales such as villages, neighborhoods, social groups, or schools. In addition to introducing you to a major set of commonly used databases, our hope is to encourage you to explore them and become comfortable seeking the data you need to create meaningful information to guide and interpret your research.

The researcher must exercise care when interpreting research findings because data observations are collected at a variety of geographic scales. Studies that make use of data aggregated to spatial units of observation are referred to as ecological studies. Social, cultural, and environmental processes are not uniform across scales; therefore, statistical correlations among data variables collected and aggregated at one observational scale, such as the census tract, can be quite different for the same variables for data collected at another level, such as the county level. Making statistical comparisons at different scales of analyses without certain caveats or reasons for doing so is known as the ecological fallacy error. Within the discipline of geography, the ecological fallacy error is well illustrated in Openshaw's (1984) and Openshaw and Taylor's (1979) Modifiable Areal Unit Problem (MAUP). Nevertheless, this issue should not preclude the use of measures for making comparisons against benchmarks or gold standards. For example, comparing individual county proportions of obese adults or children to a national proportion is a measure of disparity and provides a starting point to develop and design research questions (Ewing et al. 2003; Zhang et al. 2013), establish need-based program interventions, and guide program funding policies.

Accessing Online Secondary Data for Food and Nutrition Research

Secondary data available from most food- and nutrition-related sources are generally available in two forms based on file size: files downloadable as a spreadsheet, and more complex, large files that may require database management software. Many downloadable files available online are in text format and can be recognized by the file extensions "txt" (text), "csv" (comma separated values), "tab" (tab separated), "asc" (American Standard Code for Information Interchange), and extensions used by the U.S. Census: UF (user file) or SF1 (summary file 1). Spreadsheet programs such as Microsoft's Excel (Microsoft 2016.), Open Office

(Apache 2014), or Google Sheets (Google n.d.) can be used to read smaller data files. Many online sources now provide data downloadable in MS Excel format, which can later be exported into different formats. Data sets with large numbers of observations and variables (fields) may need to be downloaded using FTP (File Transfer Protocol) services and may later require manipulation and management using commercially available software such as Microsoft Office's Access (Microsoft 2016), SPSS (2012) or SAS (2010). Today there is a degree of interoperability between proprietary data formats (e.g., Excel, SAS, and SPSS). Although less common today, interoperability can also be accomplished by employing database and dataset translators such as Open Database Connectivity (ODBC).

Downloading data via FTP allows the user to access very large amounts of data en masse. In some cases, very large datasets can be made available on media such as DVDs and CDs. In these cases, programs like SAS and SPSS may be needed to sift through these data and organize them; however, some online data resources, like the U.S. Census and CDC WONDER (n.d.), provide graphical interfaces for filtering and querying their databases. For the more sophisticated user, the U.S. Census also allows the construction of applications programming interfaces that can be deployed via the web or on mobile devices. Such capability allows the user to drill down to specific variables (data fields) at different levels of geography and time periods. Using these facilities may take some practice on the part of the user but, once mastered, can add flexibility to research.

Increasingly, online data are spatially referenced. This allows the researcher to link fields or variables to geographic observational units such as the county or census tract. Once linked (or joined), a geographic information system (GIS) can display, manage, and manipulate features on map layers for visual and statistical analyses. Geographic data collected in the field—for example, respondent, grocery, or convenience store addresses (Jilcott et al. 2010)—can be geocoded or address-matched using a GIS and then joined to other spatial units linked to attribute data such as the percentage of food stamp recipients in a population.

Today many handheld devices such as smartphones can also provide geographic coordinates and photographic images to enhance geographic visualization and analysis, and your research.

Major Secondary Sources of Food- and Nutrition-Related Data

Table 12.2 lists several major institutional websites that can be useful for anthropological research in food and nutrition. Researchers who explore these websites will find that reference links within the website quickly ramify into many related websites. On larger, more complex websites that provide secondary data, appendices are provided for reference in the discussions that follow. Subnational and U.S. state corporate databases are not listed here. Most U.S. states provide relatively easy and direct access to the data they collect. When available for public use, these data are usually aggregated to protect confidentiality. A researcher with a government or higher-education affiliation may obtain data for research purposes by making special requests and fulfilling specific requirements for handling confidential data files.

In addition to the databases listed here, many high-income nations with well-developed data capture systems provide similar food and nutrition databases for their nations and territories. When conducting work within a nation, be sure to check its government websites and ministries for access to publicly available records. You can also request non-public data or obtain these data through a local partner. The international organizations listed here will have some data for low-income nations that are unable to collect their own data or manage databases. Also, nongovernmental organizations and nonprofits working within a specific region or nation may be willing to share data they have collected; however, be sure to scrutinize what methods were used for data collection and how the data have been vetted and verified. Due to space limitations, this chapter focuses on global and U.S. national databases.

USDA/ERS

The United States Department of Agriculture (USDA) houses a large number of public domain data sets related to agricultural production and consumption, rural development issues, and trade in agricultural goods. These data are available as time series and are geographically referenced. The USDA's Economic Research Service (ERS) collects, develops, and maintains these data while also producing reports, atlases, and other gray literature. Appendix 12.1 lists several key links within the USDA/ERS website. These links access public domain data that can be used for research and literature produced by the agency. The appendix provides links to several ERS online atlases on the food environment, food access, farm programs, and rural and small-town America. Observational units for these atlases are usually at the county level and sometimes at the census tract level. Atlas data are downloadable as MS Excel workbooks. The ERS has contributed usefully to the research community by making available a set of geographic typologies and county classification systems that can be used to develop geographical context. These ancillary datasets include the Rural Urban Continuum Code or Beale Codes, the Office of Management and Budget's (OMB) Metropolitan/ Micropolitan Statistical Areas (MMSAs), and the Core Based Statistical Area (CBSA).

The USDA also provides access to other data outside the purview of the ERS. For example, the Geospatial Data Gateway (GDG) connects users to a range of environmental and natural resources data either in downloadable form or shipped on disk media. The National Agricultural Statistics Service (NASS), for example, produces reports based on surveys on agricultural topics including crops and plants, demographics, economics and prices, environment, and livestock and animals, along with access to charts and maps. Together, the USDA and ERS also produce online literature and reports based on their research and data collection, which may help shape research ideas and questions. *Amber Waves*, for example, is an online magazine series that covers a wide array of agricultural topics revolving around the economics of food, farming, natural resources, and the rural United States. In addition to food- and farming-related online atlases and access to a range of data, occasional reports and monographs are also published on issues like food accessibility and security based on ERS data (Ver Ploeg et al. 2012; Ver Ploeg et al. 2009; Dutko, Ver Ploeg, and Farrigan 2012).

FAO

The Food and Agricultural Organization of the United Nations (FAO) provides readily accessible public domain data on global agricultural production and consumption. Appendix 12.2 lists several links to these data. Several statistical data sites (STAT) are available. These STAT links offer access to time-series and cross-sectional data on a large number of agricultural topics for 245 countries. The FAOSTAT site connects users to data and statistics on not only production, but also trade, food supply, food balance sheets, food security, prices, resources emissions, forestry, and fisheries. The FAO also provides access to two other STAT sites: COUNTRYSTAT and AQUASTAT. COUNTRYSTAT is a web-based system for food and agricultural statistics at both the national and subnational levels. This site provides quality assurance on integrated data collected from several sources. AQUASTAT is a global information system on water resources, water uses, and agricultural water management with data at different geographical scales.

Further, the FAO website allows the researcher to connect to geographically oriented sites that include spatially referenced data. This site includes a global spatial database of agricultural land use statistics and serves as an umbrella site for GeoNetwork, Climpag (Climate Impact on Agriculture), and GTOS (Global Terrestrial Observing System). These sites integrate spatially referenced agricultural data with weather and climate, collect observations, and permit the analysis of terrestrial ecosystems for the purpose of supporting multidisciplinary approaches to sustainable development programs.

In addition to databases, the FAO works with academic, governmental, and nongovernmental partners to develop a series of reports that summarize and add value to these data. These include a series of "State of" reports encompassing topics like nutrition, agriculture, food security, fisheries and aquaculture, forests, and markets (FAO 2013; FAO 2012a; FAO 2012b; FAO 2012c; FAO 2009). Literature on resources such as land and water that are key to food production and security is also addressed by the FAO in conjunction with Earthscan and made available online (FAO and Earthscan 2011). The FAO literature provides the beginning researcher with an appreciable amount of data and contextual information that can be used for studies in many parts of the world.

WHO

The World Health Organization (WHO) is a comprehensive website of secondary data, policy implementations, guidelines, standards, indicators, and gray literature with links to supporting peer-reviewed articles on nutrition, nutritionally related diseases, and global issues such as malnourishment and obesity. Appendix 12.3 lists those sites that provide data and supporting information on nutrition and nutritionally related diseases. This appendix includes data repositories that support international research, policy, and program implementation in a variety of areas such as the Sustainable Development Goals (SDGs), child nutrition, obesity, physical activity, childhood growth, breastfeeding, food security, evaluating risk factors, epidemics, health systems, injury, and environmental health.

The WHO, in addition to its partnerships with the FAO, World Bank, and the United Nation's Children Fund (UNICEF), produces a range of online publications. Examples of publications with a childhood focus include malnutrition estimates (UNICEF, WHO, and World Bank 2012) and work regarding the marketing of food and beverages to children (WHO 2012a; Hawkes 2004a), as well as childhood obesity (WHO 2012b: 54, 2012c: 86, 2009: 40). More general examples are found in areas such as regulation, food labeling and nutrition (Hawkes 2004b: 88), diet and physical activity (WHO 2008, 2003), and chronic disease prevention (WHO and FAO 2002). The data and publications produced by the WHO can assist the researcher in establishing a comparative framework and benchmarks for localized studies.

The growing availability and popularity of web-based mapping and the ubiquity of GIS now allow the researcher to make interesting comparisons among different regions of the world. Household data on health, diet, nutrition, and socioeconomic status can be recorded and tied to coordinates collected by handheld devices. These study data can then be joined to existing geographic layers, which can be comprised of administrative units, land use areas, or community health catchment areas and so on; however, the beginning researcher should keep in mind that socioeconomic data and vital and civil registration data, which are crucial for shaping development goals and measuring interventions, frequently lack consistent temporal and spatial coverage (Lopez and Thomason 2013). What is more, governmentally sponsored data collection efforts in many parts of the world are often viewed with suspicion and resistance for a variety of political reasons (Youde 2010). Nevertheless, the availability and coverage of digital international boundary data are increasing for different administrative levels. Such data can now be obtained through the Global Administrative Areas (GADM) website (see Table 12.1).

CDC/NCHS

The Centers for Disease Control (CDC) is the United States' leading public health agency. It is comprised of many centers that provide data and reports that directly and indirectly concern nutrition and nutrition-related diseases (see Appendix 12.4). County-level estimates for diabetes and obesity incidence and prevalence are available as Excel spreadsheets, with web-based mapping of these data as an automatic feature. Secondary data, charts, and maps from the Behavioral Risk Factor Surveillance System (BRFSS) are also available directly from the CDC's website. The BRFSS is a national program that collects self-reported samples on health behaviors, demographics, socioeconomic status, and outcomes for adults 18 years and older. These data and derived publications allow the researcher to study patterns and trends in overweight and obesity.

The CDC also offers downloadable Excel workbooks for calculating Body Mass Indices (BMIs) for adults, teens, and children either individually or in groups. In a classroom setting, for example, the researcher can enter age, gender, height, and weight of subjects into the Excel worksheet, and BMI and percentile for each child are automatically calculated. Excel also generates graphs showing the distributions of BMI percentiles. Excel's many database and statistical functions allow the researcher to match height and weight parameters in growth-chart tables to measurements taken in the field. Because BMI and percentiles can also be calculated in Excel, the researcher can make statistical comparisons and analyze patterns and trends over time. These data can then be summarized neatly within Excel using tables, graphs, and charts.

The National Center for Health Statistics (NCHS), as part of the CDC, develops, maintains, and disseminates the nation's health data. The NCHS houses the National Health and Nutrition Examination Survey (NHANES), a large, ongoing survey conducted in the United States that assesses the health and nutritional status of adults and children. These surveys contain questions on diabetes, diet behavior and nutrition, food security, physical activity, and weight history, among many other health related-questions. These data can be downloaded as SAS (2010) export files (xpt) for statistical analysis. Instructions, including tutorials, codebooks, and sample SAS programs, are also available from the NHANES website.

The NCHS also produces several report series on patterns and trends of morbidity, mortality (leading causes of death), births, and life expectancy. These series include data briefs produced by the NCHS, National Vital Statistics Reports, and health surveys collected by the National Health Interview Survey (NHIS) in conjunction with the U.S. Census Bureau. Data based on the Compressed Mortality

File (CMF) are available for download in Excel (csv) format through the CDC's Wide-ranging Online Data for Epidemiologic Research (CDC WONDER n.d.) website. This website provides step-by-step guidance in selecting numbers and rates by cause of death using the International Classification of Diseases (ICD) system codes. Counts and rates for individual U.S. counties and/or county typologies are possible and can be grouped by age, gender, race and ethnicity, and years. Multiple causes of death are available for some years, and causes of death can be grouped together using ICD codes. For example, diseases associated with metabolic syndrome can be combined or compared with diseases of the circulatory system, kidney diseases, and infectious diseases such as *Clostridium difficile*; however, some limitations are placed on these public domain data. If there are too few cases in a geographic area for a given year, then data suppression or a large confidence interval indicating low reliability can result. To obtain the CMF data that are the foundation of the CDC WONDER system, a written request can be made to the NCHS to obtain more detailed data on digital media.

Science-based programs rely heavily on high-quality comprehensive data with historical depth in order to make valid comparisons. The NCHS produces reliable data that can be used to set benchmarks and assess progress toward targets with the aim of reducing the nation's disease burden through programmatic interventions and policies. Several of the Healthy People objectives are concerned with nutrition-related diseases and issues. The Division of Nutrition, Physical Activity, and Obesity (DNPAO) is another health promotion website that provides information on public health efforts to prevent and control obesity and chronic diseases through good nutrition and physical activity.

Because good public health is a function of food security and good nutrition, the CDC publishes a number of reports and monographs aimed at improving the nutritional status of the U.S. population. These documents are produced in conjunction with the Institute of Medicine (IOM) and the USDA's ERS. Examples include a census tract–level atlas of the modified retail food environment index (CDC 2013); reports on children's food environment, health, and obesity (CDC 2011; IOM 2005); and dietary guidelines, nutrient requirements, and state indicators on fruits and vegetables (USDA and DHHS 2010; IOM 2006; CDC 2009). The data and literature made available by the CDC and the NCHS can provide supporting information to contextualize research projects and benchmarks for comparisons and reviewing trends.

U.S. Census Bureau

The United States Census has been in operation for more than 220 years. Originally created for the purpose of counting the nation's population for political representation every ten years, the U.S. Census also samples socioeconomic data and estimates populations on an intercensal basis (see Appendix 12.5). American FactFinder (AFF) provides access to census data and other information in a variety of formats. Every five years the Census Bureau conducts an economic census that profiles national and local economies. In addition to these data, the American Community Survey (ACS) provides 1-year, 3-year, and 5-year rolling average estimates of socioeconomic characteristics at sub-county geographies. U.S. Census data can be used as benchmarks for making comparisons or assist in establishing sampling frameworks. Another data source that can be used in research is restricted-use microdata, which include longitudinal employer-household dynamics data as well as detailed demographic and economic data. These data are accessible via several Census Bureau Research Data Centers. Access requires prior project approval.

Geography is the foundation of the U.S. Census. Census data are geographically referenced into a hierarchy of spatial units that are uniquely identified. Online mapping resources are readily available on the Census website, and digital boundary files (TIGER) for every level of census geography can be downloaded for use with a GIS.

ICPSR and IHME

The Inter-university Consortium for Political and Social Research (ICPSR) is a compendium of data sources developed over time by the social science research community. The consortium provides training in access and analytical methods to meet the needs of growing research efforts in the social sciences. It also provides a database archive that can be accessed and analyzed through such programs as SAS and SPSS These databases include data on nutrition and health surveys such as NHANES, food security, and childhood obesity at different scales of analysis and locations. This resource can give the beginning researcher examples for developing research questions and self-guided training in food and nutritional topics covered in the social sciences. These data are often the foundation for national food, nutrition, and public health policies and programs.

The Institute of Health Metrics and Evaluation (IHME) is an online resource focused on the Global Burden of Disease (GBD). Comprised of international partnerships among academic institutions and governmental and nongovernmental agencies, the IHME pursues research in the areas of health measurement, performance tracking, maximization of impacts, and innovations in measurement systems. The website features a number of innovative graphic designs for visualizing a variety of health and health-related data. Though the researcher does not have the same level of access to data as the previously discussed online resources permit, the website does provide a breadth of global research being undertaken in a variety of health topic areas. It also presents references and links to studies pertaining to obesity, malnutrition, and diabetes that can be included in literature reviews and research discussions.

Other Data Sources, Including Gray Literature

A wide range of data and information sources on food and nutrition topics are also made available through organizations such as the Pew Charitable Trust (PCT), Food and Nutrition Technical Assistance (FANTA), the Consortium of International Agricultural Research Centers (formerly CGIAR, Consultative Group for International Agricultural Research), and many other governmental and nongovernmental agencies, trusts, foundations, corporations, and nonprofits (see Table 12.1). Each of these organizations produces or has links to published reports created from secondary databases. Use of these sources can save the researcher time by eliminating the duplication of previous efforts and helping in the development of hypotheses. When using these reports, make sure that the data and reports are from trusted sources and that you understand their limitations. When possible, locate several reports that provide the same kind of information to create more confidence in the validity of the information you will use. Reports are widely available on the websites of these and other organizations, and their secondary sources of information should be named. As described above, many of these organizations collect their own data and produce their own reports, documents, and graphics.

Conclusion

As is evident from the previous overview, vast amounts of secondary data and information are available to the researcher who seeks a study context and help in shaping research questions for a project in nutritional anthropology, food insecurity, chronic disease, food preferences, or obesity/overweight issues, among many others related to food and diet. The growth and availability of secondary data available online reflects a democratizing trend in research. In the past, a certain level of programming skills and familiarity with operating systems was required to access these data, including such arcane skills as JCL (job control language), which included instructions on mounting tapes and disks remotely. The beginning researcher no longer faces such impediments to digital data. Another trend is the growth of public participation in research, which can include advocacy work on local issues with nonprofits and NGOs.

The primary purpose of this chapter is to provide the beginning researcher with entrée to valid, easily accessible data found on the Internet in the second decade of the twenty-first century. Undoubtedly, the data and the informational content derived from them will expand, accompanied by changing links and URLs. In their careers, the authors of this chapter have worked with digital data originally collected in the field as well as with secondary digital data kept on magnetic tapes since the 1980s, before they became downloadable and analyze-able on laptops in homes or available on handheld devices anywhere on the globe. Nevertheless, the beginning researcher needs a place to start when developing research questions and valid interpretations of study results. These are timeless skills, regardless of technological change or the manner in which data are warehoused and delivered.

James L. Wilson received his PhD from the University of North Carolina, Chapel Hill in 1991. He is currently Associate Professor of Geography at Northern Illinois University and Adjunct Associate Professor of Public Health at the Brody School of Medicine at East Carolina University. He teaches courses on GIS applications in public and environmental health, medical geography, maps and mapping, and environment and society. His research interests include using GIS to analyze and visualize environmental problems that have bearing on health and well-being and historical spatial epidemiology. While at East Carolina University, he worked as a research associate at the Center for Health Systems Research and Development, where he developed atlases of regional and national health disparities and conducted research on adult and childhood overweight and obesity.

Kristen Borre received her PhD in anthropology in 1990 and MPH in nutrition from the University of North Carolina, Chapel Hill. She is currently Visiting Professor of Anthropology at Northern Illinois University, where she teaches biological and cultural anthropology, nutritional anthropology, research methods, food and environment, and medical anthropology. At East Carolina University she worked as a Senior Research Scientist at the Brody School of Medicine, and as the Director of the North Carolina Agromedicine Institute, the Southeast Center for Agricultural Safety and Health, and the Growing Up FIT! Program with the Division of Research and Graduate Studies. Her research focused on childhood overweight, obesity and the health of migrant farm workers, and rural community health partnerships.

Table 12.1. Nutrition, food, and agricultural institutional websites that provide secondary data and publications that can be used in research (Descriptions, mission, mandate, and purpose statements taken from websites)

Online Data Sources	Description, Mission, Mandate, or Purpose[1]	URL
US Department of Agriculture (USDA)	Mission: provide leadership on food, agriculture, natural resources, rural development, nutrition, and related issues based on sound public policy, the best available science, and efficient management.	http://usda.gov/wps/portal/usda/usdahome
Food and Agricultural Organization of the United Nations (FAO)	Mandate: to raise levels of nutrition, improve agricultural productivity, better the lives of rural populations and contribute to the growth of the world economy	http://www.fao.org/
The World Health Organization (WHO)	The directing and coordinating authority for health within the United Nations system. It is responsible for providing leadership on global health matters, shaping the health research agenda, setting norms and standards, articulating evidence-based policy options, providing technical support to countries and monitoring and assessing health trends	http://www.who.int/
Global Administrative Areas (GADM)	GADM is a spatial database of the location of the world's administrative areas (or administrative boundaries) for use in GIS and similar software.	http://www.gadm.org/
Centers for Disease Control (CDC)	The Centers for Disease Control and Prevention is the nation's premier public health agency— working to ensure healthy people in a healthy world.	http://www.cdc.gov/
US Census Bureau	Mission: To serve as the leading source of quality data about the nation's people and economy	http://www.census.gov/
Inter-university Consortium for Political and Social Research. (ICPSR)	Provides leadership and training in data access, curation, and methods of analysis for a diverse and expanding social science research community.	http://www.icpsr.umich.edu/icpsrweb/landing.jsp

Institute of Health Metrics and Evaluation (IHME)	IHME is an independent research center identifying the best strategies to build a healthier world.	http://www.healthmetrics andevaluation.org/
Pew Charitable Trusts (PCT)	PCT addresses a variety of threats from the nation's food supply to the healthfulness of what kids eat at school. PCT projects advance science-based policies based on solid research to limit the impact of foodborne illnesses, improve the nutritional quality and safety of food sold and served in U.S. schools, curb the overuse of antibiotics on industrial farms, and assess the risks associated with chemicals added to food and its packaging	http://www.pewtrusts.org/ our_work_category.aspx?id =198
Food and Nutrition Technical Assistance (FANTA)	FANTA works to improve and strengthen nutrition and food security policies, strategies, programs and systems through technical support to the United States Agency for International Development (USAID) and its partners, including host country governments, international organizations, and nongovernmental organization implementing partners	http://www.fantaproject.org/
Consultative Group on International Agricultural Research (CGIAR)	CGIAR research is dedicated to reducing rural poverty, increasing food security, improving human health and nutrition, and ensuring more sustainable management of natural resources. It is carried out by 15 Centers, in close collaboration with hundreds of partner organizations, including national and regional research institutes, civil society organizations, academia, and the private sector.	http://www.cgiar.org/

Appendix: Secondary Data Sources Relevant to Anthropological Food and Nutrition Research

Appendix 12.1. USDA/ERS Sites

Description	URL
ERS Data Portal	http://www.ers.usda.gov/data-products/
ERS Food Environment Atlas	http://www.ers.usda.gov/data-products/food-environment-atlas/go-to-the-atlas/
ERS Food Access Research Atlas	http://www.ers.usda.gov/data-products/food-access-research-atlas/
ERS Farm Program Atlas (The database is no longer updated, but there are data available to download in Excel format)	http://www.ers.usda.gov/data-products/farm-program-atlas/
ERS Atlas of Rural and Small Town America focusing on demographics, jobs, agriculture, and county classifications	http://www.ers.usda.gov/data-products/atlas-of-rural-and-small-town-america/about-the-atlas.aspx
Rural Classifications: area classification codes, such as Frontier and Remote Area Codes, Rural-Urban Continuum Codes, Urban-Influence Codes, Rural-Urban Commuting Areas, and the ERS typology code, which classifies rural counties by their economic and policy types.	http://www.ers.usda.gov/topics/rural-economy-population/rural-classifications/
USDA's Geospatial Data Gateway (GDG) is a one-stop source for environmental and natural resources data, at any time, from anywhere, to anyone. The Gateway allows you to choose your area of interest, browse and select data from the catalogue, customize the format, and have it downloaded or shipped on CD or DVD.	https://gdg.sc.egov.usda.gov
The USDA's National Agricultural Statistics Service (NASS) conducts hundreds of surveys every year and prepares reports covering virtually every aspect of U.S. agriculture. Production and supplies of food and fiber, prices paid and received by farmers, farm labor and wages, farm finances, chemical use, and changes in the demographics of U.S. producers are only a few examples.	http://www.nass.usda.gov/
USDA Center for Nutrition Policy and Promotion: works to improve the health and well-being of Americans by developing and promoting dietary guidance that links scientific research to the nutrition needs of consumers. This site also includes a link to the *Healthy Eating Index*.	http://www.cnpp.usda.gov/
Amber Waves is an online publication on a variety of ERS topics (derived from ERS/USDA statistics, reports, and gray literature publications).	http://www.ers.usda.gov/amber-waves/

Appendix 12.2. FAO Sites

Description	URL
FAOSTAT: Statistics, large time-series and cross-sectional data relating to hunger, food, and agriculture.	http://faostat3.fao.org/home/E
FAOSTAT Beta: Statistics on production, trade, food supply, food balance sheets, food security, prices, resources emissions, forestry, and fisheries.	http://faostat.fao.org/beta/en/#data
COUNTRYSTAT: web-based information technology system for food and agriculture statistics at the national and subnational levels. In practice, it acts as a one-stop center that centralizes and integrates data coming from various sources and allows harmonization according to international standards while ensuring data quality and reliability.	http://www.fao.org/economic/ess/ess-capacity/countrystathome/en/
AQUASTAT: A global information system on water and agriculture, developed by the Land and Water Division. The main mandate of the program is to collect, analyze, and disseminate information on water resources, water uses, and agricultural water management with an emphasis on countries in Africa, Asia, Latin America, and the Caribbean. This allows interested users to find comprehensive and regularly updated information at global, regional, and national levels.	http://www.fao.org/nr/water/aquastat/main/index.stm
Global Spatial Database of Agricultural Land-Use Statistics (with data downloads).	http://kids.fao.org/agromaps/
GeoNetwork's Purpose: To improve access to and integrated use of spatial data and information, support decision making, promote multidisciplinary approaches to sustainable development, and enhance understanding of the benefits of geographic information.	http://www.fao.org/geonetwork/srv/en/main.home
Climpag (Climate Impact on Agriculture) is aimed at bringing together the various aspects and interactions between *weather, climate,* and *agriculture* in the general context of food security.	http://geonetwork3.fao.org/climpag/agroclimdb_en.php
Global Terrestrial Observing System (GTOS) is a program for observations, modeling, and analysis of terrestrial ecosystems to support sustainable development.	http://www.fao.org/gtos/
David Lubin Memorial Library: FAO information resources for agriculture, food and nutrition, rural development, plant production and protection, animal production and health, agricultural machinery, agro-industries, agro-forestry, forestry, fisheries, sustainable development, statistics, agricultural economics, and other related subjects.	http://www.fao.org/library/library-home/en/

Appendix 12.3. WHO Sites

Description	URL
The Global Health Observatory (GHO) data repository provides access to over 50 datasets on priority health topics including mortality and burden of diseases, the Sustainable Development Goal themes noncommunicable diseases and risk factors, epidemic-prone diseases, health systems, environmental health, violence and injuries, and equity, among others.	http://apps.who.int/gho/data/view.main
Portal to WHO nutrition-related databases, publications, and guidelines, as well as journal articles, including access to the electronic Library for Nutrition Actions (eLENA). Access to some of the websites described in this table can be found on this page.	http://www.who.int/nutrition/en/
The Global Database on the Implementation of Nutrition Action (GINA) is an interactive platform for sharing standardized information on nutrition policies and action. Its functions include mapping nutrition policies and action, linking policies and action to nutrition status indicators, monitoring implementation of key nutrition actions, identifying overlaps and gaps, and sharing experience on implementation practices.	https://extranet.who.int/nutrition/gina/
The Nutrition, Obesity, and Physical Activity (NOPA) database compiles information for the WHO European Member States to monitor progress on nutrition, diet, physical activity, and obesity. The country information contains national and subnational surveillance data, policy documents, action to implement policy, and examples of good practice in programs and interventions.	http://data.euro.who.int/nopa/Default.aspx
The Nutrition Landscape Information System (NLIS) is a web-based tool that provides nutrition and nutrition-related health and development data in the form of automated country profiles and user-defined downloadable data. Data presented in the country profiles are structured by the UNICEF conceptual framework for causes of malnutrition and intend to give an overview snapshot of a country's nutrition, health, and development at the national level.	http://www.who.int/nutrition/nlis/en/
The Mapping Actions for Food Security and Nutrition (MAFSAN) is a web platform to help stakeholders at country, regional, and global levels share information about their investments in food and nutrition security.	http://www.fsincop.net/community/relevant-initiatives/detail/en/c/178620/

The Vitamin and Mineral Nutrition Information System (VMNIS) assesses the micronutrient status of populations, monitors and evaluates the impact of strategies for the prevention and control of micronutrient malnutrition, and tracks related trends over time.

http://www.who.int/vmnis/en/

The Global Database on Body Mass Index provides both national and subnational adult underweight, overweight, and obesity prevalence rates by country, year of survey, and gender. The information is presented interactively as maps, tables, graphs, and downloadable documents.

http://apps.who.int/bmi/index.jsp

The Global Database on Child Growth and Malnutrition is a standardized compilation of child growth and malnutrition data from nutritional surveys conducted around the world since 1960.

http://www.who.int/nutgrowthdb/en/

The WHO Global Data Bank on Infant and Young Child Feeding pools information mainly from national and regional surveys, and studies that deal with the prevalence and duration of breastfeeding and complementary feeding. The aim is to achieve worldwide coverage in order to permit comparison between countries and regions and within countries, assessment of breastfeeding and complementary feeding trends and practices as a basis for future action, monitoring and analysis of trends over time, evaluation of the impact of infant and young child feeding promotion programs, and ready access to current data for use by policy and decision makers and other interested parties.

http://www.who.int/nutrition/databases/infantfeeding/en/index.html

Appendix 12.4.   CDC/NCHS Sites

Description	URL
Mission: the National Center for Health Statistics (NCHS) is to provide statistical information that will guide actions and policies to improve the health of the American people. As the nation's principal health statistics agency, NCHS leads the way with accurate, relevant, and timely data, as well as access to data and reports.	http://www.cdc.gov/nchs/
Interactive atlases allow the user to view data and trends for diagnosed diabetes (new and existing cases), obesity, and leisure-time physical inactivity at national, state, and county levels.	http://www.cdc.gov/diabetes/atlas/
The Behavioral Risk Factor Surveillance System (BRFSS) is the world's largest, ongoing telephone health survey system, tracking health conditions and risk behaviors in the United States yearly since 1984. Currently, data are collected monthly in all 50 states, the District of Columbia, Puerto Rico, the U.S. Virgin Islands, and Guam.	http://www.cdc.gov/brfss/
Healthy Weight provides tools for calculating BMIs for adults, children and teens. An Excel spreadsheet is also available for calculating BMIs in group settings.	https://www.cdc.gov/healthyweight/assessing/bmi/
This site is a portal to a range of vital statistics and survey data, including NHANES, National Health Care Surveys, NVSS, NHIS, Compressed Mortality File, and more.	http://www.cdc.gov/nchs/data_access/ftp_data.htm
The Wide-ranging Online Data for Epidemiologic Research (WONDER) is a menu-driven system that makes the information resources of the CDC available to public health professionals and the public at large. It provides access to a wide array of public health information including access to statistical research data published by CDC, as well as reference materials, reports, maps, and guidelines on health-related topics.	http://wonder.cdc.gov/
Healthy People provides science-based, national goals and objectives with 10-year targets designed to guide national health promotion and disease prevention efforts to improve the health of all people in the United States. For three decades, Healthy People has established benchmarks and monitored progress over time.	http://www.cdc.gov/nchs/healthy_people.htm
The Division of Nutrition, Physical Activity, and Obesity engages in strategic public health efforts to prevent and control obesity, chronic disease, and other health conditions through regular physical activity and good nutrition.	https://www.cdc.gov/nccdphp/dnpao/

Appendix 12.5. U.S. Census Bureau

Description	URL
This page lists the different types of publicly available 2010 Census data products.	http://www.census.gov/2010census/data/
American FactFinder provides access to data about the United States, Puerto Rico, and the Island Areas. The data in American FactFinder come from several censuses and surveys.	http://factfinder2.census.gov/faces/nav/jsf/pages/index.xhtml
The economic census profiles U.S. national and local economies every 5 years.	http://www.census.gov/econ/census/
The American Community Survey (ACS) is an ongoing survey that provides data annually, giving communities the current information they need to plan investments and services. Information from the survey generates data that help determine how more than $400 billion in federal and state funds are distributed each year. Variables include age, race, family and relationships, income and benefits, health insurance, and education, among others.	http://www.census.gov/acs/www/about_the_survey/american_community_survey/
Portal providing links to working papers, conferences, data, and seminars.	http://www.census.gov/research/
Access to health insurance data collected by the Census Bureau: the Current Population Survey's Annual Social and Economic Supplement (CPS ASEC), the American Community Survey (ACS), and the Survey of Income and Program Participation (SIPP). Data are available at several levels of geography over time.	http://www.census.gov/topics/health/health-insurance.html
Section 3 of the Statistical Abstract of the United States contains data on health and nutrition. (The Statistical Abstract Program has been terminated as of 2012)	http://www.census.gov/library/publications/time-series/statistical_abstracts.html
Restricted-Use Data: Some vital questions cannot be answered with publicly available data. The Census Bureau partners with various universities, research institutions, and agencies to form a nationwide network of secure Federal and Census Bureau Research Data Centers.	https://www.census.gov/ces/rdcresearch/
Topologically Integrated Geographic Encoding and Referencing (TIGER): TIGER/LINE Shapefiles, geodatabases pre-joined with selected demographic data, cartographic boundary files, kml prototype files, and TIGERweb.	https://www.census.gov/geo/maps-data/data/tiger.html

References

Apache. 2014. Openoffice 4.1.1. Los Angeles: Apache Software Foundation.

CDC (Centers for Disease Control). 2009. *State Indicator Report on Fruits and Vegetables, 2009.* Atlanta: Centers for Disease Control. http://www.cdc.gov/nutrition/downloads/stateindicatorreport2009.pdf. Accessed 8 November 2016.

———. 2011. *Children's Food Environment State Indicator Report, 2011.* Atlanta: Centers for Disease Control. https://www.cdc.gov/obesity/downloads/childrensfoodenvironment.pdf. Accessed 8 November 2016.

———. 2013. *Census Tract Level State Maps of the Modified Retail Food Environment Index (mRFEI).* Atlanta: Centers for Disease Control. http://ftp.cdc.gov/pub/Publications/dnpao/.census-tract-level-state-maps-mrfei_TAG508.pdf. Accessed 8 November 2016.

CDC WONDER. n.d. *Wide-ranging Online Data for Epidemiologic Research.* Atlanta: Centers for Disease Control. http://wonder.cdc.gov. Accessed 2 November 2016.

Dutko, Paula, Michele Ver Ploeg, and Tracey Farrigan. 2012. *Characteristics and Influential Factors of Food Deserts.* Washington, DC: U.S. Department of Agriculture, Economic Research Service. http://www.ers.usda.gov/media/883903/err140.pdf. Accessed 8 November 2016.

Ewing, Reid, Tom Schmid, Richard Killingsworth, Amy Zlot, and Stephen Raudenbush. 2003. Relationship between Urban Sprawl and Physical Activity, Obesity, and Morbidity. *American Journal of Health Promotion* 18(1): 47–57.

FAO (Food and Agriculture Organization of the United Nations). 2009. *The State of Agricultural Commodity Markets: High Food Prices, Experiences and Lessons Learned.* Rome: Food and Agriculture Organization. http://www.fao.org/docrep/012/i0854e/i0854e00.htm. Accessed 8 November 2016.

FAO. 2013. The State of Food and Agriculture: Food Systems for Better Nutrition. Rome: Food and Agriculture Organization. http://www.fao.org/docrep/018/i3300e/i3300e.pdf accessed 8 November 2016.

———. 2012a. *The State of Food and Agriculture: Investing in Agriculture for a Better Future.* Rome: Food and Agriculture Organization. http://www.fao.org/docrep/017/i3028e/i3028e.pdf. Accessed 8 November 2016.

———. 2012b. *State of World Fisheries and Aquaculture.* Rome: Food and Agriculture Organization. http://www.fao.org/docrep/016/i2727e/i2727e.pdf. Accessed 8 November 2016.

———. 2012c. *State of the World's Forests.* Rome: Food and Agriculture Organization. http://www.fao.org/docrep/016/i3010e/i3010e.pdf. Accessed 8 November 2016.

———. 2013. *The State of Food and Agriculture: Food Systems for Better Nutrition.* Rome: Food and Agriculture Organization. http://www.fao.org/docrep/018/i3300e/i3300e.pdf. Accessed 8 November 2016.

FAO and Earthscan. 2011. *The State of the World's Land and Water Resources for Food and Agriculture: Managing Systems at Risk.* Rome: Food and Agriculture Organization; London: Earthscan. http://www.fao.org/docrep/015/i1688e/i1688e00.pdf. Accessed 8 November 2016.

Google. n.d. Google Sheets. Mountain View, CA: Google Inc.

Hawkes, C. 2004a. *Marketing Food to Children: The Global Regulatory Environment.* World Health Organization. http://whqlibdoc.who.int/publications/2004/9241591579.pdf. Accessed 8 November 2016.

———. 2004b. *Nutrition Labels and Health Claims: The Global Regulatory Environment.* World Health Organization. http://whqlibdoc.who.int/publications/2004/9241591714 .pdf. Accessed 8 November 2016.

IOM (Institute of Medicine). 2005. *Preventing Childhood Obesity: Health in the Balance.* Washington, DC: The National Academies Press.

———. 2006. *Dietary Reference Intakes: The Essential Guide to Nutrient Requirements.* Washington, DC: The National Academies Press.

Jilcott, S. B., H. Liu, J. B. Moore, J. W. Bethel, J. Wilson, and A. S. Ammerman. 2010. Commute Times, Food Retail Gaps, and Body Mass Index in North Carolina Counties. *Preventing Chronic Disease* 7(5): A107. http://www.cdc.gov/pcd/issues/2010/sep/09_0208 .htm. Accessed 8 November 2016.

Lopez, Alan, and Jane Thomason. 2013. Civil Registration and Vital Statistics: Everybody's Business but Nobody's Business. *The Lancet* 381(9874): 1275–1276.

Microsoft. 2016. Microsoft Office. Redmond, WA: Microsoft. https://products.office.com/ en-us/home. Accessed 8 November 2016.

Openshaw, S. 1984. Ecological Fallacies and the Analysis of Areal Census Data. *Environment and Planning A* 16(1): 17–31.

Openshaw, S., and P. J. Taylor. 1979. A Million Or so Correlation Coefficients: Three Experiments on the Modifiable Areal Unit Problem. In *Statistical Applications in the Spatial Sciences,* ed. N. Wrigley. London: Pion Ltd.

SAS. 2010. SAS 9.3. Cary, NC: SAS Institute.

SPSS. 2012. *SPSS Statistics.* Chicago: SPSS.

UNICEF (United Nations Children's Fund), WHO (World Health Organization), and The World Bank. 2012. *UNICEF-WHO-World Bank Joint Child Malnutrition Estimates.* New York: UNICEF; Geneva: WHO; Washington, DC: The World Bank. http://www.who .int/nutgrowthdb/jme_unicef_who_wb.pdf. Accessed 8 November 2016.

USDA (U.S. Department of Agriculture) and DHHS (U.S. Department of Health and Human Services). 2010. *Dietary Guidelines for Americans, 2010.* 7th Edition, Washington, DC: U.S. Government Printing Office, December 2010.

Ver Ploeg, Michele, Vince Breneman, Paula Dutko, Ryan Williams, Samantha Snyder, Chris Dicken, and Phil Kaufman. 2012. *Access to Affordable and Nutritious Food: Updated Estimates of Distance to Supermarkets Using 2010 Data, ERR-143.* U.S. Department of Agriculture, Economic Research Service. http://www.ers.usda.gov/media/956784/err143.pdf. Accessed 6 September 2014.

Ver Ploeg, Michele, Vince Breneman, Tracey Farrigan, Karen Hamrick, David Hopkins, Phillip Kaufman, Biing-Hwan Lin, Mark Nord, Travis A. Smith, Ryan Williams, Kelly Kinnison, Carol Olander, Anita Singh, and Elizabeth Tuckermanty. 2009. *Access to Affordable and Nutritious Food: Measuring and Understanding Food Deserts and Their Consequences: Report to Congress.* U.S. Department of Agriculture, Economic Research Service, Food and Nutrition Service, and the Cooperative State Research, Education and Extension Service. http://www .ers.usda.gov/publications/pub-details/?pubid=42729. Accessed 8 November 2016.

WHO. 2003. *Process for a Global Strategy on Diet, Physical Activity and Health.* Geneva: World Health Organization. http://apps.who.int/iris/bitstream/10665/67433/1/WHO_NMH_ EXR.02.2_Rev.1.pdf?. Accessed 8 November 2016.

———. 2008. *Preventing Noncommunicable Diseases in the Workplace through Diet and Physical Activity: WHO/World Economic Forum Report of a Joint Event.* Geneva: World Health Organization. http://apps.who.int/iris/bitstream/10665/43825/1/9789241596329_eng.pdf. Accessed 8 November 2016.

———. 2009. *Population-Based Prevention Strategies for Childhood Obesity: Report of a WHO Forum and Technical Meeting.* Geneva: World Health Organization. 8 November 2016.

———. 2012a. A Framework for Implementing the Set of Recommendations on the Marketing of Foods and Non-Alcoholic Beverages to Children. Geneva: World Health Organization. http://apps.who.int/iris/bitstream/10665/80148/1/9789241503242_eng.pdf. Accessed 8 November 2016.

———. 2012b. *Population-Based Approaches to Childhood Obesity Prevention.* Geneva: World Health Organization. http://www.who.int/dietphysicalactivity/childhood/WHO_new_childhoodobesity_PREVENTION_27nov_HR_PRINT_OK.pdf. Accessed 8 November 2016.

———. 2012c. *Prioritizing Areas for Action in the Field of Population-Based Prevention of Childhood Obesity: A Set of Tools for Member States to Determine.* Geneva: World Health Organization. http://apps.who.int/iris/bitstream/10665/80147/1/9789241503273_eng.pdf?ua=1. Accessed 8 November 2016.

WHO and FAO. 2002. *Report of the Joint WHO/FAO Expert Consultation on Diet, Nutrition and the Prevention of Chronic Diseases.* Geneva: World Health Organization; Rome: Food and Agriculture Organization. http://www.who.int/dietphysicalactivity/publications/trs916/download/en/. Accessed 8 November 2016.

Youde, Jeremy R. 2010. *Biopolitical Surveillance and Public Health in International Politics.* New York: Palgrave Macmillan.

Zhang, Xingyou, Stephen Onufrak, James B. Holt, and Janet B. Croft. 2013. A Multilevel Approach to Estimating Small Area Childhood Obesity Prevalence at the Census Block-Group Level. *Preventing Chronic Disease* 10: E68.

CHAPTER **13**

Using Secondary Data in Nutritional Anthropology Research
Enhancing Ethnographic and Formative Research

Kristen Borre and James Wilson

Introduction

Nutritional anthropologists today are challenged not simply to report on particularities of dietary habits and food production, distribution, and belief systems, but to place our interpretations of food behaviors, diets, and nutritional outcomes within a global context. Anthropologists are skilled in formative research, which is needed in food and nutrition studies but often goes unstudied by policy makers and program developers. When secondary data are used in nutritional anthropology's ethnographic and formative research, the outcomes become better situated in the literature for translation into effective food and nutrition policies, interventions, and programs (Bentley, Johnson, Wasser et al. 2014). Skillful use of secondary data makes formative research better placed to impact food and nutrition research, applied policies, programs, and services. Used judiciously, secondary data provide a broader context for research significance at multiple geographic, political, and economic scales.

What Are Secondary Data?

Secondary data are defined as data that have been produced for specific purposes and are available as databases or data that are summarized and perhaps analyzed in published literature. Primary data, collected in the course of original research and shaped by the research purpose and design, are tailored to answer a specific question. Primary data become secondary data when a researcher reorganizes or modifies either the raw or processed primary data to address a question for which those data were not specifically collected.

The chief advantage of primary data is that they are tailored to address the researcher's question; the main disadvantage is the cost of collection and validation. Secondary data are widely available in both aggregated and disaggregated forms so the cost of collection and validation has already been covered; here, the challenge lies in determining whether the data are applicable to the proposed research and how to address the caveats their use may create. Potential problems arise in using secondary data when the data are derived from large and diverse populations that are not representative, or when sampling from a large secondary collection or population does not represent the group, because when the data are broken down for other purposes, the errors may become significant. In addition, the error of ecological fallacy is a real concern. Ecological fallacy occurs when processes operating at one scale are inferred at another scale. Ecological fallacy is a common problem when data are drawn out of context and used to justify a particular viewpoint, research problem, or social policy. Firebaugh (2001) and Freedman (2001) explain the problem of ecological fallacy and inference well. For a more detailed discussion of secondary data and its application to research studies, see Payne and Payne (2004).

Examples of sources of secondary data that are often used in food and nutrition research include governmental, nongovernmental, and nonprofit organizations; corporations and businesses; universities, research, and data mining organizations; and marketing and trade organizations. Secondary data can also be found in published literature using search engines. Special permissions are not usually required for use of secondary data; they are routinely de-identified in databases and the process of informed consent does not apply unless special requests are granted for the use of databases with identifiers.

Secondary data can be used within ethnographic, ethnological, formative, and longitudinal studies of food and nutrition. We address three areas: framing research questions, conducting research and providing ecological context using secondary data, and interpreting findings within the context of secondary data. Wilson and Borre (this volume) present vetted secondary data sources useful to food and nutrition research in tables with descriptions and discussion. Having read that chapter and the present one, the researcher is encouraged to consider when and how best to use secondary data at various stages of the research process. This chapter also provides some examples of how nutritional anthropologists have used secondary data and demonstrates the ease with which these vetted databases and reports may be accessed and used. Our focus is applied research, but our philosophy is that research worth doing should contribute to theory, method, and the welfare of those we study. Secondary data research is the place to begin structuring food and nutrition research projects to have the greatest impact.

Framing the Research Question

When it comes to food and nutrition research, the approaches of a nutritionist and an anthropologist differ in terms of the framing and context of the question and preparation of the research project. A nutritionist often relies on statistics derived from secondary data to shape a hypothesis and develop controls and outcome measures for the independent variable within either a particular population, a clinical trial group, or a meta-analysis (e.g., see Heaney et al. 2012). The anthropologist frames the research question holistically, often taking a socio-ecological approach (SEA) (see Bronfenbrenner 1994 and McElroy and Townsend 2015: 163–209). The anthropologist collects data using a multi-method approach and grounds the analysis within the context of the experience of the community. Secondary data provide the anthropologist with significant information about the environment, economy, social and political structures and organizations, education systems, biological exposures, and cultural beliefs.

Already familiar with seeing the big picture of food and nutrition within a community, the anthropologist can include critical secondary descriptive data to better frame research questions, data collection, and analysis. When well-regarded databases are used to frame questions and justify the multi-method approach, others outside the anthropological community are more likely to support and use research findings in their research, policy and program development, and evaluation. Nutrition and health professionals are seeking systematic, well-framed grounded research to increase the success of policies, programs, and services for improving nutritional status in global populations (Malik et al. 2014; Bentley et al. 2014; Pelto and Gove 1992).

Secondary data enrich the formation of the research problem. National and local census data can be used to target the global distribution of potential study populations and plan recruitment of participants. This is particularly important when investigating migratory populations or conducting multi-site research. These data are used in budget development for proposals and may be required by the funding organization. Agricultural and market reports will provide data on food production and distribution by region, climate, elevation, and season to guide timing of primary data collection. Incidence and prevalence of nutritional diseases within specific populations and geographic regions can guide decisions about study design, sampling, and scheduling of research protocols. Government and global reports on economic development programs, wage labor employment, supplemental economic activities, household location and size, and transfer payments to the potential research population should be investigated.

Government, nonprofit, and non-governmental organizations produce reports in which secondary data are analyzed and presented in tabular and graphic formats. Statistical modeling and hypothesis testing provide key determinants of food and nutritional behaviors and structures. Past and ongoing work in global communities can be identified through these reports. Communication with others involved in the community or conducting similar research can be done before beginning a project. The anthropologist can become aware of how his or her project might be viewed by existing program or service providers within a community. Letters of support from them may improve the chances for funding or obtaining access to geographic regions and local populations. Or the anthropologist may need to prepare ways to distance his or her research from that of other concurrent research projects to avoid contamination of results, a heavy research burden on the participants, or conflicts of interest. The quality of the relationships among organizations providing services to particular communities may enhance or limit the anthropologist's success.

In summary, secondary data from many different sources inform the scope of research and definition of the research problem, and prepare the researcher for exigencies that may occur in the field setting. Studying these data is important for constructing the research question with sensitivity to the context in which the group or population lives and experiences daily life. These data also provide information that fosters efficiency and effectiveness in project planning and field site(s) selection.

Secondary Data and Ethnographic and Ethnological Investigations of Food, Dietary Behaviors, and Nutritional Outcomes

A classic secondary database known to many anthropologists for its ethnological studies of human cultural and social life can be found in the Human Relations Area Files (HRAF). located at Yale University. HRAF anthropological researchers code ethnographic, sociological, and psychological investigations of human societies across time and space. The database is readily available online (http://hraf.yale.edu). As a research tool, this secondary data resource can be queried for information related to cross-cultural research on agriculture, food systems, food habits, nutrition, and health. The tool is useful for comparing the diversity of food production, processing, distribution, and consumption across time, geographic location, life history, and ethnic and religious group membership. Using systematic data coding done by trained anthropologists, the HRAF has assembled detailed information on over 281 cultures throughout the world across time and geographic location. Indexed at the paragraph level, it provides context for the constructed searches that often is not found in systems that use a keyword system. For example, see HRAF (n.d.) for a brief paragraph describing food taboos with links to extensive food taboo data from different global cultures.

The data are well developed for Native American and immigrant groups within the United States and Canada, but are not limited to those societies. The HRAF database also holds a valuable collection of historic research on food systems, beliefs, and behaviors. Multi-sited research projects in global studies of food habits, behaviors, and food production can be informed by preliminary research conducted using the HRAF before a research question and plan are finalized. Secondary data research can easily be performed as an end unto itself by using the HRAF for hypothesis development and testing, as it is able to provide probability samples. When using the HRAF for ethnological comparisons, caution must be taken to note the differences in the methods used for data collection, which can bias the data in unique ways. Caution must also be taken to note variation in reporting of participant-observer observations as well as methods of quantitative data collection to ensure validity of comparisons.

Secondary Data Reports and Nutritional Anthropology Research

The cultural anthropologist interested in the food system, diet, and nutritional health of particular populations should begin with published secondary data analyses that are available from agricultural, health, food, and nutrition organizations. See Wilson and Borre (this volume) for a tabular presentation of many sources of these reports and data summaries. In addition to these, meta-analyses of published research outcomes may be found through a literature search, but we will focus on the use of vetted data and research reports that are widely available. Below is an example of how these may be used to frame a research question on the effect of the global economy on the food-purchasing power of the poor.

The United States Department of Agriculture Economic Research Service (USDA ERS) produces reports on food production, distribution, marketing, regional food habits, and food security as well as summaries of these topics in publications such as *Amber Waves* (http://www.ers.usda.gov/amber-waves#.VM6zp1 rvPzI). This digital access site offers a search engine to find reports ranging from world crops and animal production, food markets and prices, food safety, food security, and farm management to the rural economy, food behaviors and health, natural resources and environment, and global markets and trade. For example, the three main predictors of food insecurity have been found to be unemployment and low wages, the effects of inflation, and the relative price of food to other household needs (Coleman-Jenson and Gregory 2014). Coleman-Jenson and Gregory present the argument that lower unemployment rates alone could have reduced the steady food insecurity rate in the United States between 2007 and 2009. Anthropologists interested in the diets of poor households and their access to food—information that is also provided as geographically referenced data through the USDA ERS (2014) (see http://www.ers.usda.gov/data-products/ food-access-research-atlas/go-to-the-atlas.aspx)—can use this information to design a formative study of the relative meaning of unemployment, unavailability of affordable nutrient-dense foods, and costs of locating and buying foods with or without government and community-based assistance programs.

Using Secondary Databases to Develop the Research Problem: Extracting Data

The U.S. Census and Food Stamp Recipients websites, which provide public access to large, complex databases and have facilities to enable the user to target and extract study data. The U.S. Census now provides population and housing data on a more continuous basis via its American Community Survey (ACS) Public Use Microdata Sample (PUMS) program. These data are available through American Fact Finder (AFF), FTP, and DataFerret, and can be downloaded en masse as a zipped file via a FTP directory. Once downloaded and unzipped, a number of separate file segments become available as text files that can be managed with SAS (SAS Institute 2010) or other DBMS. Alternatively, the Census Bureau also provides more experienced data users with an API option to enable them to develop their own census data queries in the Uniform Resource Locator (URL) address bar.

For the user who has limited experience with DBMS (data base management systems) and programming, the Census Bureau makes available a guided search using a GUI (graphical user interface) to build queries to extract specific fields (variables) from census tables. The results are a downloadable text or csv file that can then be imported into a worksheet. For studying a population using food stamps or subscribing to the Supplemental Nutrition Assistance Program (SNAP), the user would access the American FactFinder section of the Census website. The guided search allows the user to select specific variables of interest and levels of geography.

Figure 13.1, containing Figures 13.1a and 13.1b, depicts sample results using the guided steps provided by the Census Bureau in worksheets in a MS-Excel workbook. Figure 13.1a portrays the organization of the downloaded file. Column labels are defined in an accompanying csv file, Figure 13.1b. Geographic identifiers (FIPS or ANSI codes) are associated with each row of data. (The census tract is identified uniquely by an 11 digit code.) Geographic identifiers enable the joining and merging of attribute data to digital boundary files in a geographic information system (GIS). The following section is a demonstration of how secondary data from the U.S. Census Bureau can be used to provide a geographic context in food and nutrition research.

Using Secondary Databases to Develop the Research Problem: Turning Census Data into Information for Analysis

In a study it may be desirable to provide spatial context and establish benchmarks for comparative analyses. The data used in this example are estimates from the

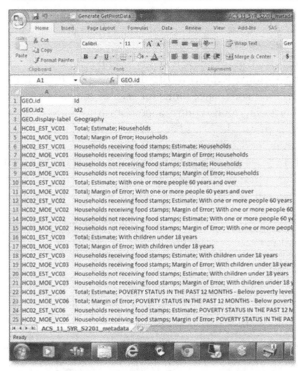

Figure 13.1a and b. Estimated household data on food stamp/SNAP recipients by census tracts, downloaded as a comma separated value (CSV) file and metadata describing the field names for the worksheet.

ACS. Depending on sample sizes, estimates will contain statistical uncertainty that makes it necessary to incorporate a measure such as a confidence interval for making statistically valid comparisons of the data. Larger sample sizes will have narrower 95 percent confidence intervals than smaller sample sizes. Table 13.1 shows ACS estimates for numbers of households and household food stamp recipients in selected geographic areas: the United States, Kentucky, Jefferson County (an urban county containing the city of Louisville with 191 census tracts), and Knox County (a rural county in eastern Kentucky with 8 census tracts). With the

Table 13.1. A comparison of percent household food stamp recipients among selected geographic regions (2006–2010)

	Estimated HHs	Est. HH Food Stamp Recipients	Est. % HH Food Stamp Recipients	95% CI
US	114,761,359	11,759,700	10.2	
Kentucky*	1,379,773	213,329	15.5	
Jefferson County (urban)	301,312	36,458	12.1	
Knox County (rural)	12,541	3,805	30.3	±0.8

*Jefferson county recipients subtracted

exception of Knox County, the estimates are based on relatively large sample sizes producing negligible confidence interval widths.

Figure 13.2 depicts the percentage of household food stamp recipients by census tracts within Jefferson County, Kentucky. The thin lines in the graph are the 95 percent upper and lower confidence limits for each of the census tracts. Census-tract households receiving food stamps range from 0 to more than 70 percent in this county. By contrast, the overall county percentage of rural Knox County households receiving food stamps is approximately 2.5 times than that of Jefferson County, with a census-tract range from over 21 percent to almost 40 percent. These comparisons appear to show greater disparity in household food stamp recipients in an urban setting than in a rural setting. A follow-up question

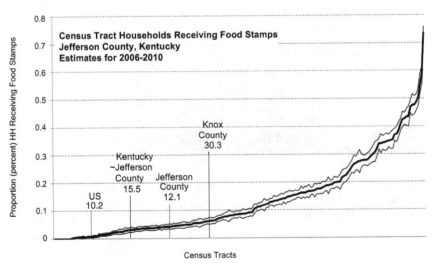

Figure 13.2. Comparison of percent households receiving food stamps between selected Kentucky geographic areas and Jefferson county census tracts.

Source: U.S. Census American Community Survey 2011

to this finding might include examining the geographic distribution of the percentage of urban households receiving food stamps.

Figure 13.3 is a map showing the distribution of percent households receiving food stamps at the census tract level for Jefferson County, which contains the city of Louisville. This area has a large concentration of census tracts, with more than 30 percent of the households receiving food stamps in the western portion of the county. Such a map can help the researcher target neighborhoods for surveying and study. For example, what is the comparative quality of diets among neighborhoods with higher percentages of households receiving food stamps? Are there differences in accessibility to different types of food venues such as grocery and convenience stores? Are the neighborhood households divided by ethnicity or age? Are preferred foods or fresh fruits and vegetables readily available and affordable in markets or produced by gardens?

The Role of the Anthropologist in Grounding Secondary Analyses: Increasing the Impact of Nutritional Anthropology Research

Although most research and development organization reports highlight research methods and statistical associations among data, they do not frame food and nutrition research within a social and cultural context. Statistical data are not

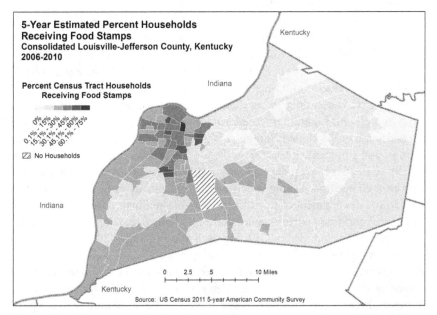

Figure 13.3. Map showing the distribution of percent census tract households receiving food stamps in Jefferson County, Kentucky, 2006 to 2010

capable of explaining how the determinants and associations in quantitative data become constructed through local and global political, economic, and social institutions. The everyday experience of families, women, children, and communities facing poverty, unemployment, lack of food availability, and the stress of choosing what can be purchased and what must be forgone is not mentioned in these secondary reports. Cultural anthropologists using a variety of theoretical approaches are needed to put a face on the secondary data, not through isolated anecdotal stories, but through systematic investigation and reporting of individual, household, and community experiences and voices. The results of the ethnographic or formative research that have been framed by statistical reports can then be discussed in light of those secondary data. Funding agencies, administrators, educators, community and government leaders, and bureaucrats are more likely to pay attention to anthropological research that has been placed within a context of familiar data. Chances for obtaining funding and expanding ethnographic research and intervention projects increase with this approach. Examples of ethnographic and formative approaches using secondary data well are discussed briefly below.

Food and nutrition policies, programs, and interventions that are grounded in community members' everyday experience have a better chance of success than those based on top-down analyses of quantitative data that may or may not be validated for application to the affected community (Bentley, Tolley, and Pequegnat 2011). Messer (1997) provides an example of an exploration of intrahousehold variation in food allocation through the relationship between the mother and her children, demonstrating that secondary-data predictions of mother-child relationships and child feeding are not universal and must be understood within the everyday life patterns of the household. Lingam et al. (2014) report on the value of multi-method formative studies targeting parenting and feeding practices regarding young children in order to develop effective interventions in India and Pakistan. International organizations such as the World Health Organization of the United Nations recognize that solutions to violence, climate change, and structural violence are rooted in the resilience of local communities (Malik et al. 2014). Yet there exist very few examples of systematic local studies that are well positioned using widely available secondary data. Using secondary data in the development of formative studies of food behaviors and nutritional outcomes provides opportunities for anthropologists to develop effective applied ethnographic research (Pelto 2013; Schensul and LeCompte 2012).

The ethnographic and ethnological testing of associations found in secondary data reports can highlight the significance of variation in the experiences and responses to food and nutrition problems across and among different groups. When anthropologists relate the results of their studies to secondary data reports used by agencies for policy development and program planning, those policies and programs have a higher rate of acceptance and success. Bogin (2012) provides an analysis using both secondary and primary research data to argue that child growth can serve as a marker of nutritional, economic, and political ecology. He incorporates secondary and primary data to build statistical and biocultural models to predict risks of obesity and growth stunting. His research focuses on the Maya and Maya-Americans, but because it is systematically designed using both secondary and primary data, the models can be adapted to other populations and ethnic groups sharing similar experiences. The models require use of a socio-ecological and evolutionary approach to link social, political, and economic environments to growth outcomes. When the research is completed, national and international agencies will be able to use the information to test hypotheses predicting poor growth outcomes and to recommend policies to reduce the incidence and prevalence of poor growth in specific populations.

Using Secondary Data for Reference: Longitudinal and Evaluation Studies

Secondary data serve the important function of providing standards, baselines, and benchmarks to monitor nutritional status, food security, hunger, and agricultural production, distribution, and consumption. When assessing food and nutritional status in a population, the results must be compared to a standard or a baseline measure for interpretation. If a condition is to be monitored, then comparisons can be made continuously to both the standard and previous results. Monitoring allows a condition or pattern of development or growth to be observed without intervention. The same standards or baselines work in longitudinal intervention trials in which data are collected as a time series. The standards or baselines are valid only when the same techniques, methods, data management, and analyses are performed. Methods must be tested for reliability and validity using standardized techniques. The two major world standards for child growth come from the World Health Organization (WHO) and the Centers for Disease Control (CDC). The relative validity of using one over the other in growth studies is widely argued (de Onis et al. 2007).

Cohort studies of children's height, weight, weight for height, and body mass index (BMI), like biochemical measures of nutrient status, all rely on standards created from secondary data analyses. Nutrition monitoring and evaluation of interventions depends on comparisons to standards. Some of the best examples of applications of baseline and standard data in child-growth monitoring and intervention studies come from longitudinal growth and nutritional status studies done in Central America. Martorell (2010) documents how longitudinal study of the growth and nutritional status of Guatemalan children over fifty years and three generations has contributed to improved food and nutrition policies and programs. Stein et al. (2004) were able to demonstrate improved length for age in the offspring of mothers who received high-protein nutritional supplements from *atole* as young children. From longitudinal data previous collected on the mother's length for age, the mother's length for age served as a baseline to assess the improvement in her own children's length for age associated with the intervention she had received as a young child.

Conclusion

Secondary data are a valuable resource for food and nutrition research. Secondary data research analyses are widely available and inexpensive to use, but they also can lead to false conclusions when employed to address research questions for which they were not designed. Nutritional anthropology research can benefit from triangulation of formative primary data with secondary data extracted at the appropriate scale.

Anthropologists use secondary data to frame research questions and project design; to situate ethnographic and formative research for translation into more effective policies, programs, and interventions; and for food and nutrition monitoring of populations and evaluation of interventions. Secondary data are widely accessible and can be found in published reports from governmental and non-governmental organizations and in published and unpublished de-identified databases. Ethnographic and formative research projects should review vetted secondary data sources as a part of the preliminary study for proposal development. Results from anthropological investigations should also use appropriate secondary data to determine the results' significance for improving policies, programs, and services to populations and communities.

Kristen Borre received her PhD in anthropology in 1990 and MPH in nutrition from the University of North Carolina, Chapel Hill. She is currently Visiting Professor of Anthropology at Northern Illinois University, where she teaches biological and cultural anthropology, nutritional anthropology, research methods, food and environment, and medical anthropology. At East Carolina University she worked as a Senior Research Scientist at the Brody School of Medicine, and as Director of the NC Agromedicine Institute, the Southeast Center for Agricultural Safety and Health, and the Growing Up FIT! Program with the Division of Research and Graduate Studies. Her research focused on childhood overweight, obesity and the health of migrant farm workers, and rural community health partnerships.

James L. Wilson received his PhD from the University of North Carolina, Chapel Hill in 1991. He is currently Associate Professor of Geography at Northern Illinois University, where he teaches courses on GIS applications in public and environmental health, medical geography, maps and mapping, and environment and society. His research interests include using GIS to analyze and visualize environmental problems that have a bearing on health and well-being. While at East Carolina University he worked as Associate Director at the Center for Health Systems Research and Development, where he developed atlases of regional and national health disparities and conducted research on adult and childhood overweight and obesity.

References

Bentley, Margaret, Susan L. Johnson, Heather Wasser, Hilary Creed-Kanashiro, Monal Shroff, Sylvia Fernandez Rao, and Melissa Cunningham. 2014. Formative Research Methods for Designing Culturally Appropriate, Integrated Child Nutrition and Development Interventions: An overview. *Annals of the New York Academy of Sciences* 1308(1): 54–67.

Bentley, Margaret. E., Elizabeth E. Tolley, and Willo. Pequegnat. 2011. Qualitative Inquiry: An End Not Just a Means. In *How to Write a Successful Research Grant Application: A Guide for Social and Behavioral Scientists*, ed. W. Pequegnat, E. Stover, and C. A. Boyce, 153–172. New York: Springer.

Bogin, Barry. 2012. Maya in Disneyland: Child Growth as a Marker of Nutritional, Economic, and Political Ecology. In *Nutritional Anthropology Biocultural Perspectives on Food and Nutrition*, ed. Darna Dufour, Alan H. Goodman, and Gretel H. Pelto, 231–234. 2nd ed. New York: Oxford.

Bronfenbrenner, Ulin. 1994. Ecological Models of Human Development. In *International Encyclopedia of Education*, vol. 3, ed. T. N. Postlethwaite and T. Husen, 37–43. Oxford: Elsevier.

Coleman-Jenson, Alisha, and Christian Gregory. 2014. Inflation and Higher Food Prices Kept Food Insecurity Rates Relatively High after the 2007–09 Recession. *Amber Waves*, 1 December 2014. http://www.ers.usda.gov/amber-waves/2014-december/inflation-and-higher-food-prices-kept-food-insecurity-rates-relatively-high-after-the-2007–09-recession.aspx#.VM7FT1rvPzI. Accessed 28 January 2015.

de Onis, Mercedes, Cutberto Garza, Adelheid W. Onyango, and Elaine Borghi. 2007. *Comparison of the WHO Child Growth Standards and the CDC 2000 Growth Charts*. Journal of Nutrition 137: 144–148.

USDA ERS (U.S. Department of Agriculture Economic Research Service). 2014. Food Access Research Atlas. http://www.ers.usda.gov/data-products/food-access-research-atlas.aspx. Updated 13 October 2014. Accessed 28 January 2015.

Firebaugh, Glenn. 2001. Ecological Fallacy. *International Encyclopedia for the Social and Behavioral Sciences*, vol. 6: 4023–4026. Oxford: Pergamon Press.

Freedman, David. A. 2001. Ecological Inference and the Ecological Fallacy. *International Encyclopedia for the Social and Behavioral Sciences*, vol. 6: 4027–4030. Oxford: Pergamon Press.

Heaney, Robert, Stephen Kopecky, Kevin C. Maki, John Hathcock, Douglas MacKay, and Taylor C. Wallace. 2012. A Review of Calcium Supplements and Cardiovascular Disease Risk. *Advances in Nutrition: An International Review Journal* 3: 763–771.

HRAF (Human Relations Area Files) n.d. https://hraf755.wordpress.com/2013/03/04/cross-cultural-studies-of-food-taboos/.

Lingam, Raghu, Pallavi Gupta, Shamsa Zafar, Zelee Hill, Aisha Yousafzai, Sharad Iyengar, Siham Sikander, Zaeem ul Haq, Shilpa Mehta, Jolene Skordis-Worrel, Atif Rahman, and Betty Kirkwood 2014. Understanding Care and Feeding Practices: Building Blocks for a Sustainable Intervention in India and Pakistan. *Annals of the New York Academy of Sciences.* 1308: 204–217.

Malik, Khalid, Maurice Kugler, Mildred Kovacivic, et.al. 2014. *Human Development Report 2014: Sustaining Progress: Reducing Vulnerabilities and Building Resilience.* New York: United Nations Development Programme.

Martorell, Reynaldo. 2010. Physical Growth and Development of the Malnourished Child: Contributions from 50 Years of Research at INCAP. *Food and Nutrition Bulletin.* 31: 68–82.

McElroy, Ann, and Patricia K. Townsend. 2015. *Medical Anthropology in Ecological Perspective.* Philadelphia: Westview Press.

Messer, Ellen. 1997. Intra-household Allocation of Food and Health Care: Current Findings and Understandings; Introduction. *Social Science and Medicine.* 44: 1675–1684.

Payne, Geoff., and Judy. Payne. 2004. Secondary Analysis. In *The Sage Key Concepts Series: Key Concepts in Social Research,* 214–219. London: Sage. doi: http://dx.doi.org/10.4135/9781849209397.n45

Pelto, Gretel. H., and Sandy Gove. 1992. Developing a Focused Ethnographic Study for the WHO Acute Respiratory Infection Control Programme. In *Rapid Assessment Procedures: Qualitative Methodologies for Planning and Evaluation of Health Related Programmes,* ed. N. S. Scrimshaw and G. R. Gleason, 215–226. Boston: International Nutrition Foundation.

Pelto, Pertti. J. 2013. *Applied Ethnography: Guidelines for Field Research.* Walnut Creek, CA: Left Coast Press.

SAS Institute Inc. 2010. *SAS ® 9.2 Language Reference: Concepts, Second Edition.* Cary, NC: SAS Institute Inc.

Schensul, Jean. J. and Margaret. D. LeCompte. 2012. *Essential Ethnographic Methods: A Mixed Methods Approach.* Lanham, MD: AltaMira Press.

Stein, Aryeh D., Huiman X. Barnhart, Meng Wang, Moshe B. Hoshen, Karen Ologoudou, Usha Ramakrishnan, Ruben Grajeda, Manuel Ramirez-Zea, and Reynaldo Martorell. 2004. Comparison of Linear Growth Patterns in the First Three Years of Life across Two Generations in Guatemala. *Pediatrics* 113(3): 270–275.

CHAPTER 14

Designing Food Insecurity Scales from the Ground Up

An Introduction and Working Example of Building and Testing Food Insecurity Scales in Anthropological Research

Craig Hadley and Lesley Jo Weaver

Introduction

Since at least the turn of the nineteenth century, when British theologian Thomas Malthus famously proposed that population growth would be kept in check by disease, famine, and limited resources, social scientists have been keenly interested in factors that shape individuals' and populations' ability to secure access to adequate food. Food insecurity occurs when an individual or a household lacks secure access to safe and culturally appropriate foods at all times (Bickel et al. 2000). Radimer's seminal work in the late 1980s (Radimer et al. 1990, 1992) underscored that a lack of food does not simply lead to "hunger"—the physical sensation resulting from inadequate calories—but also involves social and psychological elements. These include factors like anxiety about food supply, or the stigma and shame associated with having to obtain food in socially unacceptable ways. The Radimer/Cornell Hunger and Food Insecurity Scales were developed out of these initial observations. Another important finding of Radimer's work was that food insecurity operates differently at the household level than at the individual level. Spurred by a need to assess household outcomes of the U.S. government's Title II food aid program domestically and abroad, researchers associated with USAID developed the Household Food Insecurity Access Scale (HFIAS) and adaptations thereof for use among vulnerable populations in developing countries (Coates, Swindale, and Bilinsky 2007). The 2007–2008 food price crisis further reenergized interest in food insecurity, and especially in its measurement.

Research by social scientists has explored how food insecurity might be measured in a more locally relevant fashion, either by adapting the HFIAS or developing locally derived scales (Coates et al. 2006). Effective measurement of food insecurity in context is critical for understanding who is at risk of food insecurity, what factors determine risk of food insecurity, and whether programs have led to improvements in food security status. However, because the concept is abstract and context-dependent, it can be difficult to measure. To date, a consensus appears to be emerging that the measurement of food insecurity requires a toolkit rather than a single tool.

In this chapter, we walk readers through the steps that one might take to develop a food insecurity scale from "the ground up." This would represent one tool in a tool kit; others might include measures of dietary diversity (Ruel 2003), coping strategies (Maxwell et al. 2008), or measures of caloric deprivation (Headey and Ecker 2012)]. A scale is a range of values forming a standard system for measuring something. A scale should measure a specific construct or concept, like food insecurity, and all of the items or questions within a scale should measure aspects of the item of interest. To determine the effectiveness of a scale, one must assess various aspects of its reliability and validity, two concepts that we will return to shortly. We then provide step-by-step instructions on how one might use various statistical tests to explore the epidemiology of food insecurity within an anthropological study.

Semi-structured Methods to Capture the Experience of Food Insecurity

Borgatti (1999) offers an excellent overview of elicitation techniques to build locally relevant understandings of particular cultural domains—shared mental categories consisting of a set of things that are all of the same type. Such techniques would be useful, for instance, in eliciting items related to food security in a specific cultural context, which could then be converted into a locally derived food insecurity scale. Using the simple freelisting methods described by Borgatti, one could systematically elicit information from participants about the nature and experience of food insecurity, then take the most commonly mentioned items and convert them into a scale to measure food insecurity according to its locally grounded meanings. These issues as related to food insecurity are discussed in detail in Wolfe, Frongillo, and Valois (2001), Coates et al. (2006), and Frongillo and Nanama (2006). Table 14.1 gives an example of items related to food insecurity that were identified by Coates and colleagues in their qualitative study of food insecurity in Bangladesh and later used to build a food security scale. Data for scale development can also be derived from unstructured interviews or even extended participant observation, provided that these involve a sufficient number of individuals to capture the variation in the community being studied.

Table 14.1. Candidate food insecurity scale items discovered during qualitative work in Bangladesh (adapted from Coates et al. 2006).

Item description
Did behavior occur in last 12 months due to lack of resources?

Family not eat meat as part of an ordinary meal
Not give children money for snacks
Not purchase snacks for the family
Had to eat wheat (or another grain)
Not cook Bhalo Mondo ("rich food")
Ate Mishti Alu (sweet potato)
Ate Bhatar Mar (rice starch)
Ate Bon Kochu (wild taro)
Ate Shaluk (water lily)
Ate Gom Baja (fried wheat)
Ate Ata Gola Pani (flour and water gruel)
Ate Khud (broken rice)
Children ate Mishti Alu (sweet potato)
Children ate Bhatar Mar (rice starch)
Children ate Bon Kochu (wild taro)
Children ate Shaluk (water lily)
Children ate Gom Baja (fried wheat)
Children ate Ata Gola Pani (Flour and water)
Children ate Khud (broken rice)
Not eat square meals
Could not eat big fish (e.g., carp, hilsha)
Respondent ate less food
Respondent skipped entire meals
Respondent not eat for an entire day
Children skipped entire meals
Main working adult in family skipped entire meals
Children not eat for an entire day
Food stored in the home ran out
Worried about where food would come from
Family purchased rice frequently
Borrowed money from local moneylenders
Took food (rice, lentils etc.) on credit
Borrowed food from relatives or neighbors
Borrowed food to serve to Attio Shojan or Kutum (guests)
Had to seek Kurbani meat (charity meat during Eid)
Received or sought Jakat or Fitra (charitable contributions)
Not purchase something else to buy food
Sold or mortgaged things for food

How Do We Know Our Food Insecurity Scale Works?
Assessing Reliability and Validity of a Food Insecurity Scale

"Does our scale work?" is essentially a question of validity. Validity and its twin, reliability, refer to the extent to which a question or set of questions measures the phenomenon of interest. Reliability refers to the extent to which repeated measures will return similar values, assuming the underlying construct has not changed. In other words, if someone's food insecurity has not changed over the course of a month, then we would hope that our measurement of food insecurity would reflect that consistency. On the other hand, if food insecurity *did* change then we would similarly hope that our scale faithfully captures those changes (see Frongillo and Nanama 2006 and Hadley and Wutich 2009 for examples of seasonal shifts in food insecurity scales). Similarly, if our food insecurity scale is comprised of ten items, each of the items should be correlated with the other items; in other words, the odd-numbered items should predict the even-numbered items.

Cronbach's alpha, a statistic commonly used to assess internal validity of scales, is available in most common statistical packages and is a simple test of how the items on a scale predict one another. If all the items perfectly predict all other items, then Cronbach's alpha will be 1; if there is no correlation between items then the value will be 0. An alpha above 0.70 is conventionally considered an indication of good internal validity. If alpha is below 0.70, some items on the scale are not assessing the same construct and the investigator must identify which, if any, items are not relevant. Most statistical packages allow the user to specify what the alpha would be if each item was removed from the scale. In this way a user can quickly identify rogue items or even remove items that do not increase the alpha, a useful tool for identifying the fewest items required to capture the construct of interest.

We might also want to assess other aspects of validity, such as face validity and convergent validity. Face validity refers to the degree to which the items make sense in ethnographic context or to those who have an intimate familiarity with the construct of interest. Often, ethnographers will have an excellent sense of the phenomena of interest and can quickly assess the face validity of a scale. For instance, one might assess whether items that reflect more severe states of food insecurity, such as going the whole day without eating, are endorsed by fewer people than items reflecting less severe states of food insecurity, such as worrying whether one might run out of food. Investigators may also rely on local experts to assess face validity.

Convergent validity refers to the degree to which our scale correlates with variables that we expect it to; for example, we might have some ethnographic "hunches" about how food insecurity varies by social class or by season. We might therefore hypothesize that if our scale works, people should score higher (i.e., be more food insecure) in the "hunger" seasons than in seasons immediately following a good harvest. We might also predict that people who are wealthier would score lower on our scale. These propositions can be tested using simple statistical techniques described below to help establish convergent validity.

A further caveat in scale development is that one must take care to include items that are relevant to all respondents in a study. This is especially important if one is designing additive scales, where the investigators simply tally the number of affirmative responses for each participant. If some individuals are given questions to which they cannot meaningfully respond, then a simple tally no longer reflects the underlying dimension. Imagine a food insecurity scale that included the items, "Have there been days when your children complained of being hungry?" and "Have there been days when you had to limit the amount of food you gave to your children?" These two items, while seemingly tapping into food insecurity, cannot be answered by households without children. If the investigators score these as zero, then the household's food insecurity status may be artificially low (see Coates et al. 2006 for an extended discussion). This problem could be corrected in two ways: exclusion criteria could be employed to ensure all study participants will be able to respond to all questions (in this example, this would mean excluding families without children). Second, a series of validation exercises could be conducted during pilot research to ensure that all questions are relevant and comprehensible to the study population. Many techniques could be employed to accomplish this, including translation and back-translation, focus groups, and cognitive interviewing techniques (Willis 2005).

Another potential threat to validity is the "u-shaped problem," which occurs when respondents with very different characteristics give similar responses. Imagine the question, "In the last few weeks have you sold items in order to earn income?" This question appears valid, since ethnographic work demonstrates that food insecure individuals often report selling assets (Corbett 1988; Watts 1988). So do merchants, but for very different reasons that are not accounted for in the question. Another example concerns the specific dietary behavior of consumption of meat. In communities containing vegetarians, some people (usually wealthier, more educated ones) are choosing not to eat meat rather than forgoing it because they cannot afford it. Here again, similar responses may reflect very different experiences of food insecurity.

Working through an Example: A Study of Food Insecurity, Wealth, and Social Support

Assuming that our food insecurity scale adequately meets the criteria for validity and reliability, we can use the scale to explore the epidemiology of food insecurity in our study sample.

In this example, we are working with a sample of 180 households from a single community in rural Tanzania. A sample of the data for the analysis below can be found in Table 14.2. For each of the households in our sample, we collected information using a face-to-face survey on food insecurity. We are interested in two aspects of the community and their relation to food insecurity: a crude measure of household wealth, and the extent to which strong social support networks protect (or do not) from food insecurity. We assess household wealth with a simple yes or no question about ownership of a radio, and assess social support on a scale from 0 to 7, with 7 indicating the highest levels of social support.

Table 14.2. Sample of the full data set used for the analyses in the chapter (contact authors for full data set)

Household ID	Any radio?	Social support score	Household food security Score
1	1	6	5
2	0	5	5
3	1	7	13
4	1	4	6
5	0	5	14
6	0	4	8
7	1	0	4
8	1	3	8
9	1	5	5
10	1	5	12
11	1	0	0
12	0	4	5
13	1	5	5
14	0	6	3
15	0	6	11
16	1	5	5
17	0	4	3
18	1	2	0
19	1	0	0
20	1	2	2
21	0	5	8
22	1	5	2
23	1	0	1
24	1	0	0
25	1	2	0
26	0	3	6
27	0	3	14
28	0	3	10
29	1	6	4
30	1	0	0

What Is the Average Food Insecurity in Our Study Sample?

To construct a continuous measure of food insecurity from our scale we must make sure that each item is coded so that higher values indicate more food insecurity. Then, we simply add the food insecurity items together using the =SUM() function in MS Excel or the Transform → Compute Variable functions in SPSS. Once the score is calculated, we can identify the average or the mean value of food insecurity in our sample. To do this we can, in SPSS, point to Analyze → Descriptive statistics → Descriptives or in MS Excel use the =AVERAGE() function. SPSS will by default provide more information, but both methods will return the average value, which in this case equals 3.8. We can also calculate the minimum and maximum values (0 and 15) and the standard deviation, which gives insight into how variable the sample is with respect to food insecurity (3.9); in MS Excel this can be found using =STDEV(). As the standard deviation increases we know that there is more variation in the sample.

What Is the Proportion of Severely Food Insecure Households in Our Sample?

The measure constructed above is a continuous measure of food insecurity. We might want to categorize our data by the degree of food insecurity and group households into three categories: food secure, moderately food insecure, or severely food insecure. To do this we can generate cutoff points: for example, food insecurity scores of 0 or 1 will be classified as food secure, 2–4 as moderately food insecure, and scores of 5 and higher severely food insecure. SPSS can do this automatically through Transform → Recode into Different Variable, or by ranking variables (Transform → Rank Cases → Rank Type → Ntiles = 3); or one could do this in MS Excel with the IF function. Using these cutoffs with our data set, 62 households or 33% of the sample are food secure, 59 households or 32% are moderately food insecure, and 62 households or 34% are severely food insecure. Such proportions are useful for presenting data and identifying specific subgroups that might most benefit from an intervention designed to improve food security.

We now have constructed two types of food insecurity measurement: one continuous (food insecurity summary score) and one categorical (low, medium, or high food insecurity). Below, we will test basic hypotheses with each variable, and also explore how different data types can lead to different conclusions.

Is a Crude Measure of Household Wealth Associated with a Household's Level of Food Insecurity?

In our study we are interested in understanding whether levels of food insecurity differ between households that own radios experience and those that do not—in other words, if the average value of our food insecurity score differs between households that own a radio and those that do not. We previously calculated the average value of food insecurity for the entire sample, but now we must do this for the radio-owning and non–radio-owning households. This is easily achieved in SPSS by Analyze → Compare Means → Means or in Excel using Pivot Tables. This procedure demonstrates that the radio owners have an average food insecurity score of 2.7, while the non–radio owners have a score of 5.1. To determine whether this difference is statistically significant, or greater than we would expect based on chance alone, we need a statistical test. A t-test or a Mann-Whitney test calculates the significance of the difference in means between two groups. Both are available in SPSS (Analyze → Compare Means → Independent Sample T-Test). The level of significance (p-value) is reported as <0.001, which signifies that the probability of obtaining a between-group difference of this magnitude by chance alone is less than 1 in 1,000. We can therefore conclude that the food insecurity levels are indeed different between radio owners and non–radio owners. Note that this does not mean that radios cause greater food security—only that there are differences between the food security status of radio owners and non–radio owners.

We can also ask whether there are differences between radio owning and non–radio owning households in the proportion of the sample that is severely food insecure. To do so we would use the categorical variable of food insecurity that we constructed above. Because our variables are both categorical (owns radio: yes/no; severely insecure: yes/no) we can use the chi-square test, which allows us to explore between-group differences in the proportion of the sample falling into each category. Again, this test is easily conducted in SPSS (Analyze → Descriptives → Crosstabs). This test shows that there are indeed differences between radio owning and non–radio owning groups in the proportion of households in the various food security categories. Among radio owning households, 51 percent fall within the most food secure category and only 22 percent are in the most severely food insecure category. Among households lacking radios, however, only 7 percent are in the most food secure category, whereas 44 percent are in the most severely insecure category. By selecting the chi-square option in SPSS we find that the likelihood of observing a difference of this magnitude by chance is very small, as indicated by the p-value of <0.001.

Is Social Support Associated with a Household's Level of Food Insecurity?

We can also assess whether greater social support is associated with a lower level of food insecurity, as might be the case if households can call upon others in times of need. This analysis is somewhat different from the t-test example above, where the variables of interest are of two different types: whereas radio owner-ship was measured with a dichotomous variable (yes or no), social support was assessed using a 7-item list leading to a summary score that can range from 0 to 7. To examine whether there is an association between two continuous variables, in this case social support and food insecurity, we need to use a Pearson or Spearman test for correlation. For smaller samples (n = <50) and/or when the variables are not interval level then the Spearman is more often used. This test can be located in SPSS by clicking Analyze → Correlate → Bivariate and then selecting the Spearman option. Each of these statistics results in a correlation coefficient—a measure of the strength of the association between the two variables—which varies between –1 and 1. In our example, the correlation coefficient between food insecurity score and social support is a negative correlation of –0.41. This negative value suggests that as social support increases, food insecurity decreases; that is, households are more food secure. This is consistent with much anthropological theorization about social networks acting as "insurance" against periodic household shortages.

Alternatively, we can categorize the continuous social support variable into three levels reflecting low, medium, and high levels of social support and then assess whether the average value of food insecurity differs across these levels. To execute this, we first use the Transform option in SPSS to split the continuous measure of social support into three equal groups, which we will call high, medium, and low social support. Next, we will compare food insecurity levels (mean and variance) in each of the three social support groups. When comparing the mean and variance of a continuous variable across categorical variables, we use an analysis of variance (ANOVA), which in SPSS is located in Analyze → Compare Means → One-Way ANOVA. This test shows that households with the highest social support have an average food insecurity score of 1.8, the medium social support group has an average score of 3.9, and the lowest social support group has a food insecurity score of 5.7, demonstrating again that households with lower social support experience higher food insecurity. The ANOVA analysis also shows that the probability of observing these differences by chance alone is very small (p < 0.001).

What If Radio Ownership Is Also Associated with Social Support? Confounding and Multiple Predictors

The real world is complex, and it is entirely possible that radio-owning households might have higher or lower levels of social support due to some other influence. Such an association would render our interpretation of the above results quite difficult because of confounding. Confounding occurs when an association is spurious because one variable is associated with another variable, but the relationship is not causal. For example, pants size might be positively associated with blood pressure. This is not because larger pants *cause* increases in blood pressure, but because pants size is associated with adiposity, which is linked causally to blood pressure. In our food insecurity example, we can check for confounding by exploring whether radio ownership is associated with social support, and which of these two is actually associated with food insecurity. We can first do a t-test as demonstrated above to see whether the average value of social support differs between radio owners and non–radio owners. The average value of social support among radio owners is 2.5, whereas the average value among non–radio owners is 2.8; thus the t-test reveals that this difference is expected by chance alone (p = 0.15). In this case, the variables do not appear to be associated, and therefore confounding is not present. This lack of confounding means that the relationships we observed between radio ownership and food insecurity, and between social support and food insecurity, are statistically robust; in other words, radio ownership and social support independently predict food insecurity.

When two variables are associated with the outcome variable and with one another, or when we want to know the effect of two or more variables on the outcome of interest, we can use linear regression, a statistical method that allows us to identify the independent effects of predictor variables. Provided that predictor variables are not related or only moderately related, then we can use linear regression to identify their independent effects on the outcome of interest, here food insecurity. (When predictor variables are too highly correlated, a situation called multicollinearity, then they cannot both be used in linear regression.) A regression model indicates the effect of a variable, when controlling for the effects of other variables included in the model. Users can easily run a regression model in SPSS by selecting Analyze → Regression → Linear or by using =LINEST in MS Excel. Results of the linear regression using our data are shown in Table 14.3.

The intercept is interpreted as the average value of food insecurity when the other variables in the model are zero. Often, it is not realistic to interpret variables set at zero—consider, for instance, a study of adults where age is entered as a variable. The negative coefficient for the support variable demonstrates that a one-unit increase on the social support scale is associated with a 0.74 decrease in the food insecurity score, holding all other variables in the model constant. The coefficient for radio ownership demonstrates that those who own radios have, on average, food insecurity scores that are 2.0 lower than those of non–radio owners. SPSS and other programs can also indicate how much of the variation in the outcome variable is explained by the variables included in the model; this

Table 14.3. Regression Results for Food Insecurity Model

	Beta	Std. Error	Sig.
Intercept	2.89	0.52	<0.001
Social support	−0.74	0.13	<0.001
Household owns radio? Yes	−2.05	0.52	<0.001

R-square: 0.24

statistic is called the r-squared value, which in this case is about 24 percent. That is, our model accounts for just under a quarter of the variation observed in food insecurity in this sample, leaving 75 percent of the variation unexplained by our model. At this point, we might think about adding additional variables to our model to identify what might account for the unexplained variation. Depending on our philosophical approach, we can rely on theory or ethnographic knowledge to help identify variables likely to be relevant, or explore all other variables in our data set for additional relevant predictors.

We have now discussed how to build, adapt, and validate a food insecurity tool. We then walked through an example to illustrate some simple statistical analyses to test hypotheses about the epidemiology of food insecurity in a community. For many readers, this will be sufficient. Below we address three advanced topics that may prove useful for those wishing to engage in more complex analyses.

Residual Case Analysis

Residual case analysis (RCA) can be used to explore anomalous cases in one's data or scales. In the example used here, we found a strong relationship between our measure of food insecurity and social networks: those without strong networks were more food insecure overall. In RCA, we search our data for cases that do not fit the pattern; in this case, households with low social support but high food security, or with high food insecurity and high social support. One way to identify these cases is to perform a simple linear regression and specify that the residuals be saved to the dataset. A residual is the difference between the observed value of food insecurity and the predicted value, given the level of social support. A large residual indicates that our statistical model did not predict that case very well. These anomalous cases could be contacted again for follow-up research using qualitative techniques to better understand why they do not conform to the larger pattern. RCA could be used to conduct a mixed-method study that begins with a phase of qualitative inquiry to design a food insecurity scale, then a quantitative analysis of survey data, followed by a qualitative inquiry into those cases that did not fit the statistical model. An excellent discussion of RCA is given in Axinn and Pearce (2006: chapter 4).

Rasch Modeling and Differential Item Function

Rasch modeling is a quantitatively rigorous method of assessing whether the items in a scale work the same for everyone within a study. To see why this is important, imagine that we measure someone's height over three time periods and find that during time 1 the person was 160 cm, then 161 cm, and then 162 cm. We know that they grew 1 cm between each period, and that the length of a centimeter is constant at any point in time. However, if we measure someone's food security using a scale over three time points and find that they went from 1 to 2 to 3, we do not know if the unit change is the same in each period—that is, we do not know if progressing from a score of 1 to 2 is equally as difficult as progressing from 2 to 3. For some analyses, this might not matter, but for others it is very important. Imagine a study of two communities for whom the probability of endorsing item 3 on a food security score differs, and the difference is not due to underlying differences in food security. In this case, we would say that item 3 has differential item function; that is, the item has different meanings in each community (due perhaps to language issues, cultural differences in what is considered appropriate food, etc). Rasch modeling helps identify items that might be operating differently in subgroups. Identifying such bias is important because even a small difference could lead to differences in overall food security scores, and might give the false appearance that food insecurity was more problematic in one community. Excellent discussions of this issue as it relates to food insecurity scales can be found in Deitchler et al. (2010) and Coates et al. (2006).

Propensity Score Matching

Propensity score matching is a statistical matching technique that makes subgroups within a sample more comparable. In many studies, anthropologists implicitly or explicitly think about the world in terms of an experiment, asking, "How does this particular factor impact the outcome of interest?" We might wonder how participation in a micro-credit scheme affects food insecurity (using the new scale we developed), for instance, hypothesizing that micro-credit is responsible for any observed differences. We might even use regression models to control for confounding variables that could impact the results. In an observational study, however, we can never control for all possible factors, so our results are always open to multiple interpretations. Ideally, to solve this "problem," we would have two groups of people who were similar in every way, except that one participated in a micro-credit scheme and the other did not. Then, any observable difference in food insecurity would be unambiguously attributable to participation in micro-credit.

Rarely do anthropologists have the opportunity to conduct such experiments. Rather, we must rely on multiple other sources of information to make a claim about effects on food insecurity, often implicitly asking ourselves questions like, "What would this person's food insecurity status be if they had/had not participated in micro-credit (Were they rich? Poor?)?" This type of thinking is referred to as the counterfactual framework: in an observational study the counterfactual is always unobserved, so we have to make a guess at what it would be. Bernard refers to this as thought experiments (Bernard 2011).

In making such an argument we are also making an argument about exchangeability, that is, we assume that the people in our study all have the same chance of participating in micro-credit. This is a massive assumption. Indeed, many anthropologists have devoted their careers to understanding and documenting how opportunities are unequally distributed, and how structural forces produce these unequal opportunities. In these cases, no regression model can account for the lack of exchangeability. Oakes and Johnson (2006: 372) refer to this as "structural confounding," and notes that in these cases "confounding is structural since it cannot be overcome by better sampling methods or larger sample sizes. It can only be overcome by imagining a massive social revolution."

Propensity score matching (PSM) attempts to overcome some of these sources of structural confounding by making the two groups being observed (in our example, people participating in micro-credit versus those not participating) more comparable. PSM accomplishes this task using a predicted probability of group membership—in our case, micro-credit vs. control group—based on observed predictors, usually obtained from logistic regression, to create a counterfactual group. See Wilde (2007) for an example of PSM applied to a food insecurity study. In a PSM framework we would first estimate each person's probability of participating in the micro-credit scheme. Next we would match people who had the same probability of participating and identify cases where one person participated and one did not. We would then compare levels of food insecurity among the exposed and unexposed. This approach has been used recently to examine the relationship between participation in the Supplemental Nutrition Assistance Program and food insecurity (Gibson-David and Foster 2006)

Conclusion

In this chapter we tried to illustrate the steps required to build or adapt a food insecurity scale from the ground up and assess the psychometric properties of that scale. We then walked through a simple study to explore the epidemiology of food insecurity in one community. We tried to illustrate basic statistical approaches and their implementation within widely used programs, such as SPSS and MS Excel. Finally we discussed more advanced approaches to analysis, such as residual case analysis, Rasch modeling, and propensity score matching.

Craig Hadley is an anthropologist interested in health-related phenomena. He has conducted field work in East Africa and in the United States and is currently interested in designing scales to measure water insecurity. He is currently an associate professor at Emory University in Atlanta, GA.

Lesley Jo Weaver is a medical anthropologist with interests in chronic diseases, nutrition, and mental health. She has conducted mixed-methods research among women with type 2 diabetes in urban North India, and has used many of the methods described in this chapter to study the relationships between food insecurity and physical and mental health among rural Brazilian farmers. She is Assistant Professor of Anthropology at the University of Alabama.

Further Reading

Allison, Paul D. 1999. *Multiple regression: A primer.* Thousand Oaks, Pine Forge Press.

Kutner, Michael H. 1996. *Applied linear statistical models,* vol. 4. Chicago: Irwin.

Motulsky, Harvey. 1995. *Intuitive biostatistics,* vol. 1. New York: Oxford University Press.

Streiner, David L., and Geoffrey R. Norman. 2008. *Health measurement scales: a practical guide to their development and use.* Oxford, Oxford University Press.

References

Axinn, William G., and Lisa D. Pearce. 2006. *Mixed method data collection strategies.* Cambridge, Cambridge University Press.

Bernard, H. Russell. 2011. *Research Methods in Anthropology: Qualitative and Quantitative Approaches.* New York: AltaMira.

Bickel, Gary, Mark Nord, Cristofer Price, William Hamilton, and John Cook. 2000. Guide to measuring household food security. Alexandria, VA: Department of Agriculture Food and Nutrition Service.

Borgatti, Stephen P. 1999. Elicitation techniques for cultural domain analysis. in *Enhanced ethnographic methods: audiovisual techniques, focused group interviews, and elicitation techniques. Ethnographer Toolkit.* ed. Jean Schensul, Margaret LeCompte, Bonnie Nastasi, Stephen Borgatti: 115–151. Walnut Creek, CA: Altamira Press

Coates, Jennifer, Anne Swindale, and Paula Bilinsky. 2007. *Household Food Insecurity Access Scale (HFIAS) for measurement of food access: indicator guide.* Washington, DC: Food and Nutrition Technical Assistance Project, Academy for Educational Development.

Coates, J., P. E. Wilde, P. Webb, B. L. Rogers, and R. F. Houser. 2006. Comparison of a qualitative and a quantitative approach to developing a household food insecurity scale for Bangladesh. *Journal of Nutrition* 136(5): 1420S–1430S.

Corbett, Jane. 1988. Famine and household coping strategies. *World Development* 16(9): 1099–1112.

Deitchler, Megan, Terri Ballard, Anne Swindale, and Jennifer Coates. 2010. *Validation of a measure of household hunger for cross-cultural use.* Washington, DC: Food and Nurtrition Technical Assistance II Project (FANTA-2), Academy for Educational Development.

Frongillo, Edward A., and Simeon Nanama. 2006. Development and validation of an experience-based measure of household food insecurity within and across seasons in northern Burkina Faso. *Journal of Nutrition* 136(5): 1409S–1419S.

Gibson-David, C. M., and E. M. Foster. 2006. A Cautionary Tale: Using Propensity Scores To Estimate the Effect of Food Stamps on Food Insecurity. *Social Service Review* 80: 93–126.

Hadley, Craig, and Amber Wutich. 2009. Experience-based measures of food and water security: Biocultural approaches to grounded measures of insecurity. *Human Organization* 68(4): 451–460.

Headey, Derek, and Olivier Ecker. 2013. Rethinking the measurement of food security: from first principles to best practice. *Food Security* 5(3): 327–343.

Maxwell D, Caldwell R, Langworthy M. 2008. Measuring food insecurity: Can an indicator based on localized coping behaviors be used to compare across contexts? *Food Policy* 6: 533-40.

Oakes, J. Michael, and Pamela Jo Johnson. 2006. Propensity score matching for social epidemiology. *Methods in Social Epidemiology* 1: 370–393.

Radimer, K. L., C. M. Olson, and C. C. Campbell. 1990. Development of indicators to assess hunger. J. Nutr. 120: 1544–1548.

Radimer, K. L., C. M. Olson, J. C. Greene, C. C. Campbell, and J. P. Habicht. 1992. Understanding hunger and developing indicators to assess it in women and children. *J. Nutr. Educ.* 24: 36S–45S.

Ruel, Marie T. 2003. Is dietary diversity an indicator of food security or dietary quality? A review of measurement issues and research needs. *Food Nutr Bull* 24, no. 2: 231–2.

Watts, M. 1988. Coping with the market: Uncertainity and food security among Hausa peasants. In *Coping with Uncertainty in Food Supply,* ed. I. de Garine and G. Harrison, 260–289. Oxford: Clarendon Press.

Wilde, Parke E. 2007. Measuring the effect of food stamps on food insecurity and hunger: research and policy considerations. *Journal of Nutrition* 137(2): 307–310.

Willis, Gordon Bruce. 2005. *Cognitive interviewing: A tool for improving questionnaire design.* Thousand Oaks, CA: Sage.

Wolfe, Wendy S., Edward A. Frongillo, and Pascale Valois. 2003. Understanding the experience of food insecurity by elders suggests ways to improve its measurement. *Journal of Nutrition* 133(9): 2762–2769.

Index

activist scholarship, 123–124
acute respiratory infection (ARI), 69
advocacy work
    action research, 16, 31, 79–80, 86,
        88, 91, 96–98, 120, 123–125, 127,
        171, 187
    social action, 129, 131, 163, 166, 170
agroecology, 119
amber waves, 193, 204, 217, 225
American Community Survey (ACS), 197,
    209, 218–219
American Fact Finder (AFF), 17, 28–29,
    37, 63, 71–73, 82, 90, 97, 101–102,
    120, 127, 137, 150, 153, 161, 165, 197,
    211, 218, 221–222, 231, 238
analytical error, 56
Application Programming Interfaces (APIs),
    156
applied ethnography, 12, 64, 67, 78, 226
AQUASTAT, 193, 205
arts-based research, 156, 160

Beale Codes, 192
Behavioral Risk Factor Surveillance System
    (BRFSS), 195, 208
biomarkers, 10, 16, 50–51, 53–54, 58–61
Body Mass Index (BMI), 30, 195,
    207–208, 223
Bogin, B, 212

Cantor, Allison, 96
CDC, 52, 57, 147, 156, 191, 195–196,
    200, 202, 208, 210–211, 223, 225

CDC's WONDER, 1–2
census bureau research data centers, 197,
    209
census data, 197, 209, 211, 215, 218
census geography, 197
Center for Digital Storytelling, 174, 184
Cronbach's alpha, 225
chronic disease prevention, 59, 171, 194
citizen mapping, 151
Climate Impact on Agriculture (Climpag),
    193, 205
clostridium difficile, 188
cognitive mapping techniques, 67
collaboration, 80, 82, 89–91, 105, 108,
    127, 129, 136–137, 139–140, 151,
    162, 166, 179, 182, 201, 203
community action research, 16, 79, 88,
    97
community based research, 16
community food assessments, 118–119,
    124
community outreach, 127
community participation and local
    knowledge, 79
comparative analysis, 39, 218
Compressed Mortality File (CMF), 196
computer software, 144–145
confounding, 235–236, 238–239
Consultative Group on International
    Agricultural Research (CGIAR), 105,
    109, 112, 155, 198, 201, 203
Convergent validity, 230–231
Core Based Statistical Area (CBSA), 192

Correlation coefficient, 225
COUNTRYSTAT, 193, 205
Creative Narrations, 185
Cultural domain analysis, 66–67, 76, 88, 240

data analysis, 51, 88, 136–140, 142, 166, 170, 188, 217, 223
data collection, 10–12, 18, 28, 38–41, 44, 51–52, 55, 63, 65, 67–68, 78–81, 84, 88, 90, 137, 147, 166, 170, 192–194, 215, 217, 240
diet and physical activity, 194, 211
dietary analysis software, 47
dietary assessment, 51–52, 56–59
dietary diversity score, 52, 61, 93, 98
dietary exposure, 50, 53, 56
dietary intake measures, 54
dietary monitoring, 55
dietary recall, 52–53
dietary supplement ingredient database, 57
differential item function, 227–228
digital boundary files
      TIGER, 197, 209
digital storytelling, 10, 18, 136, 173–188
digital technology, 139, 141
direct action, 116, 124, 127
Division of Nutrition, Physical Actiity, and Obesity (DNPAO), 196, 208, 210

early warning systems, 17, 101–102, 110–111, 156
ecological fallacy, 190, 211, 214, 225
Economic Research Service (ERS), 16, 68, 82, 88, 118, 123, 131, 146, 150–151, 156–157, 162, 180, 183, 192–193, 195–196, 204, 210–211, 214, 217–218, 225, 228, 234–236, 238
engaged anthropology, 131
ethics, 11, 15–16, 18, 21–23, 25–27, 29, 31–34, 84, 123, 128, 164, 166–167, 170–172, 174, 188
      informed consent, 15, 22–23, 25, 27, 31, 38, 85, 128, 164, 166–167, 170, 214
etic perspectives, 16, 65–66

evaluation of interventions, 223–224
evolutionary approach, 223
export files (xtp), 187

Face validity, 230
famine, 16–17, 39, 99–105, 107, 109–111, 113, 156, 227, 240
FAO, 2, 11, 44, 49, 94–95, 97–98, 139, 147–148, 185–186, 192, 195
FAOSTAT, 98, 148, 185, 195
feminist theory, 126, 132, 163
Fieldnotes, 124, 141
film
      ethnographic film, 187
Firebaugh, G, 204
focused ethnography, 16, 75
food, 9–13, 15–19, 21, 23–25, 27, 29–33, 37–65, 67–78, 82, 86, 90–132, 135–136, 138–140, 142–161, 164, 169–170, 173–174, 177, 179–180, 182–186, 189–206, 210–241
food activism, 17, 48, 114–123, 125–128, 130–131, 151
Food and Agricultural Organization (FAO), 10, 19, 52, 57, 59, 102–103, 105–106, 111, 147, 155–156, 193–194, 200, 202, 205, 210, 212
food and beverage, 194
food and nutrition databases, 192
food and nutrition research, 16, 37, 58, 190, 204, 213–215, 218, 221, 224
Food and Nutrition Technical Assistance (FANTA), 10, 57, 61, 105, 110–111, 198, 201, 203, 240
food consumption score, 52
food deserts, 18, 115, 143, 150–151, 159, 161, 182, 189, 210–211
food environments, 142, 150
food first, 118, 124
food frequency score, 52
food insecurity, 19, 39, 41–42, 46, 74, 82, 92–96, 105–106, 110, 129, 146, 154, 198, 217, 225, 227–241
food justice, 32, 43, 117, 119, 123–124, 126, 140, 148, 151–152, 184
food landscapes, 146, 149, 154

food movement discourses, 117
food not bombs, 116
food nutrient databases, 47
food praxis, 8–9, 118–124
food security, 19, 24, 32, 42, 91–93, 98,
    102–104, 106–107, 111, 113, 117–118,
    123–124, 131, 136, 138, 140, 144, 152,
    154, 159, 193–197, 201, 203, 205–206,
    217, 223, 228, 232–234, 237–238,
    240–241
food sovereignty, 42–43, 116–117, 121,
    123, 131, 152, 159
food stamp recipitents, 183, 208–211
    cuts, 32
    website, 208
food stories, 173–174, 183, 185
food systems, 10, 32, 38, 42–44, 47–48,
    98, 124, 126, 131–132, 140, 142–143,
    148–151, 153–154, 159–160, 210,
    216–217
food systems mapping, 153–154
Freegans, 117
FTP (File Transfer Protocol), 191

geo-referenced data, 144, 147
geocoded, 191
Geographic Information System (GIS),
    10, 18–19, 135–136, 140, 142–151,
    153–158, 160–161, 191, 194, 197,
    199–200, 202, 218, 224–225
GeoNetwork, 156, 158, 193, 205
Geospatial Data Gateway (GDG), 192, 204
GIS Data, 146–147, 155, 157
GIS Software, 144–145, 148–149
    open source, 135, 137–139, 143, 147,
    150
GIS Web Resources, 154
Global Administrative Areas (GADM),
    195, 200, 202
Global Position System (GPS), 135, 140,
    147, 149, 151–152
Global Terrestrial Observing System
    (GTOS), 193, 205
google sheets, 191, 210
gray literature, 10, 19, 84, 106, 192, 194,
    198, 204

ground truthing, 148, 161
growth studies, 223
guerilla gardeners, 117

health disparities, 95, 150, 152, 154, 199,
    225
Healthy Eating Index, 57, 204
Human Relations Area Files (HRAF),
    216–217, 225
hunger, 13, 17, 39–40, 42–43, 45, 47–48,
    99–102, 104–106, 109, 111–112, 117,
    126–129, 131, 156–157, 205, 223, 227,
    230, 240–241
hypotheses, 38, 198, 223, 233, 237

impact assessment, 13, 50
indigenous groups, 116–117
infant and young child feeding, 13, 62, 65,
    71, 73, 78, 107, 207
Institute of Health Metrics and Evaluation
    (IHME), 197, 201, 203
Institute of Medicine (IOM), 54, 59, 196,
    211
Inter-university Consortium for Political
    and Social Research (ICPSR), 197, 200,
    202
International Classification of Diseases
    (ICD), 196
interviews
    children, 13, 16, 23, 40, 60, 69–73,
    77–78, 89, 98, 100, 102–105,
    108–113, 117, 130, 160, 164,
    171–172, 186, 189–190, 194–196,
    208, 210–212, 222–224, 229, 231,
    241
    group, 16–17, 19, 22, 24–25, 27–30,
    38, 41, 43, 46, 52–53, 58, 60,
    65, 76, 80–82, 84–86, 88–89,
    91, 93–94, 105, 109, 116–123,
    127–129, 146, 149, 155, 163–166,
    168, 170–171, 174, 176, 179–182,
    185, 190, 195, 198, 201, 203, 208,
    214–216, 222–223, 231, 233–235,
    238–240

Job Control Language (JCL), 198

Kentucky
  Jefferson County, 220
  Knox County, 219–220
knowledge dissemination, 82

la perruque, 121
Laboratory analysis, 54–55
linear regression, 226–227
local knowledge, 79–80, 86, 148–149

malnutrition estimates, 194, 211
mapping, 38, 67–68, 80–81, 85, 88, 91,
  97, 124, 140, 142–143, 145–151,
  153–155, 157–161, 185, 187, 194–195,
  197, 199, 206, 225
Margaret Mead, 43, 62, 131
Martorell, R, 223, 226
Maya and Maya-Americans, 223
media
  digital, 10, 18, 52, 58, 60, 85,
    136–141, 145–146, 159–160, 167,
    173–188, 194, 196–198, 217–218
  film, 165, 187–188
  images, 38, 100–101, 139, 144, 146,
    149, 162, 164–170, 172–173,
    176–177, 180, 183–184, 191
  multimedia, 185, 188
  print, 139–140, 177
  television, 162
meetings, 42, 88, 93, 119, 121–122, 182
Messer, E, 9, 12, 16, 37–38, 40–44, 46–49,
  102, 110, 112, 222, 226
Metabolic Syndrome, 196
metadata, 137, 151, 155, 190, 219
Metropolitan/Micropolitan Statistical Areas
  (MMSAs), 192
micronutrient analysis, 55
Microsoft's Access, 183
Microsoft's Excel, 190
Millennium Development Goals (MDGs),
  105
Modifiable Areal Unit Problem (MAUP),
  190
modified retail food environment index,
  188

monitoring and evaluation, 50–51, 223
multi-method formative studies, 222
multicollinearity, 236

National Agricultural Statistics Service
  (NASS), 192, 204
National Cancer Institute (NCI), 57
National Health and Nutrition
  Examination Survey (NHANES), 61,
  195, 197, 208
National Health Interview Survey (NHIS),
  195, 208
NCHS, 195–196, 208
NCI Dietary Assessment Calibrator, 49
NCI Validation Register, 49
New York City, 152, 159–160
NGO (non-governmental organization),
  13, 19, 41, 43, 57, 81–82, 92, 97,
  103–106, 108, 110–111, 116–117, 129,
  147, 155, 189, 198, 215, 224
Noble, Charlotte, 97
nutrient analysis protocols, 55, 57
nutrition analysis, 54–55
nutrition evaluation, 57
nutrition interventions, 16, 113
nutrition monitoring, 58, 223–224
Nutritional Analysis Tool (NAT), 3, 57
nutritional assessment, 12, 58, 81
nutritional epidemiology, 12, 56, 58–59,
  61, 71, 73
nutrition monitoring strategies, 8, 43
nutritional indicators

obesity, 24, 30, 75, 84, 90, 97, 124, 126–
  127, 150–152, 160, 194–199, 206–208,
  210–212, 223–225
observant participation, 120
Office of Management and Budget (OMB),
  192
Open Database Connectivity (ODBC), 183
Open Office, 182
Openshaw, S., 211
  See also Taylor, P. J.
optifoods dietary assessment tool, 67–68

participatory action research, 16, 79–80,
86, 88, 91, 96, 98, 120, 123
Participatory GIS (PGIS), 149, 158
participatory mapping, 148–149, 159–160
participatory methods, 17, 46, 91, 97
participatory rural appraisal, 13, 79–81, 86,
88, 95–98
Payne, G. and Payne, J, 214, 226
Pew Charitable Trust (PCT), 198, 201, 203
photography, 135, 163, 165, 168, 170–171
photovoice, 82, 84, 98, 135–136, 162–163,
167–171, 174, 187
PoliCultura, 185–187
practicum, 127, 130, 187
Preanalytical error, 56
primary data, 88, 136, 155, 213–215,
223–224
Program planning, 13, 64, 70–71, 189, 222
public anthropology, 131
public health, 10–11, 13, 15–16, 22,
35, 37, 39, 41, 43, 45, 47, 49, 58–59,
62–63, 66, 76, 79, 90, 92, 95–96, 98,
148, 150–151, 168, 180, 184, 186–187,
195–197, 199, 202, 208, 212
Public Use Microdata Sample (PUMS), 218

qualitative inquiry, 13, 37, 47, 225, 237
qualitative methods, 13, 37, 40, 44, 67, 81,
89, 166
quantitative methods, 81, 128

r-square value, 226–227
Rasch modeling, 237–239
real food challenge, 122
reference databases, 55
relative nutrient status, 53
reliability, 19, 40, 66, 196, 205, 223, 228,
230–231
research clearance, 117
research questions, 10, 41–42, 79, 89, 94,
117, 138, 190, 197–199, 214–215, 224
residual case analysis, 237, 239
resilience of local communities, 222
restricted use microdata, 189
risk of obesity and growth stunting, 213

Rural Urban Continuum Code (RUCC),
184, 194

SAS, 191, 195, 197, 211, 218, 226
scales, 19, 99, 190, 193, 197, 213,
227–231, 233, 235, 237–241
scholar-activists, 126
secondary data, 138, 190–191, 194–195,
198, 200, 202, 204, 213–219, 221–225
situated knowledges, 120
slow food, 40, 115, 123, 130, 132
social media, 18, 81, 85, 96–97, 131, 137,
149, 168, 177, 180, 185
socio-ecological approach, 215
spatial analysis, 144
SPSS, 191, 197, 211, 233–236, 239
statistical data sites (STAT), 193
SuperTracker, 57
Supplemental Nutrition Assistance Program
(SNAP), 157, 218–219

Taylor, P. J., 182. *See also* Openshaw
Trials of Improved Practices (TIPS), 75, 77
turnkey nutrition analysis, 47

United Nation's Childrens Fund
(UNICEF), 12, 41, 103–106, 113, 194,
206, 211
United States Department of Agriculture
(USDA), 43, 55, 57–58, 118, 123, 147,
150–151, 153, 156–157, 192–193, 196,
200, 202, 204, 210–211, 217, 225
United States Food and Drug
Administration (FDA), 58
urban food deserts, 189
US Census, 200
US Center for Disease Control (CDC), 52,
57, 147, 156, 191, 195–196, 200, 202,
208, 210–211, 223, 225
US Department of Agriculture (USDA),
43, 55, 57–58, 118, 123, 147, 150–151,
153, 156–157, 192–193, 196, 200, 202,
204, 210–211, 217, 225
USAID Food and Nutrition Technical
Assistance (FANTA), 10, 57, 61, 105,
110–111, 198, 201, 203, 240

validity, 27, 66, 198, 217, 223, 228,
230–231
Via Campesina, 115
videovoice, 18, 162–163, 165–166, 170
visual, 18, 38, 67, 82, 84, 86, 92, 137, 140,
144–147, 162, 164–165, 171, 173–174,
178, 180, 186–188, 191
visual research, 174, 188
Vitamin A deficiency, 8, 62, 68, 97,
100–101

web-based mapping, 147, 149, 194–195
weighed food records, 52–53
Wide-ranging Online Data for
Epidemiological Research (WONDER),
191, 196, 208, 210, 238

World Bank, 59, 79, 98, 157, 161, 194,
211
World Food Programme (WFP), 57, 103,
106, 147, 156
World Health Organization (WHO),
10, 13–14, 17, 19, 22–24, 29–30, 32,
39–40, 44–46, 58, 65–66, 68–70,
74–78, 84–85, 89, 91, 93–94, 99–100,
103–104, 110, 112, 115, 117, 119–122,
127–128, 130–131, 137, 139, 147, 152,
157, 160–161, 163, 167–168, 171,
174–182, 191, 194, 198, 200, 202,
206–207, 210–212, 218, 223–226, 228,
230, 236, 238–239

Printed in the USA
CPSIA information can be obtained
at www.ICGtesting.com
LVHW081746031123
762986LV00046B/1042